DI005783

CROSSFIRE EDUCATION

Metaphor, Cultural Evolution and Chaos in the Schools

William A. Jordan

University Press of America, Inc.
Lanham • New York • London

Copyright © 1996 by
University Press of America,® Inc.
4720 Boston Way
Lanham, Maryland 20706

3 Henrietta Street
London, WC2E 8LU England

Library of Congress Cataloging-in-Publication Data

Jordan, William A. (William Amos)
Crossfire education : metaphor, cultural evolution and chaos in the
schools / William A. Jordan.
p.   cm.
Includes bibliographical references and index.
1. Education--United States--Aims and objectives. 2. Education--
Social aspects--United States. 3. Educational anthropology--United
States. 4. School management and organization--United States. 5.
Educational change--United States.   I. Title.
LA217.2.J67   1995   370.19'34'0973 --dc20   95-44353 CIP

ISBN 0-7618-0168-5 (cloth: alk: ppr.)
ISBN 0-7618-0169-3 (pbk: alk: ppr.)

DEDICATION

This book is dedicated to teachers. They work harder and with less recognition than any group ever should have to. Specifically, I want to dedicate it to:

Hoover Jordan, my father, Professor Emeritus at Eastern Michigan University who made grammar a game as we did the dishes together.

Charles Meyers, a brilliant inspirational former fifth grade teacher at Estabrook Elementary School in Ypsilanti, Michigan.

Mark Papworth, former professor of anthropology at Oberlin College whose lectures attracted crowds.

Elizabeth Cowan, former professor of rhetoric at Texas A&M University who brought rhetorical discovery procedures into classes and lives.

Contents

Preface

I am a fifth generation teacher, and happy to have the title. My great-great-grandfather, Benjamin Harding, a frontier merchant, helped build a log schoolhouse in Kansas and taught in it until a regular full-time teacher could be found. His daughter, Clara, born in 1851, lived to be 106. She was acutely aware of time and children and the passing of generational knowledge as she told my brother and me stories of wagon trains, indians, and life on the prairie. One evening we stood holding hands by her picket fence in Missouri and watched a jet as it flew high overhead, aluminum glinting in the evening sky, contrail streaming behind. She spoke to me of the 'miracles' that occurred in her lifetime: Conestoga wagons giving way to rail, automobiles and roads, planes and now jets. She turned to my brother, Tom, telling him, "When I was a little girl, I met an old man who was a youth during the Revolution and he told me that I should always remember that I knew someone who had been alive in those times. Tom, you're going to live into the 21st century, and you can always say that you knew someone who knew someone in the Revolution."

In this present period of nine month product cycles and the doubling of information every few years, I like the idea that I knew someone who knew someone in The Revolution - not the Industrial Revolution, or the sexual revolution, or the computer revolution, but, The *American* Revolution, complete with Washington and Franklin and Jefferson. It is a constant reminder of how close the past is and how fast our rate of change. From the Massachusetts Militia and muskets to Conestogas and Colts to the moon and MIRVs: but where is education?

This book owes its existence to the Supreme Being of Education. There has never been a day in my life from Mrs. Skeels' Kindergarten class to the final sign-off on my dissertation to the present moment that I have not been self-consciously aware of the special nature of education, of classes, of classrooms, of teachers, students, staff and administrators. Perhaps it is a direct genetic endowment from Benjamin Harding to me; perhaps it is spiritual past-life information brought into present time as Wordsworth notes in his Intimations of Immortality:

> The Soul that rises with us, our life's Star,
> Hath had elsewhere its setting,
>   And cometh from afar:
> Not in entire forgetfulness,
> And not in utter nakedness,
> But trailing clouds of glory do we come
>   From God, who is our home:....

Teachers are both the luckiest and most God-forsaken people on Earth. Not unlike saints, they are expected to create miracles - *with* nothing and *for* nothing, just to please the unbelieving hordes.

Educational theory should help us. We know better though, as little has changed since Thomas Moore, the Irish poet, commented on educational theory in the 1830s as:

> Closet dry marrowless theories of unattainable perfection, which have all the dullness of matter of fact, without its substance, and all the unreality of imagination, without a single gleam of its light.
> (from Jordan, H., 1975, pg. 414)

I wrote this book to pose questions - not solve problems. Intuitive, gleaming, imagination becomes our greatest need and indeed reality in a time of change when there is no substance on which to stand. This book is about the greatest change in communication since the Greeks, and how that change is affecting our culture and schools. The solutions I have given are obvious once the Matrix is set up. You will certainly find other solutions.

The real solutions will come from the grassroots, from the people, not from the theorists and not from on high, but from people who care about their children and their community - people who band together to make schools part of their lives. People in communication. The change will be revolutionary, just as the change was for the man my great-grandmother knew: from a subject ruled by the absolute authority of the King to becoming a free being.

Acknowledgments

The Author would like to thank a number of people beyond those noted in the dedication. The first four readers - brother, Tom; late wife, Jeanne Marie; and friends, John Moran and Joe Kryzyanowski - gave enough hope to continue the project. Thanks Tom for the initial two hour midnight talk/walk at minus four degrees in Durango, CO as I expostulated evolutionary theory at a ski resort; Jeanne Marie for a keen proofing eye, putting up with my getting up at 4:00 am to write, and a lot of common sense about the nature of school; John for keeping the book in good hands and disabusing me of pride of authorship; and Joe K. for steadfast theoretical and rhetorical criticism, and for being the best teacher I've ever had the priviledge to work with. Thanks gang.

In California, thanks to Alec Brusca for a sense of humor; Harry Smith for absolutely unforgiving discussion, Diane Stillman for final proofing with all three eyes, and the crew at BPI for energywork.

Many thanks to my dissertation director, Bob White, for formative discussions over burritos and beer at the Quarters. Other committee members unwittingly contributed - Dean Brodkey for discussions on metaphor and teaching in TESOL and George Stoumbis for an inspired examination question on periods of education.

Thanks to Chris Griscom and the Light Institute of Galisteo for the Macintosh used in the project.

And finally thanks to the people at the University Press of America for their patience in seeing the book come to life.

Part I

SETTING
THE
ANALYTIC
FRAMEWORK

School
as a
Cultural Phenomenon

CHAPTER 1

Incentives for Change

One of my clearest memories of elementary school occurred in "reading class" in first grade. I had read 75 pages ahead in the basal reader on my own and then got stuck on a word. When I went to the teacher for help, she told me I was to stay with the class. I told her I just wanted to know the word, but she was adamant that she would help me when the class got to that part of the book. I was furious because my Mom and Dad always helped me with words. I couldn't see why the teacher wouldn't help me. I still can't

In that moment, however, I clearly comprehended that I wanted to change the way schools worked. I also understood that school was not about learning, it was about the teacher being right. It was only one of many incidents in my educational life, but it had gemlike purity in illuminating narrowness and ignorance.

Children examine their world through new eyes and without the labelling and categories of adults. When a child likes ducks or horses or dogs and sees one in a coloring book, the response is not "Did the artist give a faithful rendering?" or "I'm seeing the advent of cubism in that sketch." No. The response is, "I like it; I'm going to color it - and then the child reaches for a favorite color and begins scribbling. If blue is the favorite color, then a blue duck or dog or horse emerges with great satisfaction. A nice duck and a nice color - until the teacher tells the child, probably very sweetly, that ducks are brown, implying that the child doesn't know colors or ducks. A success becomes a failure, and the child wonders why. While school may stifle personal initiative with the conscious control inherent in basal readers, it stifles creativity by demanding conformity for the sake of conformity. Just as students become locked into having to see the way the teacher does, administrators march in lockstep pattern. This book looks at some of the issues surrounding education and will try to suggest ways of moving from the grainy black and white of our past to seeing and riding a horse of many colors.

Criticism of the present system is easy. There is more than enough blame to go around and like the Middle East, each faction claims to be right and points to the other factions as wrong. The real risk in taking such a limited position against the others and assigning blame is that, rather like fighting the Tar Baby, one simply becomes stuck and dirty while clarifying nothing.

In 24 years of teaching elementary, middle, and high school as well as undergraduate and graduate students, writing instructional materials, developing curricula, administering educational, corporate and grant programs, and performing academic research, it seems clear to me that the only important aspect of education is the interaction between students and teachers. Everything else is peripheral and should be supportive of that activity. Whether a class meets in an olive grove with Socrates, in a closely guarded military base, or in an inner-city school is irrelevant: the defining characteristic is that students are working with a teacher.

This book will work from that simple premise - we need teachers working *with* students: communicating. Afterall, the only reason for education in the first place is having students learn knowledge deemed important by their own culture.

Rarely have I seen the distinction with such clarity as when I was finishing my doctoral coursework. I took a class with students from many different realms of education. When I mentioned that student and teacher interaction was the only important entity in education, the educational administration people called me naive, citing money and politics as the factors which govern education, and are, therefore, most important. I am, perhaps, naive, but not on this issue. Just as people in the federal bureaucracy mistake money and politics for policy whether domestic or foreign, the people in educational administration mistake money and politics for education. That is a fundamental issue in changing the direction of education. The educational establishment with superintendents, state finance accountants, curriculum designers, school boards, regents, colleges of education, and book writers and publishers should be present only to support the teacher and student in the endeavor of teaching and learning. However, they all seem to have their own agendas, most of which have little to do with the student in the classroom learning anything.

I'll be the first to acknowledge that I do not know what learning is or how it occurs. It is a mental process that cannot be measured. We can measure facts, and we can measure skills, and we can measure behaviors, and we can even measure the moment that learning occurs with an EEG and circle the brainwave shift as an "event," but none of these is learning.

The very notion of "learning" is anathema to many in education because it cannot be measured. They speak of intended learning outcomes (ILOs), or learning as "changed behavior," and specify these behaviors and outcomes in "objectives." We can measure behavioral objectives and that seems to make a large segment of society quite happy. To the reductionist mentality, if it can be measured, then it is real. If it can't be measured, then it isn't provable, and is, therefore, not important or not worth discussing.

Our belief in testing is as pervasive as it is extraordinary. In many ways, school shouldn't be called school, it should be called the test center. Teachers have competency tests and teacher exams; students get formative, summative, diagnostic, remedial, personality, IQ, competency, criterion, aptitude, and achievement tests, and now many schools are instituting drug tests. School seems to be more about measurement than it does about learning, meaning and the search for those abstractions. But then, abstractions don't fit the multiple-choice format.

The central problem in trying to discuss education in an analytic manner is that when one examines a single part in isolation, one is necessarily ignoring other equally important aspects of the whole. We cannot discuss teacher education without framing the subject in the larger light of what curriculum the teacher is going to teach, under what classroom conditions the material will be taught, and how the students will be selected, instructed, and evaluated. In like manner, to discuss the curriculum, without reference to the goals of the students, the education of the teachers, or the outlook of the community is to present a limited, and quite distorted view of the situation. We could go through all the component parts of education, citing the interrelationships as we briefly did with teacher education and curriculum; however, we must be aware that education as a cultural phenomena does not occur in isolation and that any effort to reduce the whole to components must only be done with the understanding that we must fit the discussion back into the whole at the end - keeping the larger vision intact.

When looking at education, the popular press has a problem because it tends to express the issues in simplistic terms and have these ideas exemplified by catch phrases such as "back to the basics," "educational accountability," and "traditional values." In each case, the expression takes the form of looking back to the good old days of rigor and backbone. While sympathizing with the general confusion over present-day education and the ease of looking at the past instead of trying to think about, and plan the future, I think that we really should step back and examine the way we view it.

Frank Smith, the reading theorist, makes the point that we have, in the last 30 years, tended to use a military, "project" mentality when viewing education, as though the same system analysis which brought together thousands of small isolated units to form the whole of the moonshot was the only way to conquer educational problems. Modern America is unique in thinking that the parts of education can be divorced from the whole and still retain meaning.

In traditional American education, whether in the one room school house or the Latin grammar school, the teacher was "right" and the student learned what the teacher had to offer - not unlike education throughout the ages. The community, the larger culture, the administration, teacher education, curriculum, and testing all were embodied in the teacher and transmitted directly without intermediaries.

With the advent of mass education, the teacher was no longer the sole arbiter but had to fit into the larger administrative plan as laid out by the school board, specifying the curriculum to be taught and the testing to be done under what circumstances. With the isolation brought about by using "technical experts," education could, and did, become insulated and isolated from the very cultural forces which must guide and shape it. The experts of education, just as experts in any area, erect walls to guard their special knowledge.

As we move into a new era of connection and communication, the organization of education must change to reflect differing needs and expectations. Education will show students the relationships between various aspects of the world as they interact rather than in isolation.

Current discussion of education rages with heart-felt conviction, not-so-much discussing issues as issuing polemics from deep within the confines of hardened bunkers. From Hirsch's traditionalism seeking to institutionalize a monocultural national curriculum, to Bloom and Schlafly arguing for absolutism, Schor charging the conservative restoration with oppression of minorities, or Smith railing against bureaucratic imposition in the schools, little consideration is paid to the larger issue of the redefinition of education in a *changed* society.

Hirsch in *Cultural Literacy*, Bloom in *Closing of the American Mind*, and Schlafly with the Eagle Forum all know that change is upon us, and all want to go back to a previous "golden age." Hirsch uses the findings of cognitive psychology that one must have a core of knowledge in order integrate new information in a meaningful manner to argue his case for returning to 19th century monocultural education. When one notes that only 10 percent of people graduated from high school in 1920, we realize how exclusive and limited in every facet the education of the period was in reality. It is an exclusivity which we would find neither practical, possible, nor desirable given the nature of current society.

Bloom and Schlafly would have us go much further back in seeking an adequate model. Bloom finds Plato to be the solution while Schlafly finds educational salvation in an idiosyncratic reading of the Bible. Neither can abide a relativistic world despite more than one hundred years of philosophical relativism and nearly one hundred years of physical relativism. Despite the temptation to dismiss these two as anachronisms, the very response they receive from their constituencies demands that they be dealt with seriously.

Schor in *Culture Wars* and Smith in *Insult to Intelligence* each consciously choose a limited discussion of education, Schor examining the politics of mass education and Smith the implications of teaching and learning within a bureaucracy. There are, of course, many other critics, but these five represent the major schools of criticism in American education: monolingual/monocultural, classical, religious, political, and psychological. Overlaps occur, but the patterns of thought are relatively distinct.

Each of these five writers argues from the existing educational framework, rather than seeing the current situation in the larger light of cultural evolution with changed demands placed on education. For examination, we must change the frame of reference, then we can redefine the issues themselves.

When we change the frame of reference, the dominant question changes at the same time. Instead of asking, "What must we do to improve American public education?", and looking for a simple, unilateral answer, we should ask whether American education serves the needs of the society. We have to be aware that the result of such a question might demand that we restructure the system. Current writing tries to find the problem on a troubleshooting chart as though the educational system were an automobile starting system. Instead, we need to step back and ask if the automobile itself is the ideal mode of transport. We cannot even ask the proper question unless we are dealing with the proper level of abstraction.

Bertalanffy and the general system theorists show how an analytical framework of examination must be large enough to encompass all aspects of the system under scrutiny and yet small enough to retain meaning. That is, one can say nothing about everything, or one can say almost everything about almost nothing. The named critics select one aspect of the educational issue, take supportive pieces of history and theory and posit the combination as an elucidation of, or the solution to, our current problems. In each case, they say more or less about an issue, depending on the scope of their argument, but the actual argument itself is framed within a very narrow focus.

By raising the current discussion to a more abstract level, perspective may be gained and the limitation removed on what may actually be debated. Rather than a point-by-point examination of the merits of traditional education vs. progressive education, open vs.closed classes, standardized testing vs. individual achievement or the myriad other issues, this book will investigate cultural change in education. As such, the purpose is not to make specific curricular suggestions, or to praise or disparage specific authors or ideas, but to try to redefine the discussion itself, giving it some perspective and direction.

The book began as a series of thoughts about three metaphors used to describe and view education in America. The first metaphor of mind as muscle shows an elite, limited, traditional education in which the mind could be disciplined as a muscle to become stronger by hard work. With the second, industrialism, machine imagery took over from physical body imagery while currently, the third, the mind as a neural network is being compared to a computer network. The latter is as yet only partially accepted as an educational metaphor and as such is much less well-defined than the other two.

By showing the relationship between the three metaphors, and the progression from one to the next, I hope to show how cultural evolution has left the schools in metaphoric emptiness - and that the consequences are resonating with increasing violence.

As a teacher/curriculum developer in scientific and technical language areas (electronics, mechanics, and health occupations to name a few), I see a great deal of frustration when technicians are forced to examine language. Technical people, especially engineers, see the world in vertical, "If...,then..." terms. With mathematics as a base, such people know that one must add and subtract, before moving to multiplication, algebra and higher math. Language has no such direct progression. Spelling is not related to grammar. Syntax is largely independent of semantics. Rhetoric stands alone in general usage. Furthermore, one can begin language study almost anywhere as long as one studies all the parts and most importantly realizes that each part is essential to the whole. In fact, the whole cannot exist as isolated parts - you take one component out of language and you are left with nothing.

Anyone who has ever seen a stroke patient with aphasia knows this first-hand. In Wernicke's aphasia, the patient has good syntax but little semantic control, i.e., the patient babbles "good English" but with little sense. In contrast, Broca's aphasia leaves semantic control but not syntactic, i.e., the person has something to say and knows the words, but has trouble putting the thought into a coherent sentence, stuttering and omitting words.

Discussing education is rather like discussing language. We can look at individual parts, but in so doing, we must make sure that we keep in mind that those parts have little meaning separated from the whole. Thus, it makes no difference whether one examines curriculum before teacher education before school administration etc. as they are all simply parts of the larger unit.

When we specify that one sector of the educational establishment is most important, we are falling into the trap of industrial linearity where there is always a hierarchical top-down classification structure. Freed from that constraint, we can examine educational issues which form a whole rather than viewing the information in a limited sequential process.

Additionally, in order to perform this examination, we need to analyze the prejudices of own worldviews, see where education has been, and, most importantly, where it is going. This process involves seeing cultural evolution in present day America and how the educational establishment reacts to change while at the same time helping to shape the change. In short, we must move from the heat of the battle to a more dispassionate, philosophical environment where issues can be examined without accusation.

In late 20th century America, scientific technology has outstripped philosophy - and education reflects the turmoil of a society accelerating into change with no idea of direction and no guidance. We need to find a place where science and philosophy can be reconciled.

Historically, when philosophy and science concur, the product of the conjunction will not only be influential, but enduring. In the West, such a conjunction has occurred only three times: in Greece, in 17th century Rationalism, and at the turn of this century. Philosophically, the Greeks examined the nature of truth with Plato and truth of nature with Aristotle. Greek science joined philosophy in seeking immutable laws of mathematics and physics as well as a confirmable definition of man and his reason. With the advent of Rationalism, Newton defined the mechanics of physics, and God was portrayed the Master Clockmaker of the Universe. In the 19th century, German philosophy concluded that relativism was necessarily all that was left, just as the theory of relativity and quantum physics showed that Newtonian mechanics were inadequate to discuss particle and wave theory in the electromagnetic spectrum. The implications of a non-static, non-permanent, vibratory, probablistic universe are still being defined, refined and integrated at varying rates in our own culture as well as the rest of the world - and causing a great deal of tension as a result.

An illustration of this shift from a fixed to a variable universe comes in the area of testing: nuclear bomb tests and standardized school testing. Tying these two widely separate types of testing together Sternglass and Bell in the *Phi Delta Kappan* in 1983 found that the decline of scores on the Scholastic Aptitude Test (SAT) correlated to the kiloton yield of the open-air nuclear testing done 17-18 years earlier. While others such as the Wirst commission cite other 'more direct' explanations Sternglass and Bell make a convincing case. Not only did the scores correlate inversely with the nuclear kiloton yield (higher radioactive output with lower scores on the SAT), but they correlated in intensity as well (years with a sharply higher radioactive yield later gave sharply lower scores on the test). These results fly in the face of conventional educational wisdom which account for lowered SAT scores by citing drug use, family breakdown and the increased testing of all students, including many minorities, who traditionally do not score as well as white middle class students.

What's more, the greatest declines in test scores occurred in Utah which is directly downwind from the Nevada open air nuclear test sites. This is especially interesting in light of the fact that Utah, with its Mormon population, has not had many of the social events blamed for a lowering of test scores - from drugs to family breakdown to minorities lowering school standards. Coincidence? It would not appear to be, especially because Sternglass noted in 1979 that 1980 would be the year that scores turned around if their study was correct as it would be 17-18 years after the signing of the open air nuclear test ban. They were correct. Furthermore, they not only showed which radioactive isotopes caused cognitive impairment (Iodine 131) and why (hypothyroidism - the thyroid controls fetal and infant cognitive development and ability), but also show the same correlation for fetal death, infant mortality, and congenital birth defects on a state by state basis.

The interesting aspect of a correlation between SAT scores and fallout is not so much the SAT scores themselves, which are subject to criticism from any number of angles, but what it means as to the ability of a whole generation of minds. To what degree have the nuclear powers affected the cognitive abilities of people worldwide?

We are the first generation who have to think on global terms because the world is interrelated in a way it never has been in the past. Nuclear fallout knows no political boundaries whether from bombs or reactor meltdown as in Chernobyl. We cannot hide behind national boundaries when satellites can see everything. Russia's policy of glastnost may have been the the desire of Gorbachev and Yeltsin, but it is also the reality of their not being able to hide anymore. Satellite pictures tell us of dramatic events such as a nuclear meltdown in visual, infrared, and radioactive terms. Coercion, denial, and persuasion, historically three staples of diplomacy and statesmanship, are rendered meaningless in the face of the evidence from satellites. The Soviets had to admit to a serious nuclear accident when confronted with evidence from radiation sensing posts in Scandinavia, and satellite photographs from both the French and U.S.

In other aspects of global interrelationship, communication technologies have superceded purely national borders and have damned the jingoistic ethnocentric thinkers as relics - dinosaurs awaiting their death. In other words, satellite photos and sensing devices really do have a great deal to do with the price of beans. Just as there is no denying a dramatic event such as a nuclear meltdown, there is no denying the effects of nature. When it rains in Brazil, the price of coffee changes in Chicago, Tokyo, and London. Drought in Argentina changes the price of soybeans in Des Moines. Raising the prime lending rate in Japan not only raises our interest rates, but lowers the value of the dollar, affecting our ability to pay for French wine or German cars.

Acid rain, nuclear waste disposal, and groundwater contamination do not admit of arbitrary borders based on nationality and culture. When the U.S., English and Dutch dump their plutonium waste in the ocean there is an absolute certainty that the effects will be felt by all for thousands of years. Europe's waste is already poisoning marine mammals in the North Sea. The cutting of tropical rainforests affects climate worldwide.

One could think in culturally absolute terms in the past and get away with it - no longer. One can criticize cultural absolutism as ethnocentric, if one believes in the relative value of cultures, or as anachronistic if one believes in progressive politics, but both arguments pale to the greater need of caring for the earth and mankind in the larger sense. For survival, we need to change our approach.

CHAPTER 2

The Blinding Light of Greece: Their Light, Our Blindness

While the brilliance of the Greek Golden Age is undisputed, one should not simply accept the Greeks as the pinnacle of civilization and, uncritically, wish to return. With slavery as the basis of production, pederasty as the basis of education, and animal baiting as a popular form of entertainment, we may admire aspects of reasoned Greek thought without necessarily accepting the cultural entirety as some neoclassicists would have us do.

In fact, it is the very quality of reasoned argumentation which separates the Greeks from those civilizations which went before. Jaynes in his work *The Origin of Consciousness in the Breakdown of the Bicameral Mind* argues that Greek perception of the world was qualitatively different, allowing separation of self from world. Using different arguments, Ong argues that oral society must be organized differently from literate society. Conscious, reasoned, persuasive argumentation - rhetoric - became the key subject in Greek education, and the subject of great debate among the thinkers since.

Say the word "rhetoric" and people envision empty speech, vacuous politicians, or invidious, corporate PR mannequins. Rhetoric has had this bad name ever since Plato called it empty flattery which, like cosmetics, covers the truth. In spite of Plato's criticism, rhetoric has always been central to education when ideas have needed expression. Dynamic thought demands to be heard in effective terms.

As communication needs changed so did rhetoric. For democratic Greeks and Romans, free political expression demanded persuasive speech. St. Augustine adapted classical, pagan rhetoric to his evangelical Christian need. A thousand years later, after the invention of the printing press changed communication, Peter Ramus adapted rhetoric to reflect the new reality of print.

Of late, rhetoric has again shifted - from traditional, classical persuasion and arrangement to the more philosophical position of discovery and identification. Psychologists adapted rhetorical discovery techniques to help patients realize and assert their identity. Academicians use these psychological discovery procedures to help student writers find and refine ideas. Popularly, in the most modern advertising, we no longer hear sports figures say, "Wear this shoe, and you'll score the way I do." As in Nike shoe ads, we simply find images of the athlete performing, intercut with the corporate logo. In contrast to advertising, schools have not embraced the idea of communication, discovery or identification.

Despite the noise in the popular press about new learning and new education, we are hardly the first to have faced educational change. Greek students learned literature, science, and philosophy as the "new learning" with rhetoric, poetic and mathematics as the basics. A look at rhetoric in the Greek Golden Age, while not exactly parallel to our present educational situation, is still most instructive.

Athens brimmed with new ideas. Change became the norm as the Athenians expanded the notions of politics, philosophy, music, poetry, drama and science. Communication of ideas became paramount in the open forum of the agora. The rise of the democratic assembly and courts demanded effective speech and rhetoric because of the premium on the eloquent man able to persuade others of the justness of his position. Those ideas from the agora and assembly which did not stand up to scrutiny faced scorn and public ridicule from Aristophanes and the other satirists. Rhetoricians of all stripes taught speech to the burgeoning democracy of Athens, and as in any growth industry, there were good and bad, ethical and unethical practitioners.

To say we need to go back to the Platonic conception of education and apply his absolutes to regenerate American education is both limited and inappropriate. While Allan Bloom makes an urgent case for reinstituting the absolutism which marks Plato's *Republic*, we would be well served to remind ourselves that Plato was only one voice in his own time. Aristotle had a different view.

Plato objected to rhetoric because it was more interested in appearance and effect than truth. However, at the end of the *Phadreus*, he admits that if the rhetorical discovery mechanisms were to be used to find the truth, then rhetoric would be of value. He is not sanguine that discovery of truth is at the heart of most men though as they plead their case before the ignorant masses, striving for advantage.

In contrast, Aristotle said the goal of rhetoric was finding, "the available means of persuasion in any given case" i.e. useful and morally neutral. Following his line of reasoning, a rhetor must have a broad and deep education if he is to use the "available means." One must thoroughly know the subject matter being discussed, know the available means of presenting the subject matter, and finally know the audience in order to shape the discourse. Because absolute proofs are often not possible in everyday life as they are in science, Aristotle notes that we must deal with what people believe to be true in persuasion. In what is the basis for all further discussion of rhetoric and logic, as well as the foundation of psychology, Aristotle's *Rhetoric* presents topics for argumentation and proofs useful for persuasion.

The tension between these two men is still with us: moral education versus value free, the Platonic absolutes held as belief versus the probability of belief of the Aristotelian proofs, and the Socratic dialogue as the means of education versus the completely written handbook as the means for learning.

Plato, Aristotle, Euclid, Pythagoras, and the historians, poets, and dramatists of Greece literally wrote a new book. In both quality and quantity the nature of Greek communication was different from that which preceded it. From the Egyptians and Sumerians to the early Jewish texts, writing was purely for business or religion and guarded as power. As Athenian democracy extended power to the populace, the need for literacy and communicative ability became extended as well. By introducing writing into philosophy, establishing rhetoric as a formal course of education, interpreting history rather than simply recording it, and writing poetry and drama formally rather than simply having extemporaneous oral presentation, the Greeks demonstrated self-consciousness in action. Their use of literacy in philosophy, education, history and entertainment demands separation of the self from others on the immediate task - new ground in the Old World. This separation of self from subject encouraged intensity and vertical depth of learning not possible in the oral tradition which is broad in its comprehensive ability to record all that is necessary. The very breadth of an oral system precludes the depth of a literate one. Oral culture is concerned with the narration of naming. Whether affixing of genealogical lineage, the recitation of the history of events and heroes, or the learning of the edible from the non-edible, persons, places, and actions have dominance. Oral recitation or narration answers the question of "what is" or "who is," and necessarily uses horizontal, parallel, compound syntactic and rhetorical development. Horizontal development is needed because the oral tradition is broad rather than deep, i.e., every person in the group must be included by oral connection in contrast to a literate culture where the individual is connected by print but may in fact be physically and emotionally isolated. Oral culture demands personal connection for continuance where literate culture has libraries. When the last Indian of a tribe dies without having the tribal stories recorded, the history of the tribe disappears. We can look back at Greece or Rome and read what they thought at a given time - their societies are gone but their story lives in print.

Orality needs parallelism for its development because of memory constraints. In the *Iliad* one finds well-defined conventions often repeated whether in character introduction, reintroduction by epithet, or description of events. Such parallelism tends to be developed with repeated compound syntactic structures rather than subordinate structures. The narrator can take as much time as necessary and repeat as much information as is necessary in order for his audience to understand. This spaciousness of talk over print occurs because the orator speaks immediately with no physical separation to an audience to convey his point, in contrast to the author who writes blindly and hopes the audience can interpret his meaning.

With the advent of self-conscious literacy by the Greeks, conditional analysis could be applied to the linearity of naming: the "if this..., then that...." sentence. This complex subordination allowed the development of formal logic and applications such as philosophy and engineering predicated on highly involved definition and classification schemes. Subordinate structure in both syntax and rhetoric is so common in the engineering thought process of industrial culture that we rarely think about it.

As computers gain popular acceptance, the use of databases and spreadsheets extend a new element to mental consideration. Able to handle vast amounts of information, one can not only simultaneously examine various levels of naming and schemes of classification, but also check conditions applicable to each in a manner impossible to do by solitary mentation without computers. Functionally, the computer combines the compound naming inherent in the breadth of orality with the complex depth of conditional analysis in literacy. The combination of broad, deep analysis results in a compound-complex structure with the ability to ask,"What if...", representing a three dimensional model integrating both the breadth of naming and the depth of analysis.

Graphically, we can examine this progression in a four-way grid with a simple description of the cultural periods and some of their attributes. Greater depth will be added in succeeding chapters as the grid becomes an interactive Matrix. The cultural periods will move from the upper-left with Oral/Emergent Literacy, Traditional/Classical Literacy, Industrial Literacy, and Post-Industrial/Communicative Literacy:

Table 2.1 - Four Cultural Periods

Oral Culture	**Traditional Literacy**
Self Represents Culture	Self Consciousness
Truth as Wholes	Conditional Analysis
Coordinate Syntax	Subordinate Syntax
Post-Industrial Literacy	**Industrial Literacy**
Self Seeks Identity	Self in Isolation
Comprehensive Analysis	Organizational Analysis
Compound-Complex Syntax	Subordinate Syntax

Where the Greeks began a system that allowed separation of self from others on a task for the first time, present day America has come to the logical endpoint where industrial specialization has so separated people that even the educated have trouble communicating. The isolating depth of learning is so great that there is virtually no breadth of knowledge. The engineer cannot talk to the doctor who cannot talk to the lawyer.

This isolation comes at a time when we are facing a communication revolution as great as that which the Greeks faced because virtually any fact in existence can be ascertained by anyone with a computer and modem almost instantaneously. Where the Greeks had a blank slate in beginning their endeavor to understand the world with knowledge and the written word, our slate is virtually full and yet doubling in size every few years.

Clearly, education for specialty is futile. However, rather than viewing us as an endpoint or deadend of the Greek tradition, we might better relate our cultural position with the Greeks. They were the endpoint of oral tradition; they had gone as far as the breadth of oral tradition allowed; their oral slate was full so they reversed and went from broad to more specialized education. We have reached the endpoint allowed by the specialized use of literacy, and we too must change direction.

However, we can not simply move from our narrow specialized learning back to broad learning, pretending that we are just changing emphasis while keeping other aspects the same. When the Greeks moved beyond the oral tradition, the world changed. It will do no less in this shift. Education will become more broad no doubt, but it must take into consideration past learning as well which is deep. Just as the Greeks built on the inclusive breadth of oral learning to reshape the world with their new classification schemes (impossible in oral culture), we must build on the present vertical depth of learning in reshaping the world. Rather than call for a new breadth as opposed to present depth, we must look for an integration of the two in comprehensiveness. The combination of the two planar forms must result in a three dimensional model having both broad and deep capacity: a hologram. We find a ready example in the recent study of chaos, the study of non-linear phenomena, which demands the extended analysis allowed by the computer. Events, such as fluid turbulence, too vast in scope to be analyzed by single human brains can be analyzed with the broad depth of computers.

However, firmly caught in the hierarchic specialization of complex, *subordinate* structures, education appears unable to see that the integrating conjunctive link of broad knowledge is missing. Specialists probe the patient ever deeper with reductionist programs and technology, failing even to see the problem.

Our task is to tame the new communicative power with the grace, insight, and effect with which our Greek forebearers tamed literacy.

CHAPTER 3

Communication and Society - The Shifting Gears of Awareness

In addition to expanding the idea of different types of syntax representing cultural plateaus and educational needs, we need to examine the idea of human communication and the implications in mankind's development, focusing on directions in education. Where the very complexity of communication may distinguish humankind from the rest of the animal world, the differing means of communication distinguish the cultural periods discussed in the last chapter: the pre-/emergent literacy before the Greeks, the developed literacy of the Greeks, and modern, post-industrial communication. In particular, we must examine the organization of communication in these periods in more detail to develop a clearer model of cultural evolution, keeping in mind the precept that broad oral education allows for little depth of questioning the status quo while specialized literate education demands such questioning, but with little breadth or connection of ideas.

Communication Allowed Survival

By emphasizing the word communication in the electronic sense rather than the simple use of symbol or signal, I want to by-pass tedious discussions of animal behavior - whether the warning signals of animals such as a fearful beaver slapping its tail on the water, or the clearly informative dance of honeybees in giving directions to pollen, or the fascinating, but little understood "languages" of whales and dolphins.

We might begin by examining the fundamental basis of communication and build a functional model. The most basic concepts of communication are that there must be a purpose for communication between two entities which are in some manner connected in a bidirectional fashion with a shared code. Purpose and shared code preclude simple randomness, or noise, while bidirection ensures that the message can have a response rather than being dead-ended. In simplest form for individual humans, this means two people exchanging information in a common language.

Applied to mankind in general, we find that communication is the only specialty given us by nature. Without the cheetah's speed, elephant's strength, lion's claws, shark's teeth, or bear's fur, we have succeeded as a species by our generalization and the cooperative effort allowed by communication. We are demonstrably a success. At least, so far, we are a success; however, if we do not change our specialized use of communication for war and war materiel, we may go the way of the mastodon, sabre-tooth tiger, and dinosaurs who despite massive offensive and defensive tools were doomed by over-specialization and lack of adaptability.

Man needed to cooperate to succeed evolutionarily if only because of his extreme inadequacy in physical departments. The identification of shared meaning established the culture of coordinated hunting and gathering society and compensated for the lack of physical attributes. We are simply later versions of that society, grown larger.

Aspects of Literate Communication and Cultural Evolution

At the hunting and gathering level, we find society that is basically integrated. Although, from an anthropological perspective, one may identify a big man, a shaman, a hunter, and a jokester, all four participate in all aspects of life, connected by the communality of oral tradition. They all hunt; they all participate in religion; and rule is largely by consensus. Orality insures that each member of the group is fully informed of its history, lineage, and educated in the necessities of life. The all-inclusive breadth of such education guarantees integration with the group, but provides little or no means of questioning and discovering the larger world.

As noted previously, where the Greeks introduced self-conscious literacy for the first time, their use of writing blossomed from a gradual increase of awareness throughout the Middle East. The Old Testament of the Bible gives clear evidence of the shift. The rules listed so exhaustively in Deuteronomy are not unlike the rules listed on stelae in Babylonia or Egypt. These are simple prescriptions, expected to be obeyed, not questioned. By the time Moses receives the commandments (circa 900 B.C.), his wandering tribe asked Moses what was in it for them. In contrast, Isaiah and Amos, writing at the same time as Greek culture flowered, share the awareness of self though from a different perspective. This growing awareness was not individual breakthrough but rather a gradual accumulation of knowledge and people - a critical mass had formed.

In brutal contrast, we find an example of oral culture shift today in the U.S. Amerindian groups are having to make conscious decisions as to how their oral cultures proceed. The Navajo have officially decided on an alphabet and literate culture whereas some pueblos along the Rio Grande have consciously decided against literacy, viewing it as the destruction of their cultures. Two issues glare incandescently: how can the Navajo teach literacy, especially bilingual literacy, and retain their wholistic culture intact? versus how can the pueblos endure in isolation, both cultural and economic?

Specialized Communication with Industrialism

Interestingly, where communication allowed development of society originally, and literacy provided for specialization of production means into agrarian and urban society, the very enlargement of specialization in industrialism has fragmented society to the point of non-communication. We are back to the tower of Babel where scientist cannot talk to humanist, or layperson to any "expert" be he doctor, lawyer, biologist, physicist, literary critic, or educator. The specialized languages of any field define not only who is in the field, but necessarily, who is not in the field. Perhaps we have come back to a neolithic primitivism, where the only shared symbols are those relating to the primal urges which drove man to procreative success in the first place. If so, then perhaps, "I Can't Get No Satisfaction" is a fitting anthem to the period.

To Everything There is a Season

Fortunately, just as we have pushed specialized non-communication to its logical end, the gyre returns and changes the face of reality.

Through the industrial period, increasing control of information demanded ever-increasing specialization of job knowledge. Now, however, we find electronics taking the world two separate directions.

The area of transportation provides a clear example. The agrarian wheelwright, the industrial railroad mechanic and the post-industrial diesel mechanic need, acquire and use information in dramatically different manners. While the amount of information per se certainly has increased at each level, the important aspect is the nature of the information needed. Where the wheelwright learned his trade as an apprentice and needed no formal schooling to size and shape a wheel for a Conestoga wagon, the railroad mechanic had to have formal training to be able to service the complexity of a steam locomotive. Without such training, the mechanic was a mortal danger to himself and to the entire train. Fixed procedures for training, service and maintenance had to be established to assure uniformity of work. Still the mechanic could service the whole locomotive, or any part, as it sat in the roundhouse.

In contrast, in a present-day diesel truck garage, a mechanic cannot service an entire tractor rig. The electronic controls on a modern truck preclude comprehensive knowledge of repair. The electronically monitored governor requires the same type of repair as any other computer, but diesel shops are not computer repair shops. One cannot apply the needle probe and volt meter used in standard wire electrical repairs, and thus the mechanic has a choice of sending the component to a specialty shop or simply by-passing the controls with an old-style copper wire.

At the same time that computers are changing the nature of diesel engine repair, they are making the job of diesel mechanic increasingly like other jobs. It used to be that much of mechanics was seat of the pants work - "this sounds about right," or, "look at that white smoke, the fuel injectors must be out of sync." Now the engine is hooked to a computer analyzer which gives a printout almost instantaneously, telling what needs repair and to what degree.

Thus, the modern diesel mechanic no longer needs the fundamental mechanical sense of his predecessors in spotting needed repairs while at the same time he cannot repair the entirety of the unit. This is not unlike the architectural drafter who no longer draws, but interprets the architect's ideas and directions by using a computer keyboard to assemble architectural icons into what constitutes a drawing on the screen and then has the computer print out the "draft." The secretary writes with the word processor, justifying syntax and spelling by computer program; the nurse examines patient treatment on the computer, with deviations from the norm flagged by the program;

refinery operators control oil flow through digital instrumentation; and professors grade tests with a computerized scanner which prints out grades and class means.

Does it sound as though the diesel mechanic and professor are in similar businesses? They both control information. Just as industrial society separates the diesel mechanic almost as far as possible from the professor, the two are thrown back together by new technology. The vertically isolated industrial tower of Babel transforms into a communicative, connective, network.

Communication Must Be Complementary - Not One-Way Hierarchy

The full, isolated, power of industrialism was the extreme focus of physical materials at a given point in time. The assembly lines of Detroit are perhaps the best example of this hierarchical, industrial power. Henry Ford did not have the best car aesthetically or mechanically, but he had the best production technique. The assembly line moved, the supervisors supervised, and cars rolled, but when workers decided to strike, Ford called in muscle and created some of the worst labor riots in U.S. history in order to carry out his will. He dictated policy in an autocratic hierarchical pattern. The many worked at the bottom, each layer up had fewer, and he sat at the top, not unlike an Egyptian king or Persian emperor. The only significant difference was that he controlled an industrial empire which could assure that iron ore from Duluth arrived in Detroit at the same time as coal from Pennsylvania, and rubber from Akron. Raw materials rolled into one side of the River Rouge Plant, and, voila!, cars rolled out the other side.

Hierarchy dictates in a top down fashion; each layer supervising and rating those layers below. Each level knew that it was accountable to the layer above from the lowest floor worker to the vice-president. Messages were simply dictated downward, as response was not expected and certainly not desired. Ford ran his company, and John Smith, the water pump installer on the line, was not expected to comment on policy.

Within the industrial paradigm, information, knowledge and power were accounted for in the same economic terms as the total production of goods: in zero sum fashion. If Ford sold more cars, then Chevrolet sold fewer as there were a finite number of car buyers. If I moved up the hierarchical power ladder of the Ford company, then someone else was not going to climb, or they would climb in "my footsteps." If I held power, then someone else did not. Sharing is impossible in a vertical structure; competition is the only reality.

When one speaks of "working over", rather than "working with", the connotations of superiority are inescapable. The vertical industrial metaphor of superiority and inferiority clearly marks corporate position as in, "climbing the ladder", "moving up", "on the bottom rung", "going upstairs", "rising to the top", "in on the ground floor", and "working your way up."

Information as an Absolute - The Captains of Industry

Ford was not unlike other "Captains of Industry", Rockefeller, Morgan, and Carnegie to name a few, who ruled autocratically with physical control of ideas and materiel. At first, it seems curious to put J.P. Morgan, a financier, in with the steel, oil, and automobile men, but not when one considers that finance until the critical period of the turn of the century meant control of gold.

Morgan controlled international transaction by keeping a solid gold base. The only problem with gold as a base is that it is so limited in quantity that even before the turn of the century, we could realistically no longer use it as a standard for currency because currency need was far ahead of gold production and reserves. William Jennings Bryan could see clearly enough that we were going to be "crucified on a cross of gold" if we didn't change. Once finance is removed from a specie base, it is no longer a zero sum entity subject to control by a single person.

Thus the "Captains" controlled industry by controlling the fundamental commodities of oil, gold, iron, coal and rubber. They rose to power with physical control of materials and information. What information they used, they used as a commodity. "If I have it, they don't." They controlled absolutely in monarchical terms and sentiment arose against the abuses of power. It is interesting to speculate on what would have happened had they been allowed to proceed, unfettered by trust busting regulation.

The Inevitability of Autocratic Demise

Where Henry Ford was an autocratic innovator and changed the nature of car production by bringing it all under one roof, his absolute personal control brought the company into dangerous trouble by hanging onto the Model T long after it was obsolete. In its time the Model T was only an adequate car, made popular by the price. There were better cars available when it was introduced, and by the time it was discontinued, it was a relic. The point is that Henry Ford's genius was in the initial control of commodities for production - not in understanding carmaking and marketing - and by not relinquishing control to those who understood, he almost ruined his company. He had moved beyond his observable world. His company survived as a modern corporation, not as his personal fiefdom.

Just as the world economy grew quickly beyond the limits of the gold standard at the turn of the century, changing the nature of the world of finance, the other "basic" industries changed as well - all moved beyond the simple observable world. The steel industry no longer meant cast iron and soft steel; it became chrome steel, and nickel steel and high-carbon steel - items which were no longer directly inspectable by the magnate who had to remove himself from absolute control and believe someone else. A similar change occurred in oil.   Simple observable fluid separation gave way to catalytic crackers where hydrocarbons could be reshaped by heat, pressure and additives. The boss in both steel and oil is the process engineer who controls the forces. Thus, the giant personal companies of the "Captains of Industry" would have been transformed without the trustbusters, simply in different ways. Ironically, the companies which came to symbolize the industrial might of America, came to true power as the engine of the economy only after the founding autocrats had given way to the continuing institutional corporate control of industry, rather than the previous personal control.

Transformation of Information Control

The transformation from autocracy to corporate entity represents one change in the control and use of information. However, the basic idea of a top-down patriarchal hierarchy with a zero sum mentality remained firmly intact. With competition as the espoused ideal, the corporations and individuals within corporations fought for dominance like so many baboons in a troop, or roosters in a coop - no matter that the Darwinian analogy of natural struggle for survival was inappropriate for humans. We initially succeeded by cooperating, not competing. The cost of "winning at all costs" is nearly "all cost" at present. In human terms, the damage is uncountable; in environmental terms, we are at the point of not being able to breathe the air, drink the water, or dispose of the garbage. Yet people even now hark to the Lombardi adage of a time past, "Winning is not the best thing, it is the only thing." Of course, as a concept, winning is relative and subject to redefinition, and I think we are fast approaching the point where cooperatively cleaning up our act and working for survival will be considered winning.

Nature demands that the leader of the animal pack be the most physically dominant individual as a means of passing successful genes into the genetic pool. However, for humans, who lack the teeth and claws of the animal world, success has always been predicated on teamwork, facilitated by communication. The dominant was the one who could skillfully communicate and convince the others to do his bidding. Thus, from the beginnings of formal education, rhetoric - the art of effective communication - was the key subject. Other areas of study might be added, but they were peripheral to the necessity of communication.

Vertical versus Horizontal, Connected Structure

With the advent of industrialism, generalized education and generalized communication were not only not needed, they were not desired. Specialization for jobs demanded specialization of education and the fragmentation of communication so that soon only those in a given field could understand one another. With such isolation, lack of communication soon meant attributing a lack of importance to other areas and a disregard of the consequences of actions in toto. Having lost a view of the whole, we see the present chaos.

As noted, communication demands bidirectionality, taking into account, for effectiveness, the audience of the communication - contrasting with industrial hierarchy, where orders are given and response is not desired. However, just as actual jobs are currently seeing a convergence in the form of computer use, whether for architectural drafters or diesel mechanics, the managerial organization of corporations is shifting. The vertical structure of smokestack industries is giving way to a webbed, network structure, led by the information technologies. In a vertical structure, orders are given monodirectionally from the top; in a webbed structure, information is exchanged for mutual benefit.

Where this is most obvious is in information technologies. The development of software demands only access to, and language knowledge of, a computer. The software developer needs a business operations manager for marketing, and the relation between the developer and manager is mutual; both need the other and must communicate. Because neither is tied by space or time, they can work according to their own schedule and dominance cannot be enforced from the top down. With a disagreement, one person would simply say, "I'll find another manager (or software developer)."

Less obvious horizontal structure comes in the form of employee owned organizations such as America West Airlines. When each person is enfranchised by the operation, each has a stake in smooth operation and all people become important, not just those "at the top". Reservations people are important as are baggage handlers, pilots, managers and attendants: each depends on the other for job continuity and therefore, none can be more important. This contrasts sharply with General Motors buying out its former director, H. Ross Perot, at a huge premium (while trying to get union concessions with a poverty plea) because they did not like a maverick voice saying the organization was poorly run.

In short, information is not zero sum, but rather additive. The software developer and business manager both gain by the sharing and cooperation of their communication. Likewise America West does not have labor trouble because "labor and management" work as one integrated unit and share the profits. Playing off the old maxim of "what's good for General Motors is good for America", one might speculate that when GM becomes a consensus organization, then America will have turned a corner.

Adding to the grid established in the introduction, we find that type and organization of work shifts with each period:

Table 3.1 - Four Cultural Periods

Oral Culture	**Traditional Literacy**
Self Represents Culture	Self Consciousness
Truth as Wholes	Conditional Analysis
Coordinate Syntax	Subordinate Syntax
All connected in work	Specialization of jobs
Unified in work	Development of hierarchy
Post-Industrial Communication	**Industrial Literacy**
Self Seeks Identity	Self in Isolation
Comprehensive Analysis	Organizational Analysis
Compound-Complex Syntax	Subordinate Syntax
Reconnecting of Job Skills	Isolation of Jobs
Network Accountability	Vertical Hierarchy

It appears that we are coming back to a realization that integration is more productive than dis-integration. A good case in point is Harley-Davidson, the American manufacturer of large motorcycles. Until the Sixties, it was the dominant motorcycle in the U.S. With the Japanese entry in the Sixties, Harley had to redefine itself. It seemingly could not compete with the high-performance, low cost Japanese bikes, and it increasingly lost market share. Having been bought by AMF, a corporation which knew nothing of motorcycles, it came close to extinction. The bikes were so shoddy in construction that showrooms had to put cardboard under brand new bikes because they already leaked oil. With a buyout from AMF by motorcycle enthusiast businessmen, Harley management asked the workers how to improve the product. The answer was simple, "Let us build good bikes." Workers know good from bad in parts and construction, but if they are told to use all parts good or bad so there is no waste, pennies may be saved at the expense of the company. With workers taking an active role in advising the company, Harley rebounded so strongly that it asked that government sanctions against large Japanese bikes be lifted early.

The integration of a Harley-Davidson, America West or the myriad small software companies shows the benefit of communication and bidirectional accountability. Because that structure is not vertical, we should not think up and down accountability, but rather around, connected as equals: each part accounts to the other - not the bottom rung to the top. The needs of each must be viewed for mutual benefit as each part is one within the organization. Such mutual accountability carries the feel of symbiosis such that the organization sees its needs as organic.

Where in mankind's beginning, oral communication allowed societal organization and survival, the introduction of literacy allowed specialization of knowledge which eventually led to isolation in industrial hierarchy. That very isolation has led to a search for better means of communication on the personal, corporate and societal levels, and we find a new pattern emerging: the network. The complementary integration of parts of the network has not spread evenly throughout the culture however.

CHAPTER 4

Network Culture:
From Melting Pot to Salad Bar

Throughout the postwar period, the United States has led the world, though not with the imperial hegemony of the Greeks, Persians, Romans or British. With the most telephones, biggest houses, most televisions, most cars, most energy consumed per capita, the most consumption, the greatest production, we set an example which the rest of the world has been striving to duplicate and now the largest question facing that world is, "What next?" It cannot continue.

A funny thing happened though. As our economy prospered, the relative unity of the depression and war years gave way to fractiousness in economic, religious, and racial terms. Mirrored in our schools, the lack of consensus has destroyed the notion of the common good, and with it, many of the images which previously united the country. Whether or not these images were good, or right, or true, or really the ideal is of little import in this discussion; the fact they came to be questioned is the import.

If the Melting Pot is the American ideal, then perhaps we need to examine the cook and kitchen. Anyone who has ever attended a large cooking pot has seen the white froth covering a layer of fat over the body which sits on a burnt base at the bottom. The economic and racial suggestions contained in the analogy are inescapable with the white and fat at the top and the brown and black at the bottom, but such a simplistic horizontal separation does little to clarify current educational discussion.

Nationality

The cliche of the Melting Pot, made of English, Irish, Dutch, French, Spanish, Italian, German, and Slavic blended into a happy monocultural family by the blessings of the New World, sounds so sentimentally appealing that it is hard to attack. We have always been multicultural - and not just in the superficial category of national origin, but in the more important category of expectation and outlook.

As to national origin, the blending in the U.S. of the various groups is virtually unparalleled in history. Just read the names on football jerseys, in the credits at the end of a television show or movie, or on the faculty of large universities. Demonstrably, we have a fair cross-section of the world as to nationality. Furthermore, the majority of the football players, show business workers, and university faculty members belong to the dominant "culture" - that is, that ill-defined Anglo-based agreement which binds the U.S. legally, linguistically and, in broad terms, culturally.

In essence, those who wanted to participate in the U.S. learned the rules, learned the language and got on with life whether or not they kept their native language and culture alive or not. Being a part of Senn Fein, LULAC, the Sons of Italy, the NAACP, or the Hamtramack Polish American Club, did and does not preclude one from participating in mainstream America. Linguistic subcultures do not interfere with nationality if the nation and its participants accept variety. Switzerland has been a peaceful, prosperous nation for 800 years despite having three linguistic cultures. On the other hand, the Irish have been at war for just as long. Monolingualism is clearly not sufficient to sustain a nation just as cultural pluralism will not destroy a nation.

Expectation and Outlook

On the other hand, if we examine expectation and outlook, rather than nationality, we find a quite different picture. Dating from the very beginning of the New World, the participants had different goals and different means for reaching those goals. The Protestant English, Dutch and Germans came for commercial reasons; the Catholic Spanish and French came for the greater glory of God and King, and, whatever money they could make, so much the better. Nobody asked the Indians, who got taken for a ride, or Blacks, who got brought along for the ride.

Colonial   Assimilation

Assimilation demands interaction with two different groups finding a mutual point of identification where the lesser group blends with the more dominant. The English colonies easily dominated the East Coast with the British Empire's support and the assimilation by trade of the other groups.   Because the Dutch and Germans were there for commercial purposes, it behooved them to trade with the dominant power whomever that might be.

In the Western U.S., the story was different. With the Crusades to the Holy Land a thing of the past, Spain put its Catholic zeal into converting the New World with the same fanaticism which marked the Crusades and Inquisition. Conversion or death leaves little room for negotiation or assimilation.   At the time John Smith founded Jamestown, Virginia, Santa Fe, New Mexico had already been the regional capital for several years. The King of Spain made land grants just as did the King of England, but there is a major difference: many Spanish land grants have remained and are still legally binding in areas such as New Mexico.   Portions of Albuquerque, as well as large segments of the state of New Mexico still have the grants in effect, with benefits accruing to those who are decendants of the original beneficiaries. People possessing kingly title to their land and speaking their own imperial language find little reason to assimilate with those considered invaders - despite the fact that Native Americans view both as invaders.

Recent Immigrants

On the other hand, the recent immigrants, legal and illegal, are not invited to become members and have formed a semi-permanent subclass of menial laborers. Many Anglos snidely comment on the situation by saying, "When the Irish, Italians, Polacks, and Swedes came over, they went to work, took jobs 'at the bottom', rolled up their sleeves, got their hands dirty, learned the language and 'worked their way up'." Of course they did, but virtually everyone else got their hands dirty with hard work at that period too. One does not move up from cleaning bedpans in a hospital in the 1990s by simple apprenticeship to a doctor or nurse. One does not move from sweeping a K-Mart floor to management trainee just because a kindly manager sees promise, Dickens and Horatio Alger notwithstanding. Years of learning a language before education can commence, while at the same time having to support a family, precludes the good jobs that need education.

The major problem for immigrants is demonstrably that the family must be supported no matter whatever else happens. If education interferes with support, then education must go. Minimum wage jobs leave little leeway for extras such as education, even if that is really a necessity. Forty hours a week, 50 weeks a year means the wage earner gets a pre-tax $9,000 a year at $4.50 an hour. And we expect them to learn a language and get an education while keeping a family going on $6700 a year? Even at the least expensive state colleges, tuition, room, and board considerably exceeds $9000 for a single person, but we expect a whole family of immigrants to live on it, get educated, prosper and be thankful for the chance America is giving them.

The Disenfranchised

Historically, the dominant culture has not invited Indians and Blacks to assimilate, and now it seems hurt and affronted that many do not want to assimilate. After centuries of being shot, hung, herded, imported, sold, lied to, and excluded, in a ten year period, people of color moved from being in the back of the bus to being courted to fill job quotas for legalistic, Anglo-based, affirmative action. And white folks are surprised that children of color have a hard time learning "rational" Anglo culture? Branded disadvantaged or learning disabled, the children once again get shunted off for "special" education.

Where linguistic culture will not, of itself, divide a nation, the separation of people from the dominant culture by their frame of reference can. The 1990s are not the 1890s. A present day Spanish-speaking farmworker in California's central valley is not in the same position as a Norwegian farmworker in Wisconsin in the 1890s. The Norwegian had hopes of working hard and someday getting his own farm, or going into business for himself selling to other farmers. The Spanish-speaking farmworker of California will never save enough money to buy land for a farm; he's lucky to have enough to eat and a beat up car, forget a house, medical insurance and retirement. As for business, can he get a bank loan with no experience? no collateral? no education? As a nation, the U.S. must decide whether it will break the cycle of the disenfranchised and provide the education and incentive to participate more broadly.

Stirring the Pot

Though the simplicity of the previous discussion necessarily leaves out many subtleties, it identifies the large horizontal race and class based segmentation of modern America. It says nothing, however, about the far more divisive vertical segmentation. At a time when the U.S. is coming to terms with the legal realities of inclusive egalitarianism rather than simply mouthing platitudes of all men being equal, many people are choosing exclusive, divergent ways of life.

The divergence of lifestyle goes far beyond the rekindling of ethnic spirit often expressed at city festivals with slogans such as "Erin Go Bragh" or "You Betcha Dupa, I'm Polish." In like manner, it goes beyond the rebirth of regionalism whether on bumper stickers such as the Texas oil patch comment, "Let the Yankees freeze in the dark." The new divergence is in the choice of cultural time.

The Cultures of Time

The Reagan era saw a schism in time. When Reagan took office in 1980, his ascension marked a new period. He came into office speaking of the need to hold dear the traditional nuclear family and the traditional values associated with it, while at the same time speaking of secret technologies and laser beam wonder weapons. No matter that the traditional father, mother, and their own kids type family was not the most numerous type of family anymore or that Reagan's several families bore no resemblance to his talk. Nor that the wonder weapons were only scientific musings at the time. Once before in this century for similar reasons, a leader took power by praising the myth of the past while simultaneously appealing to the technology of the future. Hitler brought us the world war; fortunately Reagan only presided over cultural conflict. Clearly, reality has little to do with one's perception - rather perception has everything to do with one's reality.

By appealing to the distant past, Reagan tapped into current malaise by projecting that the old days must have been better. When? Vietnam? Civil Rights actions? the Cold War? Korea? World War II? The Depression? Coolidge, Harding,& Hoover? Sounds like a lot of laughs when the Hollywood/Washington PR machines are turned off. Perhaps we need to go back to no plumbing or electricity, complete with polio, anthrax, plague, and smallpox to find the good old days. However, as writers and orators have known since Greece: reality doesn't sell, perceptions do. People perceived the present as lousy and figured the past must have been better without a second thought.

The second temporal conflict of the Reagan era was the promissory materialism of Star Wars. Not only was a weapon system named for a movie by the Hollywood President, but it was sold as much on the benefits to be derived by the technology as for the defensive reality. Just as Teflon emerged as a product of the race to the moon, similar untold products were promised if only enough defense research money was spent to foil the "Evil Empire." People believed the good old days of the past: they bought the promise of material good in the future - the Teflon President had arrived.

The Three Bifurcated Cultures

Part of the success of Reagan was the timing of his Presidency. The turmoil of the Sixties had given way to the listlessness of the Seventies. There was no revolution, but neither was there resolution. Protest may have died with the students at Kent State, but Blacks, Hispanics, women, and gays would not go back in the closet and pushed America to face the its racism and inequality. The global village and future shock became terms of common parlance. It was not the good old days.

The "culture of the future" sought ultimate communication but found itself split between the physical and metaphysical worlds. On the one hand, micro-electronics opened new vistas in physical communication. Not since Gutenberg had such a revolution occurred. On the other side, global computer and television networks, demanded a redefinition of the way in which man thought of himself. The one-ness of humanity is evident when the nightly news broadcast in Peoria comes live from China with commentary from Moscow, London, and Washington. The one group viewed the future as the technology of communication where the other saw it as human communication.

The "culture of the present" is equally split within the industrial worldview. One group pushes for a more inclusive definition of industrial social democracy while the other insists on industrial measurement - system design. While one faction of the Senate debates the merits of catastrophic health care, the other side insists that the effects are impossible to measure. The debate goes on.

The "culture of the past" babbles of the good old days with three voices. There are old-fashioned conservatives interested in preserving the good for our progeny rather than blindly accepting present untested gobbledegook. Then there are the truly reactionary religious groups who want to go back to the ideal of the "City on the Hill" with God, country and home. Finally, there is an emerging group dedicated to the Tory ideal of an orderly society where everyone knows his place and firmly remains there. The past is clearly present in the U.S.

With the past, present and future all contending for the limited space of the American psyche, many subgroupings and admixtures could be cited. The mixture of any ethnic, age, economic, or language group with the three time cultures yields a distinct variant suitable for newspaper or dissertation discussion, or maybe a sitcom on TV, depending on your preference.

Variety Within the Culture

The variety available in the U.S. at present was unimaginable only a few years ago. Economics and communication have worked together to bring the change. The prosperity of the middle class has ensured a discretionary income great enough to propel service industries into being the largest employers in the country. Alvin Toffler notes in *The Third Wave* that industrial civilization peaked in the decade surrounding 1955 when white-collar and service workers outnumbered blue-collar workers for the first time. And at the same time that communication technology has allowed custom design of physical products, human communication has assured an awareness of the world. Just look at the restaurant page of any large city. Oriental food used to mean generic Chinese. Now, in Oriental, just within Chinese cuisine, one must know Mandarin, Hunan, Szetchuan, and Cantonese, not to mention several types of Japanese, Indian, and Thai cuisine, Korean, Vietnamese, Mongolian, and Malaysian/Indonesian. Similar expansions have occurred with Middle Eastern, and Latin American - Carribean foods, as well as U.S. regional cuisine.

Examples abound: TV used to mean the three networks. Now for non-cable houses it means twice that, ten times that many for cable houses, and hundreds of channels for dish owners. Jeans used to mean one or two cuts of Lee or Levi, but now one has every size and cut possible for men, women, boys and girls whether normal, large, tall, petite, fashion, work, or depending on personality, with or without sequins, rhinestones or crystals. Should we look at the vegetable and fruit counter at the grocery store, the vacations advertised at travel agencies, or the range of financial instruments available?

Within the smorgasbord of cultural variety, why should we expect education to remain fixed in the 19th century, the 1930s, or 1950s? Education is no more a static product than any other aspect of culture whether, culinary, couture, or financial. People look at education and bemoan the lack of a central core, or comment on the variety of courses offered which has given rise to the term "shopping mall schools," but they fail to look at the underlying reality of the educational system. A single program of study has not been part of mainstream American education this century on the one hand, and the proliferation of courses in shopping mall schools is not true variety, rather it is like adding items to the menu - all within the Mandarin cuisine. True variety in education will recognize multiculturalism and the need for comprehensive, connected education and use it for greater understanding of the individual in the world, not simply add another divisive track to the already splintered "standard" curriculum.

Temporal Cultures and the Schools

Strident mouthpieces representing the cultures of past, present and future all lay current claim to the schools, saying that America depends on them to remain great, good, progressive, strong and a host of other adjectives. The traditional, industrial, and communicative cultures at work now, however, did not arise in a vacuum, but rather within a historical context. Perhaps by stepping back and examining in greater detail the cultures, their operative metaphors, and interactions as they developed over time, we might see a clearer course for the schools.

CHAPTER 5

Defining Educational Metaphors: The Traditional, Industrial, and Communicative

Having looked briefly at the multiple cultures at work in the United States at the current time, it would be well to look at the development and interaction over time of the traditional, industrial and communicative cultures with regard to education. One means of examining the three areas in a meaningful way is to look at the operative educational metaphor for each. When we compare the metaphors, many of the current conflicts in education become clearer both in the overt view of the condition of education as well as the underlying assumptions about what education is and should be. First, though, we should clearly define our terms.

First and Second Level Metaphors

Metaphors are generally considered figures of speech in which one entity stands for another in an implied comparison, illuminating or amplifying the given item beyond what can be understood with pure denotative exposition. In simplest form, what I call the first level, metaphors are confined to a single sentence, as in "John is a bull of a football player"; however, metaphors can easily be extended to form the structural basis of a poem or prose work. While often studied formally in poetry or writing classes, metaphor occurs equally in common speech. The sports pages are filled with metaphors such as "the bomb" in football or "the slam" in basketball. In fact, both of these expressions have been so used that they carry little metaphoric impact in and of themselves, but are quite representative of the larger, or what I term, second level, metaphors of their respective games. These larger metaphors operate in a fashion which tends to shape not only the way an activity is described by writers, but how it is even viewed by spectators.

In the sports analogy, the metaphors both describe and shape the game, with football terminology tending to military metaphor: the bomb, the blitz, the defensive stand, field generals and trench warfare. Basketball, on the other hand, uses terminology of intimidation: the slam, in your face, dominating the paint, rejecting the ball, driving the lane, and charging.

Virtually every sport or activity can be similarly typed by an operative metaphor. The point in discussing sports is to show that the very metaphors used to describe the game actually help to define the game for participant and spectator alike. The metaphors do not occur by accident. Football is a strategic game with set plays, rather like military campaigns. The offense makes a move and the defense counters, causing the offense to reassess and continue the same strategy or change. In contrast, basketball is a game of domination whether played on the street or in the NBA. The team that "drives the lane" or "dominates the glass" will probably win. "Going to the iron" insures that your team will score baskets, shoot free throws, and put the other team in foul trouble. Players and fans have learned the operations of each game and interact, giving the home team an advantage.

The learning of such metaphorical information is part of enculturation whether that information is knowing the proper time to shake hands, the succession of British monarchs, or the line-up of the 1968 World Series Champions. In each case, the information known or not known will determine acceptance within certain groups and/or guidelines. For shaking hands, sex, age, ethnicity, and education are all mediating factors, determining whether hands will be shaken after a short or long period of absence, several times during the day or never. Such basic cultural information is assumed, and awkwardness only occurs whenever a person is not familiar with the expected custom: whether through ignorance or shyness. In contrast to knowing the British monarchical succession or the 1968 World Series Champion's line-up, where the information is overtly learned, hand shake information is learned through social observation and interaction. However, equally gauche to shaking hands incorrectly in some circles would be to think that James I established the Restoration or, in others, that Al Kaline played second base. Whether overtly learned or simply observed, information must be used meaningfully to fit the appropriate social circumstance.

Social information such as handshaking is usually learned with a few gaffs and then reduced to automaticity - to be used on the appropriate occasion. Overtly learned information such as monarchical succession or player line-up rarely reduces to such automaticity and needs the use of mnemonic devices for reproduction, however inexact. Appropriate use of information, however, is always expected and means metaphorically that one belongs; incorrect usage labels one as an inferior or outsider and is greeted with jeers of derision for misplacing ballplayers or subtle knowing looks if one misses the order of monarchs.

Sociologists and psychologists have known for years that people are guided by metaphors at both conscious and unconscious levels. The luxury car or second home stand as metaphors of success in the material world while dream symbols represent another aspect of reality in the unconscious. It is important to note that metaphoric representation occurs at both conscious and unconscious levels, shaping the ways events are both perceived and integrated.

Learning theorists have understood only too well the ramifications of multilevel processing and have embraced or denied such mentalist conceptions. Behaviorists, by assuming only that which can be measured is valid, reject the reality of the metaphor as a mental construct leading to further understanding. Cognitivists, on the other hand, see such mental constructs as schemas which help to organize otherwise random information into logical patterns for current knowledge and later retrieval.

Such schematic representation guides not only the acquisition of explicit information about education (or any other subject), but, to a large extent, controls how we use that information, thereby turning information into knowledge. The metaphors used in reference to schools and learning have changed as schools and the idea of learning themselves have changed.

The Metaphors of Education

Traditional Education:
Physical Exercise or Mind = Muscle

School has traditionally been the conservator of cultural experience. The Paideia of Greece was literally the enculturation of Athenian values; the trivium of grammar, rhetoric and logic preserved classical ideals well into the Middle Ages; and finally, the veneration of the classics in the modern world established the Latin Grammar School as the curricular ideal. In this latter model, Latin was construed as the basis of English as well as good training for the mind. No matter that no one ever used Latin in normal communication - it was the mark of an educated man. As conservator of experience, traditional education reified the values of the society, reflecting a static view of the world (sometimes only conservative as in Greece, sometimes backward as with the Scholastics in the 12th and 13th centuries in Europe). Because traditional society is largely unchanging, and possesses a static view of the world, traditional education concentrates on learning the body of material which makes one "educated"; therefore, the instructional emphasis is on rote memorization of the fixed curricular corpus of cultural information whether in the oral tradition of Homeric Greece, the 1000 years in Europe after the height of the Roman Empire, or America in the 18th and 19th centuries.

Traditional learning meant memorizing large quantities of information however difficult or pointless. Education was not meant to be entertainment; in fact, it was felt that if work was congenial, then it had no educational value. In 19th century America, children were routinely given "grinders" or difficult problems to solve, based on the belief that assiduous tasks developed different faculties. Geometry was supposed to develop logic just as Greek and Latin were felt to develop language ability. Such development was based on the Lockean notion of faculties of mind and character which could be augmented by sufficient discipline or dissipated by a similar lack. It was felt that repetitious drilling built discipline and character much as repeated exercise built strong muscles. Thus "good students" persevered in sometimes meaningless, always arduous, tasks while others eventually left school.

The principle of discipline is central to traditional societies because of the power structure which dictates that the elite rules over the many whose sweat and muscle keep the society producing. Whether one examines tribal life with one strong leader, religious life with one ruling prelate, or the ruling elite of the European monarchies of the previous centuries, absolute power is concentrated at the top and the rest of the populous is expected to obey. Thus, in organizational terms, one finds an individual or cluster over the other people mediated only by groups such as the military. At the bottom, people have the rough equality of little power and little hope of gaining it.

The Physical Exercise Metaphor

Traditional education in the U.S., with the tenets of faculty psychology and the idea of mental discipline, operated as though the mind were a muscle which developed by repetition of exercises. When combined with the static nature of information in traditional society, the exercise metaphor ensured that information was memorized rather than synthesized. Thus Latin, for example, could be looked upon as an important subject even though it had little bearing upon daily life in America. English has Latin words, but English as a word order language has almost nothing to do at the syntactic level with Latin, a declined case language. Furthermore, because of the influence of the classics, English rhetoric also came to be modelled on Greek and Latin although that was a particularly ill fit. The great periodic Latinate sentences of Lincoln at Gettysburg had little to do with the vernacular being spoken by members of his audience.

In traditional society, powered as it is by human muscle, the individual has a responsibility to work for his, as well as society's good. It is not surprising, therefore, to find discipline as an important aspect of school. The elaboration of discipline as a tenet of schooling came about with the support of faculty psychology which said that strong mind and character was built by hard work, whether or not that work had meaning. To this end, the teacher stood as the arbiter of good with both the student and content being subject to his authority or whim. Thus schooling stood for a moral good in developing character, and exercised the mind as though it were a muscle in achieving its goal.

Industrial Education:
Industrial Behavior or Mind = Machine

Outside of the elite Latin grammar schools, traditional education in America has been characterized by the same utilitarianism that shaped the rest of America. Locke's philosophical materialism, Darwinian laissez-faire economics, and a wide-open frontier dictated that most people got enough education to perform a job, earn a living and support a family - in short, to survive.

However with the growth of industrialism, marked by the specialization of the workforce, urbanization, and the increase in knowledge, intensive education for the elite and minimal education for the masses was no longer feasible. With the need for a change in the educational system, the metaphor changed as well. The physical exercise metaphor of mind equals a muscle, reflecting a human powered society, gave way to the mind equals machine metaphor of industrial society. Furthermore, we must keep in mind that machines are created for special purposes and have a limited use.

This shift is most clearly illustrated by two reports. The report of the Committee on Secondary School Studies, commonly known as the Committee of Ten, in 1893 stressed mental discipline, holding that education should contribute to "strong and effective mental training." Furthermore, they recommended that education in high school should be geared toward college, even though fewer than ten percent of students even graduated from high school. In contrast the report published by the Commission on the Reorganization of Secondary Education in 1918 said that the Seven Cardinal Principles of the high school curriculum should be: health, command of fundamental processes, worthy home membership, vocational efficiency, civic participation, worthy use of leisure time and ethical character. In 25 years the entire orientation of American education had changed from the use of subject matter to develop mental faculties to having the individual fit into society with civic, moral development and productive job ability. The nebulous "fundamental processes" is the only hint that school is for book learning of subject matter, the rest is social accommodation whether for ethical development or vocational use.

Curriculum design in the new era went in two directions: the first being the business-efficiency or management orientation which stressed the utilitarian needs of a growing commercial society. The second group was the Progressive Movement, characterized by a belief in individual development within the framework of democratic social competence.

The business model curriculum embraced the American ideals that hard work and individuality will create success and that education should provide the vocational competence for productive citizenship. As part of the new industrial paradigm, the business model made use of "science" by applying statistics to the new field of psychological measurement. While promulgating the idea of upward mobility by education -- stay in school and get a better paying job -- it tended to reinforce the status quo with its social stratification. Under this model, workers just became more efficient workers or were taught the skills needed for corporate America

The influence on curriculum centered at the high school level in developing a track system. Where high schools previously had had tracks, there had been no special curricular emphasis for those students for whom high school was terminal. The assumption in the traditional model was that the material designed for college was good for everyone. The business model redefined the purpose of the high school, splitting the tracks for the college bound and the vocational. In particular, the Smith-Hughes Act of 1917 provided federal funds for vocational education and set up regulatory boards for inspection of schools receiving funds, reflecting the business rather than the educational tone of the endeavor. No longer was education an end in itself as it had been under the traditional model: education was to serve the industry of America. The definition of education in traditional society where one became "educated" to one's level gave way to the notion of one becoming vocationally competent as part of being a good citizen.

With Dewey's *Democracy and Education* defining the broad scope, progressives espoused education as a part of life rather than exercise in preparation for life, content that is not simply organized data but gives meaning to social life, learning as reorganization of experience, and interest as the basis of learning. While progressive curriculum aims appear quite different from traditional aims, in fact, they are a redefinition of existing structures rather than a revolt. Traditional education had maintained that a good citizen should be able to read, write, have a good moral character and a disciplined mind; progressives redefined the citizen as showing individual growth and exercising democratic skills.

Progressive instruction redefined the nature of the classroom with its participatory learning and emphasis on the learner learning rather than the subject matter being memorized. This redefinition, a movement away from mechanical rote ingestion of information to a demand that the student understand material, required that material be presented in a fashion so that students could form wholes. Traditional disciplines were replaced by units or projects integrating various aspects of a subject. Thus a unit might be "Where you live" with discussion of geography, climate, work, and sociology, using teaching activities such as games, trips, and group discussions.

Given the changes after the Civil War, but coming into focus after the turn of the century, it was inevitable that evolutionary redefinition of schools would take place. The business-efficiency model demanded that education fulfill the needs of industrial society with a content-centered curriculum, eschewing study for the sake of becoming educated. With strict measurement for maximum efficiency, they saw behavioral psychology as the means for increasing productivity in the school. The

Progressives changed education by introducing a student-centered curriculum, and emphasizing the enfranchisements of all the people forming a democracy. Together they discredited faculty psychology and the concomitant idea of mental discipline.

The reality which came out of the combination of the two reform movements created conflict right into the 1960s. Curriculum change occurred but not in a uniform fashion. The track system of the business model was accepted as was the concept of top-down control by mental measurement and the behaviorist specification of testing observable learning behaviors. Thus, the infrastructure of schools was determined by the business model of education for the obvious reason that it was custom designed for efficient mass administration. Large school systems needed the industrial administrative hierarchy as they increasingly became businesses. Each aspect of school was reduced to the quantitative boxes favored by administrators who want uncomplicated decisions. On the other hand, some of the teaching and curriculum ideas of the Progressives were adopted: student-centered classes and material presented in a manner conducive to student interest (in contrast to the "grinders" of traditional education).

Conflicts arose between administrators who sought the neat package promised by business and teachers who realized that a neat package was not necessarily the best education. The conflict was fought as usual in the classroom. Were teachers teaching students or content? If they taught to student need, what of the standard tests? Teach to the test? That was the usual answer enforced from the top. The battle continues.

This was education by hierarchy. Traditional education was decentralized in the sense that teachers ruled their classrooms, and students knew they had no recourse. There was not a fixed curriculum or standardized testing because it was not needed. Essentially everyone knew that becoming educated meant being familiar with several hundred books and the concepts contained therein. In looking back, the decentralized education of traditional times seems so simple and direct, it is little wonder people desire to go back.

In saying that industrial education is hierarchical education, the point is that it is administered in industrial fashion. Each state set up a Department of Education which set certification guidelines for teachers, administrators, and schools alike. Teachers answer to principals just as floor workers answer to the shop foremen. In turn, principals answer to the school system supervisors as foremen answer to production supervisors. The school superintendent answers to the state administrators as production supervisors answer to corporate management. Very direct, and *very* unidirectional. Student> teacher > principal > school supervisors > school superintendent > state board

>state superintendent.   There is little provision for downward accountability.

The Industrial Metaphor

As industrial society needed industrial workers in great quantity, a relatively uniform product had to come from schools. Furthermore, the future workers must possess a uniform outlook which was suited to industrial life. Simply expanding the traditional form of education was neither desirable or practical. Study of Greek and Latin was both time consuming and of little practical use for industrial workers. Additionally, liberal arts education was not conducive to keeping people working at repetitive jobs which offered little chance for advancement. Thus, the small scale one-room school house or private academy gave way to the factory-like brick block school with students in lines and classrooms in lines, mirroring the assembly-line mentality taking over America.

In like manner the psychology of schools changed with the physical plant.   The faculty psychology of traditional education, which emphasized personal character development through disciplined work, gave way to the twin cults of mental measurement and behaviorist psychology. If students were to be an industrial commodity, they must be measured and sorted by objective, observable standards. No longer could a teacher say that a student learned something, but that the student demonstrated a measurable behavior. The teacher moved from the arbiter of the good in traditional education to measurers of bodies for retention of subject matter content.

The industrial metaphor of mind as machine applies to the business-efficiency and progressive movement differently but equally effectively. For the business group, the notion is obviously assembly line education (or in many cases training) in order to get parts to build the industrial machine. Just as people were assigned roles in a factory, working on lines, at a certain measurable speed, so were students assigned classes, molded to a certain form, measured and stamped with the inspectors' approval or not - all with the greatest possible speed. Little heed was paid to the individual; he was just a cog in the system. The traditional curriculum was replaced for utilitarian reasons to free up time for more useful commercial subjects - not as a rejection of the essential values of the society. Thus the college bound moved ahead with little change of studies while the workers tracked into commercial subjects. The industrial metaphor evolved from the traditional as societal need showed itself from the first modern high school after the Civil War to the pinnacle in the 1950s.

For the progressives, the industrial metaphor is useful as the movement rose with urban industrial democracy. Before industrialism, the point of view emphasizing individual development for the masses could not have occurred because individual development was the passtime of the upper-class. With a rising middle-class, the development of the individual went in hand with democratic socialization, mirroring the events of the society where the labor movement pushed for worker rights and participation in democratic dialogue.

The industrial metaphor stands to the physical exercise metaphor as a simple outgrowth of the new educational needs of the society on the one hand and the social needs of the changed society on the other. No longer was the physical exercise of man what moved society; industrial machine might took over for the strong arms of the ploughman and smith. The individual of strength had been subsumed into the organization.

Communicative Education:
The Computer or Mind = Electronic Network

Growth in communication has signalled each new cultural plateau, with each era becoming shorter than the previous. Mankind was preliterate for hundreds of thousands of years. Self-conscious literacy has existed for 2500 years, and communicative literacy only for forty.

The ancient empires ruled by dint of the monarch having messengers bring news from the outlying areas and then dispatching them with instructions. On foot or horseback, by chariot or boat, the empires labored to communicate. Rome brought system to this kind of communication, building roads and developing the infrastructure to facilitate the movement of messengers. However, even at its peak in Rome, this system was ponderous in operation, elitist in nature, and limited in scope.

Despite the drawbacks, no alternative to the use of trained scribes existed until the printing press in the 1440s. As has been well documented, the printing press changed the nature of communication, by providing the means for universal literacy. Increasingly, with information available to the masses, power came to those who controlled the flow. Thus within a generation of its invention, Luther and Calvin led the reformation in changing the view toward the church; Columbus and Magellan changed the view toward the physical world; and Copernicus showed the earth as part of the universe and not the center. The growth of knowledge fueled the rise of modern nation states with their colonial ambitions, the divorce of church and state, and the analysis of the universe with the scientific method.

Where the invention of the printing press began mass communication, the advent of electrical devices initiated practically instantaneous mass communication. With the invention of the telegraph (1830s), the telephone (1876) by Bell, and radio (1895) by Marconi, space was collapsed by the temporal immediacy of information exchange. However, not until the development of the transistor (1948) and computer (1946) d4id this communication take on its current importance.

Historically, communication has meant talking, writing, or transportation or the means by which people could accomplish those activities. Present personal communication has been augmented by numerous devices from computer modems to fax machines to cellular telephones and satellite TV. However, the commencement of electronic communication has added a new meaning to communication and meant a revision of the way the world is organized. Electrical devices provide instant signals; electronics provide control to communication. This cybernetic dimension of communication demands a two-way circuit: information is sent out and a reassessment is made when the signal returns. The input- output reassessment is control and is the basis of computer circuitry in operation, made possible by the speed of transistor switching. Certainly, people can speak more easily and inexpensively over long distance now than in 1935 and television is better than in 1948, but the defining characteristic of this "information age" is that virtually every occupational field and seemingly every new object has communication and control devices. Not only do we find on the personal level, remote control TVs, home computers, electronically controlled fuel mixture of cars, the temperature controls of refrigerators and stoves, and the product identification bars at the grocery store, but virtually every level of industry from personnel processing, to automatic control of industrial instrumentation devices and robotics is guided by electronic measurement and control.

When people say the U.S. is an information economy, it does not mean we have stopped industrial production, though service jobs now outnumber industrial jobs, it means we now have a new principle by which we are organized. Just as industrialism outmoded the physical efforts of people and animals and reorganized society, communication and control devices have changed the organization of industry and, necessarily, society.

The Communicative Metaphor

The communication metaphor of the electronic network is appropriate at several levels. Just as industrial muscle displaced physical exercise as the engine of society so communication in computers and electronics has displaced purely mechanical industrialism. Furthermore, the awareness brought about by communication has shown that we are in relation with other people and other groups whether we like it or not. The two concepts of physical communication and human communication unite to form the central issue in the change going on in schools - that of the variety occurring in the U.S. As noted in the last chapter, from food to dress to financial instruments, Americans face a barrage of choices brought about by a greater awareness of the world and the communication devices needed to buy those items. Schools cannot remain static amid such change. They must create an ability in students to know how to learn in order to adapt to the change.

Conservatives, such as Hirsch, counter that students need facts in order to learn more facts, citing cognitive psychology. Most learning theorists would agree with such a statement in pure laboratory form - they call it "the given-new paradigm," i.e., one uses previously learned "given" knowledge to integrate new information. I note lab form because of the presumption that the fact to be learned is worthwhile and has meaning to the person learning it. If the student sees no relation between school facts and his/her life, the chances of learning are remote. That is the side of cognitive psychology that the educational conservatives miss - facts do not equal education - learning must revolve around meaning and the relation of that meaning to individual lives. Finding that meaning should be the central task of those currently working in education.

For example, if we take a fact such as "In 1492, Columbus sailed to America," what is the meaning? I originally wrote "discovered" but that shows my schooling and proves the point I am making here: we have a fact - what is the meaning? and why should someone know it? From the point of view of my Navajo students, Columbus could not discover something which Indians already occupied, but furthermore, the date signals the beginning of the end for the American Indian's traditional life. For the Spanish, it marked the beginning of a glorious new imperial chapter. For geographers, it further disproved the flat Earth theory. For navigators, it set new benchmarks. For epidemiologists, it sets the stage for massive epidemics. All of these answers have meaning because they put the fact in relation to other facts - rather than simply holding a fact in isolation as multiple choice formats do in school. Meaning demands relation, not just facts - or to paraphrase Frank Smith, "If you want facts, read the phone book, it has a lot of facts."

The Challenge of Filling the Communication Metaphor

The challenge of the communication metaphor of mind as neural network in the schools is that it is, of itself, a void - it is a set of relations. Just as language itself has no meaning, it is a vehicle for communication, a neural network only sets a pattern for communication.

In contrast, the traditional era's physical education metaphor of mind as muscle implicitly carries the message of known action for development. If one is to repeat an exercise, one must know the exercise, just as one knew there to be a corpus of material to be learned. Furthermore, in physical exercise even though inequality is a given, development is good for all. The child entering such a system knew what lay ahead at each step and could take some comfort or umbrage that others had suffered the same slings and arrows.

The mind as machine industrial metaphor limits expectations: man did not think; he behaved. He was shown to have a range of action, just as education specified limited behavior. This statistical observation obviated the individual, subsuming him into the larger societal unit. Again, the child entering such a system knew the choices, limited as they might be.

When we specify the communicative metaphor of mind as neural network - a set of relations - we do not have the idea of known action for development that was prevalent in traditional education, or the specified behavior of the industrial period. We are instead left with a void from which we must define a reality. Creating one's own definition demands a different kind of knowledge, a different set of skills than those which have gone before. Just as facts in traditional education gave way to measurable behaviorism industrial education, those behaviors are currently giving way to relations. We have moved from the traditional naming of the "thing" to the industrial measuring how the "thing acts in a given condition" to looking at "If the 'thing' acts this way now, what happens if we change conditions, and then what does it mean in larger scale, and finally, what are we to do with it?" It appears we are getting more abstract - less concerned with "thingness" and more concerned with "the spaces and relations between things" as we move across the different cultural plateaus.

Clearly, the move from physical reality to ideational reality changes the role of the school in several fashions: the role of information versus knowledge, the role of the school in the community and the role of the individual in relation to the community.

Concrete Examples of Communication Shift

Before industrialism, craftsmen created individual "things." These items were expensive and demanded careful attention in the making and the owning. One could not afford to waste "things" when they were individually produced. The individual design and building gave great artistic value to the best and functionality to the ordinary whether in the making of silverware, guns, or wagons.

Industrialism created mass "things", not so finely wrought at the top, but much more accessible to the general populace. Machine stamped eating utensils were not of the quality of the Revere Silver Works, but they were usable and available. Gunsmiths created individual artistic works, but even the common gun was expensive until Colt began mass producing them. The saying in the Old West, "God made man, but Sam Colt made them equal" was only possible when guns were readily available. In like manner, the Model T brought individual transportation to the masses.

Currently, we are witnessing a revolution in which we can have individual design on mass items, allowed by communication. As computer aided design (CAD) and computer aided manufacture (CAM) have moved from the rarified atmosphere of top-secret military installations to small business applications, we have gained the ability to specify desires and have them created automatically. The speed and efficiency of such processes allow greater specificity of design than previously possible as well as custom or near-custom production.

The additional benefit is the "what if" factor of computer modelling. When one had an idea in the past, one would have to build a prototype and test it to find how it would work. Now when one has an idea, it is possible to test it on a computer, saving the time and expense of creating the actual physical item. By saving both time and money, many more ideas can be examined - in fact, the variables themselves become the basis for design changes - that is, they can be held constant against secondary characteristics.

The automobile companies are a case in point. From the inception of a design idea, computers allow for modelling and prediction of each system of a car. For example, given an interior and exterior limitation, the CAD systems can not only give the most efficient shape, but indicate appropriate component assemblies and predict such items as fuel economy, braking distance, and handling characteristics for each given grouping of components. Now, if a person desires a larger engine for a given car, necessitating a change in front end size, then the computer can redesign that car with the new limitation. If, on the other hand, one adds a functional design limit such as a fuel economy, then the CAD system can show what is allowable to that limit.

When the CAD designed automobile is ready for production, computer controlled inventory assures that the proper parts arrive at the designated point at the precise time. Robotics often assemble large parts of the car and are integral to quality assurance of the final product.

In a different field such as architectural design, the human architectural drafter has been replaced by the computerized drafter, a computer operator, trained in drafting fundamentals. Where traditionally the drafter took the architect's specifications and drew up the appropriate blueprint by hand with a T-square and triangle, sometimes taking a day or more depending on the complexity, the drafter now controls a computer in which symbols can be manipulated on a screen to create a blueprint. The great saving of time and increase in productivity comes in the multitude of revisions which need to be done in construction projects. Rather than redrawing the blueprint each time, taking a day to do it, the drafter reloads the computer, puts the appropriate template over the keyboard and inserts a new window placement, heating duct, or handicap doorway. The computer justifies the new drawing and prints it immediately with no erasures or smudges, allowing the drafter/operator to move onto the next assignment.

In the examples of automobile and architectural design, we find the dual actions of communication. The client receives a product created to his personal specifications, created by the use of communication devices.

In other fields we see an equal move toward communication. In psychology, the value assumptions of faculty psychology were replaced by the authoritarian dictates of either Freudian analysis or behaviorism which in turn were supplanted by cognitive psychology in the form of, among others, Rogerian non-directive therapy, gestalt psychology, and transactional analysis -- all of which are client-centered. In language, the prescriptivist right and wrong of traditional English teaching moved to the behavioral descriptivists who said, "this is the way it is" and were in turn replaced by the transformational- generativists and discourse analysts who are still attempting to explain language function. The cultural movement appears organic in that, in each case, static product yields to active communicative process - the cultural plateaus revisited.

Table   5.1 - Four Cultural Periods

Oral Culture	**Traditional Literacy**
Self Represents Culture	Self Consciousness
Truth as Wholes	Conditional Analysis
Coordinate Syntax	Subordinate Syntax
All connected in work	Specialization of jobs
Unified in work	Development of hierarchy
Acceptance of Belief	Faculty Psychology
Group Transmits Culture	Teacher Sets Good/Bad
Education as Enculturation	Prescriptive Teaching

Post-Industrial Communication	**Industrial Literacy**
Self Seeks Identity	Self in Isolation
Comprehensive Analysis	Organizational Analysis
Compound-Complex Syntax	Subordinate Syntax
Reconnecting of Job Skills	Isolation of Jobs
Network Accountability	Vertical Hierarchy
Cognitive Psychology	Behaviorist Psychology
Teacher as Facilitator	Teacher Measures Skill
Explanatory Teaching	Descriptive Teaching

Toward Organic Education

Just as education was transformed at the beginning of the century by the demands of an industrial society, education must come to grips with the emerging reality of change in post-industrial society. The present structure of education resembles the more primitive smokestack corporations with bloated, top-heavy, individual domains, protected at the expense of the whole. If education were a motorcycle, it would be leaking oil on the showroom floor, destined never to get its motor running and head out on the highway.

The obvious, and easiest, answer is to say that education will follow the lead that the more progressive corporations are presently taking, just as education followed the corporate lead at the turn of the century. That is rather simplistic, given the changes in the structure of knowledge going on at the moment and the accompanying self-consciousness of the changes. This metarecognition predisposes one to try to shape and extend naissant organization rather than simply react to what is already past tense. Reformation is inevitable.

CHAPTER 6

Cultural War in the Schools

While the culture warriors fighting for the schools may argue for different cultural perspectives, or different cultural times, they use the technology of communication and, indeed, only need to fight because of the cultural shift occurring at the moment. The battle for the schools is not being fought in the agora or one room schoolhouse of traditional times. Neither is it being fought in the typical daily print media of the industrial period. It comes nightly on the television with statement and counterpoint from the principals at the national, state, and local levels. With the exception of a few articulate voices, demagoguery reigns in the new forum, just as it has in past forums.

Having discussed the temporal views and their metaphors within the larger trifurcated cultural milieu, we should move to a more focused examination of their position vis a vis present day schools. Each cultural time period views the role of school quite differently; and furthermore, reflective of the schisms within each time period, there is no more consensus about schools than about other subjects.

The role of the school has usually been examined in one of three ways: as conservator of the culture, reconstructor of the culture, or finally, as change agent/critic of the culture. While useful in a historical sense, such examination looks backward instead of illuminating the future. By examining the three relationships together, perhaps we can prepare to look at future direction.

For our purposes at present, because quick definitions will be expanded by further discussion, I will define the school in the role of conservator as one which seeks to keep the tradition of previous times alive in the present. The school as a reconstructor of the culture will be viewed as one which changes education but works within the established society and does not advocate a revolutionary approach -- literally reconstructing society from what is present. The school as critic of society wants to change not only school but society, usually, outside of the norms of the present society.

The Traditional View - School as Conservator of Culture

School has traditionally taught children cultural knowledge in both information and attitude. As such they taught the information that was deemed correct or appropriate at the given time. The choice of words here, "correct" and "appropriate" reflect the monitoring effect the schools put on thought. Unorthodox thought has never been allowed in traditional education. Knowledge and information tend to be virtually synonymous in the traditional view whether 19th century American, the Middle Ages in Europe, or Amerindian: the child being Locke's tabula rasa which should be filled correctly, according to societal prescription.

Tradition and traditional education may be viewed on a number of levels within and between cultures. On the oral pre/emergent literate, tribal level, consensus is a must. Education becomes learning the collective wisdom of the tribe, including the history and rules. The first books of the Old Testament of the Bible, an example of transcribed orality, provide a clear picture of the completeness of how one must live: the history and lineage of the tribe, when and how one can eat or pray, who and how one marries, what one can and cannot do, and the appropriate punishments for each. Conservation of culture is not so much the point as continuation of culture, there being little difference at the tribal level.

In a different sense at the pre-/emergent level of literacy, the Babylonian Empire for instance, with emergent literate specialization, education served as an elitist sorting function, selecting some for priesthood and others for government or army. In such a system, early education sorts while later education is vocational in becoming a part of the continuing existence of the institution to which one has become apprenticed. Education is the conservator of the entire culture here in that limits are placed on what may be studied within each occupation for the benefit of the whole.

Conservation of culture often takes quite another tack in literate societies - suppression or repression of knowledge or individuals. For example, in Republican Rome, people needed rhetoric in the courts which were active much as the Greek courts had been several hundred years before. The rhetoric of Cicero is an active system of logical argumentation and when he speaks of rhetoric as "a good man speaking well" he is thinking of someone schooled in ethical behavior and argumentation. Later, after the fall of the Republic, in Imperial Rome, when the Emperor became the law, the courts were not used and rhetoric slid into mere words. Real education in ethical behavior and speech was regarded as a dangerous activity in Imperial Rome - dangerous to the state as well as to the individual. In other times, conservation of culture meant ignoring scientific fact for preservation of church dominated culture as with Galileo and Copernicus, or the reinterpretation of history to present the given system in favorable light as in the case of slavery.

With the advent of industrialism and its compulsory mass education, the sorting function continued and became formalized in the track system, where "bright" children were selected for the college track while "others" went into vocational training - all within the same school. Previously, the sorting function had been far more demographic as elite children went to elite schools and others got what they could where they lived.

As industrial change forced schools to redefine their purpose, conservation of high culture became a focus as traditional ways were clearly passing away. Where the high culture of the arts had existed in the "natural elites" of the upper class simply as a part of existence, high culture now became part of "proper education." This change is reflected in terminology. Where one used to be an "educated man," before industrialism, which assumed knowledge of high culture, in the industrial period that same person began being called a "cultured man" to reflect a difference from those who were merely educated professionally.

In the communicative era, high culture is largely unknown, protected by the upper-class as an endangered specie. The real question before the schools is how much knowledge is needed in order to make the vital connections necessary to gather other knowledge. In other words, what is the critical mass at which point one can continue to learn on one's own? The question is still very much open and with us.

The Industrial View - School as Reconstructor of Culture

School as reconstructor of the society/culture is a recent phenomenon, predicated on sufficient food and supporting goods to allow individuals to develop apart from society. Traditionally, only the upper classes had time for self-development and society as a whole was not tolerant of individuals who differed from the norm e.g., Socrates in Greece, Christians in early Rome, or almost any minority in the Inquisition.

The primary force in education as reconstructor in America has been the shift to urban industrialism from an agrarian base, pushing education to become relevant to the needs of industrial society instead of catering to an elite, Latin grammar school segment, and giving minimal education to others. America needed people well-enough educated to run and repair the machines, balance the books, and keep the paper moving. Where in agrarian society, a wheelwright could hew a wheel for a conestoga wagon by sight and experience and install it with no formal education, the railroad mechanic had to know the torque values for a wheel bolt and be able to apply those values. Too tight and the wheel cracks; too loose and it falls off.

The business efficiency reconstructors were interested only in training able workers. Their interest was not in changing society even though they had that effect. Curriculum theorists such as Tyler instituted the formal track system in high school insuring that the class system in place would not be upset while at the same time providing bodies for industrial development.

In contrast to the business model of education which grew out of utilitarian need, the Progressive Movement was philosophical in nature, examining the futility of traditional education. The Progressive Movement grew out of the work of 19th century theoreticians Rousseau, Pestalozzi, Froebel, and Herbart. Rousseau viewed education as the means by which mankind could progress from the barbarism of absolute authority to a free independence. As a result, Rousseau held that children should remain free as children rather than be treated as mini-adults. He noted that children are wonderful learners when left to their own devices and that such innate ability should be used in school rather than suppressed in artificial formalism. In like manner, Pestalozzi held that sympathetic understanding by the teacher is more conducive to student learning than punishment and that concrete sense impressions developed student awareness much as they learned from their own concrete needs (150 years before cognitive and developmental psychology). Froebel continued Rousseau's and Pestalozzi's ideas that education must grow from the individual needing to learn. He founded the kindergarten as a means for children to progress in learning while at the same time remaining children. He felt that such spontaneous activities helped the self-expression of children while providing a basis for later learning. Herbart formalized many of these Romantic views stating that education was the means for a person to form a comprehensive and harmonious life, echoing Aristotle and Cicero. Such a comprehensive end could only be achieved by systematic educational methodology, and thus the development of his five step teaching method which is still widely used.

Although never agreeing with each other, the business efficiency and Progressive movements together discredited traditional education, allowing great diversity, if not great harmony to enter education. The change is still being felt.

Critics - School as Change Agent

The school as critic of the society assumes a very different posture by reacting against the society in contrast to the previous two concepts. Where the school as conservator reflects what the society has been, and the school as reconstructor is trying to make schools become what the society has already become, the school as critic is trying to change the very nature of society rather than working within the system. Where the two previous concepts may have individuals who lead them, their growth is based on large groups working within the society. The school as critic, however, is almost always based on an individual's work. Men such as Freire, Goodman, Illich, Holt, and Neill represent education outside of the societal norms. I chose these five as being categorically representative of most of the criticisms of public education - the same five categories that I noted in citing Hirsch, Bloom, Schlafly, Schor, and Smith who are all currently trying to reconstruct the schools.

In *Freedom and Beyond* Holt takes a position very similar to Neill's *Summerhill,* saying that mass bureaucratic education cannot work given the uniqueness of each child. Both agree that children must seek their own education; opportunities must be provided, but education will occur when it is needed.

Freire takes a political view of education as a means for oppression or freedom, depending on the use. Insomuch as education is a consumer item supplied by governments worldwide, it is a tool used for manipulation of the masses and is used for suppression of the general population. Freire suggests that through education and literacy the peasant masses can gain the ability to *know* and therefore act upon that knowledge. For him, illiteracy, as the culture of silence, must be broken before other actions can be taken. Therefore, education is the means to a political end.

Where Illich starts with the same assumptions as Freire, he suggests a Christian communalism in *Celebration of Awareness* as a means to third-world development without the problems of industrialized nations.

Goodman represents the most eclectic side of criticism, positing an anarchistic psychological view of desired education. Decrying the politics of educational consumerism and industrial bureaucracy, he reflects the political awareness of Illich and Freire while from his own gestalt psychological background shows, rather like Neill and Holt, how the schools negate creativity and force individuals into playing roles within the system.

The common thread holding the critics together is that all find their truth in places other than in the bureaucratic representation of educational hierarchy in present society. For the critics, whether the truth resides in the individual or the collectiveness of society, education begins in awareness, responsibility, and the ability to communicate.

Cultural Time and Present Schools

The past, present, and future temporal schisms and the physical exercise, industrial machine behavior, and interactive communication metaphors broadly represent the traditional, reconstructive and critical concepts used so far in this chapter, respectively. The adverb "broadly" is used as the fit is not complete as posited so far here. Traditional and reconstructive roles fit well with the physical exercise and industrial metaphors, but clearly the critics have fallen short in communicating their revolutionary change of society. Whether the "communication" of the critics was too early for society to deal with, or the politics were unacceptably leftist, or the self-righteous proclamations were too iconoclastic, the net effect, other than for Freire who continues to have influence, was to cause discussion in intellectual circles, to start some projects, and never to develop fully. That is not to say that there is no effect - simply that the effect has not taken the immediate personal turn desired when declaimed. One cannot over-estimate the effect of the critics if one looks at the five reconstructors: Hirsch, Bloom, Schor, Schlafly and Smith, all of whom look moderate and responsible by comparison.

The examination of the three periods drawing on appropriate writings should further show the relation of the concepts and should lead us to possible extensions of the train of thought.

Traditional - The Conservators

> Intellect is the capitalized and communal form of live intelligence.....Intellect is at once a body of common knowledge and the channels through which the right particle of it can be brought to bear quickly, without the effort of redemonstration, on the matter at hand. Intellect is community property and can be handed down.
> (Barzun, 1959)

> Parents have the right to assure that their children's beliefs and moral values are not undermined by the schools. Pupils have the right to have and to hold their values and moral standards without direct or indirect manipulation by the schools through curricula, textbooks, audio-visual materials, or supplementary assignments.
> (Schlafly, 1984)

While both Barzun and Schlafly view schools as the conservator of experience, their ends differ sharply. For Barzun, preservation of experience means that knowledge will be guarded, valued and passed on as our inheritance. Schools should act as the source of this transmission of knowledge because it is the cumulative knowledge of a culture which allows understanding and integration of new phenomena with old. Schlafly, on the other hand, wants no part of the heritage of communal knowledge as she has found truth elsewhere. School will teach only the information she wants taught rather than what is at large in the society. This static view of conservator is at the traditional level in that information must fit what already exists as there is not a growing corpus of information in such a society.

The dichotomy posed by these two is hardly new. In fact, the same situation arose in Roman education. The Roman model of education was based on the Greek, carrying on the tradition of classical knowledge, and it emphasized the rhetoric of Cicero and, later, Quintillian along with mathematics and physical education. The Christians of the second and third century A.D. had a problem in that they tried to avoid the pagan system, sometimes at pain of death. However, by avoiding Roman education, just as Schlafly's group tries to avoid pagan America, they deprived themselves of the education so necessary to carry on their evangelism.

The resolution came later when St. Augustine realized that he could modify the Roman system, add the cumulative knowledge of the church and have a new entity. In the process, rhetoric was rejuvenated as an active entity in use for preaching instead of being taught as a dead subject looking back to the days of Cicero and the Roman Republic.

Thus the conservator can be viewed as a protector of knowledge to be passed along to the next generation or as a censor ensuring that present values remain unchanged. In either case, the conservators have their eyes firmly on the rearview mirror.

Industrial - The Reconstructors

> What are the roots that clutch, what branches grow
> Out of this stony rubbish? Son of man
> You cannot say, or guess, for you know only
> A heap of broken images, where the sun beats,
> And the dead tree gives no shelter
> (Eliot, The Wasteland)

> The Tree of Knowledge is not that of Life.
> Philosophy and science, and the springs
> of wonder, and the wisdom of the world
> I have essayed, and in my mind there is
> A power to make these subject to itself-
> But this availed not"
> (Byron, Manfred)

The metaphor of the insufficient tree used by Eliot and Byron fits the period of the primary reconstructors, not only from the point of view of organic social growth, but the inadequacy of previous knowledge. Industrial progress is just not enough. The "stony rubbish" and "broken images" appropriately describe the educated western world after the First World War. Perceptions of the world had changed, necessitating changes in social institutions -- not the least of which were the schools. "The wisdom of the world...availed not." Certainly the wisdom of the world did not help in World War I or in the aftermath. While "The Tree of Knowledge is not that of Life," can be taken as a Romantic credo, it is equally apropos for the Progressive Movement which derived many of its precepts from the Romantics -- the worth of individual development being primary. The other aspect of Byron's statement is the idea that true knowledge is not static; one does not pick it off a tree; it is not something which can be acquired as a unit, but must be lived.

The school as reconstructor can take numerous forms, depending on the kind of change which is desired. It is fitting that out of the vacuum created by the fall of traditionalism, two American ideals emerged to lead American education: the business-efficiency model and the Progressives. The self-reliant, self-made man of commerce or the soil, conservative in thought and powerful in action, contrasts with the enlightened men of thought who framed the Declaration, the

Constitution and the Bill of Rights, bringing Jeffersonian democracy to fruition. The two have always been in conflict in America, and nowhere is it clearer than in the two models of education. School can be viewed as a vocational training ground or as a source for passing on the knowledge and ideals of the society, but rarely will they both occur together.

These conflicting views of the school shape not only the content of the curriculum, but also the way in which the material is taught. The business-efficiency model stresses the observable, growing as it does from materialism. Psychologically, it is in tune with behaviorism, the creation of objectives stated in measurable terms and, is conducive to a rigid structure, fixed material content, a tight time frame, little creativity, and focus on the material rather than student.

The Progressive goal stresses the possible, based as it is on idealism. Because it emphasizes the thought of the learner over the content, it is in tune with cognitive psychology. This means that the school will have a more open atmosphere with students having a say in the affairs and courses.

Just as these positions became defined by the two models in the post-World War I period, it is an on-going concern in each school system and classroom. To what degree can the teacher emphasize material or student, and structure or freedom and still remain within the guiding principles of the given school? And how does the system itself define a position, given that both are active views within society? The positions are in constant flux. The Progressive demise in the late Fifties when Sputnik was launched gave rise to behavioral efficiency and discipline- centered curriculums of the so-called "new math" and "new English" in the early Sixties. In turn, in the late Sixties, discipline-centered schools were called irrelevant, and "open" and "free" schools came in, only to be supplanted by back-to-the-basics people in the Seventies. Both sides claim to have what is necessary, and it can only be hoped that "the wisdom of the world" will not yield "a heap of broken images."

Communicative - The Critics

> Turning and turning in the widening gyre
> The falcon cannot hear the falconer;
> Things fall apart; the center cannot hold;
> Mere anarchy is loosed upon the world,
> The blood-dimmed tide is loosed, and everywhere
> The ceremony of innocence is drowned"
> (Yeats, The Second Coming)

> I saw the best minds of my generation destroyed by
> madness, starving hysterical naked,...
> listening to the crack of doom on the hydrogen jukebox...
> who were burned alive in their innocent flannel suits on
> Madison Avenue amid blasts of leaden verse & the tanked-up
> clatter of the iron regiments of fashion & the nitroglycerine
> shrieks of the fairies of advertising & the mustard gas of
> sinister intelligent editors, or were run down by the drunken
> taxicabs of Absolute Reality. "
> (Ginsburg, Howl)

Yeats' fear of anarchy and drowned innocence in 1920 becomes "Absolute Reality" for Ginsburg in 1956. The world had moved from horse cavalry in World War I to the "the crack of doom on the hydrogen jukebox" while schools had only moved to a discussion of a classical education versus a business or progressive emphasis. As society fragmented, education increasingly has become a subject of criticism.

The extreme end of the critical point of view is revolution, be it political or educational. The critical groups (Holt and Neill, Freire and Illich, and Goodman) move from a discussion of the school as presently conceived to reveal how it might be seen in a changed and, for each of them, better society. Each has a program in which the school is viewed differently. Broadly, these can be grouped two ways, viewing the school as an instrument of individual development or of societal development. Both ideas naturally come into the classroom at every level, but as posited by these critics, the ideas become the focus of education itself. In a typical present-day classroom, individual development is touted as the ideal, but, in fact, when it must go hand in hand with societal norms and expectations (compulsory education, well-behaved children, a well-rounded curriculum, fixed times for school etc.) the individual is subsumed into the whole. Clearly, extremes of any type are viewed with suspicion, and the median is celebrated. As an example, test scores in formal reports are reported in terms of deviation from the norm while the popular press touts the average as increasing or decreasing without regard to what that means.

Holt, Neill and Goodman hold that school should be an individual affair, not in the sense of the individual within the system as noted above, but the individual free of the system and able to make Byronic choices about the totality of his education and life. The implications are immense. If the individual is completely free, then one either has "the center cannot hold" and "mere anarchy" as a result, *or* those unknowing souls "who were burned alive in their innocent flannel suits."   Certainly, for Goodman, saving people from unwitting conformity, "innocent flannel suits," is preferable, just as it is for Holt and Neill. For people in mass state education, anarchy is not worth the trade-off; in fact, it is completely unacceptable.

For the social/political critics, the school is an instrument of power by which the masses can be awakened to fulfill their destiny. The individual, while touted as the key to education, is, in fact, subsumed to the mass idea of a raised political consciousness, capable of bringing about change. Such a view is anathema to public education which is beholden to public opinion and therefore reflects popular rather than revolutionary thought.

Both of these critical views of education can be parts of any classroom in public education, but only parts. Because of the conservative nature of public education shaped as it is by Ginsburg's "iron regiments of fashion" in the form of school boards and the "mustard gas of sinister intelligent editors" in the form of superintendents, we have innocence drowned and where, taking Yeats' next line, "the best lack all conviction, while the worst are full of passionate intensity."

Resolving   Conflicts

All is not hopeless in resolving the issues raised so far, but we have to find common ground on which to build. That is the premise of modern rhetoric and modern psychology. Change is inevitable, but then it always has been - what has been lacking is the breadth of vision to unite the disparate sectors of the temporal cultures. We have been so busy looking for answers by deep thought and intense analysis, that we seem to have forgotten that perspective is useful sometimes. We can pull the parts into a coherent form, answering some of the questions posed in the first chapter by pulling the plateaus of literacy, the time cultures and the metaphors together into a single unit: the Matrix.

CHAPTER 7

Communication, Cultural Evolution and the Schools

Having identified three cultural plateaus by thought pattern and syntax, examined three cultures of time, three metaphors of education, and the varied roles of the school, we now need a mechanism for uniting these aspects of cultural change into a coherent whole. The four part grid that has been developing throughout the book can provide the basis for an interactive Matrix that will serve our purposes very well for integrating historical data and showing future direction. People of all cultural periods and in all parts of the world have independently developed four part systems for explaining phenomena. From the naturalistic four directions, four winds, four seasons, and four elements (earth, air, fire and water) to the intellectual fours of Plato, Jung and Yeats, four has a long history as the explanatory number. If we frame the Matrix with two items on each side, we should be able to gain some insight into communication, cultural evolution, and the schools.

The *Myers-Briggs Personality Indicator (MBTI)*, used in counseling, is based on the Jungian model of a four part compass of the psyche, and provides a clear view of personalities in education. The Myers-Briggs posits Introversion/Extroversion, Perception/Judgment, Sensation/Intuition and Feeling/Thought as binary choices in a fourpart schema. This Jungian model proved workable, but ponderous, in looking at cultural and educational evolution. William Irwin Thompson in *At the Edge of History,* used Yeats' four part schema from *A Vision* and John Marshall's anthropologic film *The Hunters* to look at cultural movement far more elegantly than I had been able to do using Jung and the MBTI alone. Bringing these two models together proved most useful, but our purposes being different, I end with quite different results, due in most part to my imposing an external four part order as opposed to Thompson's looking for the order to emerge from within.

Definition and Overview of the Matrix

As we set up Plato and Aristotle to illustrate fundamental differences in views of education, we will use them as the columns of our matrix and label them for their dominant characteristics: "The Ideal" and "The Real," respectively. Much recent controversy in education has centered on the absolute versus relative values being taught in the schools, and, in that these values contrast the Ideal and the Real, we will be label the rows: "The Absolute" and "The Relative." The interaction of these four should provide a basis for examining literacy, cultural evolution, and the position of the schools.

Figure 7.1

The Matrix: Cultural Overview

	Ideal	**Real**
A b s o l u t e	Oral	Literate
R e l a t i v e	Communicative	Industrial

The left side represents the ideal, interior world while the right side is pragmatic and exterior. In short, the ideational Platonic world rests on the left in contrast to the operational Aristotelian world on the right.

The line between the top and bottom halves separates the absolute and relative. The absolute will be characterized by inflexible limits. These limits can be as different as Platonic forms and God in the upper left quadrant or social and physical limits such as absolute monarchy or the gold standard, respectively, in the upper right sector. The relative half of the grid is not defined by such absolute limits, but rather by definitions which have been set by man and can be changed as desired.

As we have seen in earlier chapters, chronologic time has moved in a clockwise manner from the upper left quadrant of orality through the upper right sector of classical literacy to the bottom right sector of industrial literacy to the present communicative period in the lower left. To limit the discussion, when we speak of cultural change, we cannot cover all change and so we will restrict discussion to aspects which we can apply to education such as ideation, leadership, and psychology. However, first we need to define the four sectors and look at the larger patterns they reflect.

The Absolute-Ideal   -   The Inspirational

If we examine the upper left sector, the Absolute-Ideal quadrant, labelled the Inspirational, we find a bounded world where limits are non-negotiable and tend to the spiritual or intellectual. Pragmatic action has no more place than relative values. Furthermore, leadership comes from the divine, charismatic, inspired, person - the prophet or intellectual speaking the truth. Moses is a good exemplar, speaking absolutely and ideally, certainly not with the relative values of committee decisions. In like manner, he did not have power from the "real" side of the grid, i.e., he had no army or institution backing him.

Here, in the Inspirational, there must be a unity in being - not divided by pragmatic self-interest, or the relative good set by the few. We will assign the pre-/emergent literate cultural period to this quadrant because a preliterate society must be governed by the wholes of orality, not with the divisions implied in full literacy after the Greeks introduced literate self-consciousness with its independence of thought and action. None of the other sectors give us such wholes.

With culturally accepted wholes, there is no psychology as such; there is acceptance with belief and Godly judgment of good and evil. Psychology works on the premise of accomodation which is not part of such an all-or-none proposition.

The Absolute-Real   -   The Authoritarian

The shift from the Absolute-Ideal to the Absolute-Real, labelled the Authoritarian, begins with the introduction of full literacy by the self-consciousness of Greek writing. This quadrant is pragmatic and concerned with real worldly power; therefore, we find politics and the formal thinking needed to establish lines of authority and control.

The cultural period for the Absolute-Real, Authoritarian Period is roughly from the Greek Golden Age to the 20th century. The end point of the Absolute-Real falls at the beginning of the 20th century because so many significant artistic, psychological and scientific events occurred close to that date. Conveniently, Planck's formulation of quantum theory, fracturing the absolutes of Newtonian physics and the death of Nietzsche, who postulating the inevitability of relativity in philosophy fall in the year 1900.

The leader in the Absolute-Real quadrant is a true authoritarian, absolute, leader, ruling as military head or a king who controls military power. Lines of authority are clearly drawn and always return to the central personage. This kind of a leader could be the head of state, the head of a religion, or the head of a company. Where Moses led by Godly authority, men such as Alexander the Great, Henry the VIII, and John D. Rockefeller ruled by worldly fiat in the realm of Absolute-Real.

Psychologically, such a period is marked by belief in discipline for following the established order - with a variety of rationales to back up the belief. Whether one believes in the balance of the four basic elements in the classical period, the humors of the Middle Ages, or the faculty psychology begun in the late 17th century, the result is that there is a seemingly rational way to explain human behavior.

The Relative-Real   -   The Physical

Moving down to the lower right hand quadrant, the Relative-Real, labelled the Physical, power is defined by organization; ideas are not paramount and communication is not bidirectional. Here, one finds the pragmatic, uninspired mass world of farmers, factory workers, the military, and technical and service workers as well as government and corporate functionaries. The cultural period for this era is the first half of this century, bounded on the one side with the demise of the Authoritarian era and, on the other, by the beginning of the Communicative era in the 1950s.

Characteristically, the individual of power from the previous period is subsumed by the organization man and the hierarchical industrial production system. The absolute rule of the autocrat is lost in committees, just as absolute responsibility is lost in the non-individualistic decision-making process where no one person receives credit or blame. Management by objectives rules this quadrant with the company striving to limit the personal - valuing instead the organization. Where Henry Ford founded a company, took it to success, and almost lost it by his own decisions, the present corporate entity known as Ford Motor has no one person so in charge. It has layers of administration, a Board of Directors, banks, investment houses and outside counsel to keep it operating properly. In like manner, where government in the previous period meant an absolute ruler such as Henry VIII, government in the Relative - Real is represented by a vast bureaucracy. One hierarchy is elected to leadership and power, but the bulk of government simply continues in the form of functionaries in the civil service.

In the realm of the Relative-Real, only clearly defined observable behaviors are important, with judgment based on conforming to the stated behaviors. Therefore behaviorist psychology is the norm. Industrial training thrives in this atmosphere of stated objectives whereas less clearly defined mentalist conceptions such as mind are dismissed as non-observable, not to mention absolutes such as "the good" and "the truth."

The Relative-Ideal - The Communicative

Completing the Matrix, we come to the Relative-Ideal, labelled the Communicative, where we find context-sensitive entities and the rise of the individual en masse. These two items seem unrelated, but they are easily derived by looking at the parts of the Relative-Ideal. Firstly, in contrast to the Physical sector making judgments based on stated objectives, the Authoritarian making rational power decisions, and the Inspirational making value judgments on absolutes, the Communicative sector tries to avoid judgment, preferring interpretation, identification of common ground, and accomodation for mutual benefit. Secondly, with the ideal defined in relative, rather than absolute terms, each person or group can set its own self-defined ideal. The emergence of identification and self-discovery in psychology explains the rise of the current human potential movement. Client-centered psychology stresses the personal discovery of identification and self-realization as the means of not only coping, but of growing in contrast to the authoritarianism of Freudian analysis or the definition of behavioral goals in behaviorist therapy. To Rogers, Ellis, and Perls in psychology, and Burke, Booth and Pike in rhetoric, discovery and self-realization are central.

Clearly, the Communicative cultural period is mature in the intellectual and media parts of society now with the study of cognitive psychology and communication, but lagging in the institutional (including education) and political arenas.

Figure 7.2

The Matrix: Descriptive Overview

	I d e a l	**R e a l**
A b s o l u t e	**Inspirational** Preliterate Divine Charismatic Ethical Moses Godly Judgment Jung's Intuition	**Authoritarian** Urban literate Individual of power Formal, logical Alexander the Great Henry the VIII Henry Ford Faculty Psychology Jung's Thought

R e l a t i v e	**Communicative**
	
	Sensitive
	Decentralized
	   Power Structure
	Carl Rogers
	Peace Corps
	Client Centered
	   Therapy
	
	Jung's Feeling
		Physical
		
		Industrial literate
		Bureaucratic
		Pragmatic
		U.S. Government
		General Motors
		B.F. Skinner
		Behaviorist Psychology
		
		Jung's Sensation

Application of the Matrix

Having viewed each quadrant, we should look at the applications of the matrix. First, we need to examine the evolution of cultures through time: moving from oral to literate to computer culture. Second, we need to examine and amplify the concept of cultural evolution in one period, that is, viewing cultural change beginning in the Inspirational and moving through Communicative, Physical, and finally into the Authoritarian sectors. Finally, we need to apply both patterns to our central idea: education.

Persona and Cultural Progression through Time

While not stated explicitly each of the quadrants has a persona. The explication of these personas will help illustrate the evolution of culture at one time, its evolution through time, and the application to education.

The Absolute-Ideal

The Absolute-Ideal takes the persona of the Inspirator: the individual taken by the spiritual or intellectual magic of revelation, finding wholeness - pure knowing without words. The quality of wordless wholes links this quadrant with either preliterate society or intellectual creative vision.

Religious prophecy is literally the inspiriting of the prophet. Whether in the commanding Old Testament terms of Moses, Abraham, and Isaiah, the Koranic dream revelation of the world and heaven to Mohammed, or the searching for enlightenment by Gautama under the Bo tree, the moment of spirit comes as an entirety.

Similarly, intellectual inspiriting often occurs in one moment of discovery: the "a-hah" moment which connects previously unconnected information. Such revelation is as wordless as the Godly possession of the religious prophets even though it usually occurs after extensive work on a subject lays the foundation for the breakthrough. Mendeleev finding the organizational key in the Periodic Chart of the Elements, Newton watching the apple fall and seeing gravity, or Kekule, in a dream, connecting a snake biting its tail to the circular construction of the benzene ring, all show people who were well versed in a subject making the final connection in a moment of inspiration.

The Inspirator takes different forms in different cultural times. In pre-literate society, he is the shaman, representing his group to the non-physical, non-human universe. In classical times the Inspirator's job splits, and the intellectual is divided from the religious. Thus, he moves from the Greek priest of the oracle to the Roman soothsayer and, finally, to Christian priest in the religious sphere while in the intellectual sphere, the Greek scholar expands the fundamental knowledge of mathematics, logic, and philosophy. With industrial development, the religious inspirator becomes the philosopher a la Kierkegaard, while the intellectual inspirator becomes the physical scientist a la Faraday. Finally, in the communicative era, the religious side becomes personally religious whether in New Age psycho-religious terms or going back to traditional fundamentalist belief. The intellectual side turns to information science in the broadest sense, including electronics, lasers, cognitive structure, and recombinant genetics rearranging biologic information.

Figure 7.3

The Matrix: the Absolute-Ideal

Ideal	Real
  A **b** **s** **o** **l** **u** **t** **e** Personal Religion Information Scientist Philosopher Physical Scientist Priest Logician **Shaman**	

The Absolute-Real

The Absolute-Real, the Authoritarian, takes the persona of the Leader with the control of power as the central theme. The Leader controls a given situation by whatever means are necessary. In preliterate time, the leader was a "big man," a dominant warrior or charismatic personality. With the advent of literacy and the formalism of hierarchy, the big man was supplanted by an emperor or king who ruled in absolute fashion. The absolute ruler was replaced in turn by the rule of law which meant that the men who would have been "big men" or kings in a different era then had the alternative of being in business or constitutional government. Thus, we see the rise of the industrial autocrat paralleling election or appointment to government as a means to power, in contrast previous periods. The bifurcation of power continues in communicative times with some power people still becoming government officials while the industrial autocrat who reigned with lines of authority has been replaced by the entrepreneur who rules with ideas, initiative and money outside of typical bureaucratic rules and moves on to new endeavors when constraints get too close.

Figure   7.4

The Matrix: the Absolute-Real

	Ideal		Real	
A b s o l u t e	Personal Religion	Information Scientist	Bureaucrat	
				Entrepreneur
	Philosopher		Government Official	
		Physical Scientist		Industrial Autocrat
	Priest	Logician	**King**	
		Shaman	Big Man	

The Relative-Real

The Relative-Real, labelled the Physical, is the realm of the drone and has the persona of the Worker. They produce what society needs, according to the definitions of the society. They are not leaders, or inspired, and, with their pragmatism, they are not particularly concerned with communication. They live to live: survivors.

In preliterate society, the producer is the hunter, the one who produces food for the group. With agrarian society, the producer becomes the farmer. In industrialism, factory workers take over from the farmer while in the communicative era the factory worker becomes the technician or service worker. Industrial assembly which used to be manual now uses a great deal of automation, monitored by technicians. For example, sheet metal welding on automobiles used to be done by people, but now robotic spot welders perform the operation. On the other hand, support/service workers now outnumber all others, being the secretaries, restaurant workers, store clerks, janitors, mechanics, and others who keep daily life going.

Figure   7.5

The   Matrix: the   Relative-Real

	Ideal	Real

A b s o l u t e	Personal Religion Information Scientist
	
	Philosopher
	
	Physical Scientist
	
	Priest Logician
	
	Shaman
		Bureaucrat
		
		       Entrepreneur
		Government Official
		     Industrial Autocrat
		King
		
		Big Man

R e l a t i v e		Hunter Farmer **Factory Worker** Technician Service Worker

The Relative-Ideal

The Relative-Ideal, labelled the Communicative, is the sector which brings to light the ideas of a given time. The persona is clearly that of the Communicator. It is ideal as it tries to enlighten the other sectors, but relative in that it expresses that enlightenment in a form which is comprehensible to each of the other sectors in their own terms. Where the Inspirator wants to inform the other sectors of the discovery of his own truth in his own personal terms, the Communicator frames a given "truth" in the terms of the other sectors so that they understand for themselves.

In preliterate times, the communicator is the jokester. He leavens the moment, keeping the big man from getting too pompous, entertaining the hunter and providing a counterpoint to the seriousness of the shaman. With literacy, the jokester becomes the artist, again entertaining, satirizing, and enlightening as playwright, poet, sculptor, and painter. With the coming of corporate industrialism, the artist becomes the media while keeping the same functions. In the communicative period, these functions are taken over by education. In such a period, one must keep in mind the breadth and growth of education from its original scope of enculturation. Enlightenment has been a function of education for all time; entertainment is a recent function as people realize life-long learning - continuing education means people exploring new avenues and interests for their own enjoyment; and criticism is increasingly a function of scholars observing the workings of society.

Figure 7.6

The Matrix: the Relative-Ideal

	Ideal	Real

A b s o l u t e	Personal Religion Information Scientist
	
	Philosopher
	
	Physical Scientist
	
	Priest Logician
	
	Shaman
		Bureaucrat
		            Entrepreneur
		
		Government Official
		            Industrial Autocrat
		
		King
		
		Big Man

R e l a t i v e	Jokester Artist Media **Education**	Hunter Farmer **Factory Worker** Technician Service Worker

Cultural Evolution through Time

With the matrix, we can examine cultural evolution over time in two manners. The first examines each quadrant as its own period of time. Using a clockwise rotation from sector to sector on the matrix, we look first at the Absolute-Ideal as the preliterate, and then move on to the Absolute-Real as the literate, the Relative-Real as industrial, and finally the Relative-Ideal as the communicative period.

The second method examines the concentric lines forming increasingly larger blocks from the center. Thus, we see the preliterate shaman, big man, hunter, and jokester in the inner block. The second ring of blocks has the priest/logician, king, farmer and artist in the literate period. The third block, the industrial, has the philosopher/scientist, government official/industrial autocrat, factory worker and media. The fourth block, the communicative, has the cognitive psychologist/information scientist, bureaucrat/entrepreneur, technician/service worker, and education.

Figure 7.7

The Matrix: Cultural Evolution through Time

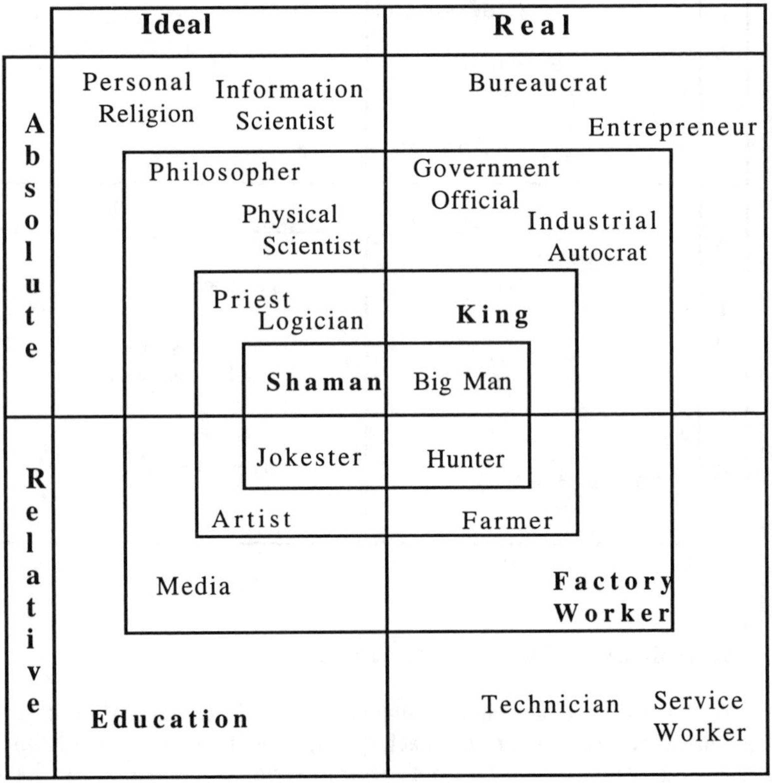

Interestingly, in looking at the matrix, job functions split in the time period after exemplification. Thus, in the pre/emergent literate period where the Shaman exemplifies the dominant characteristics, the next exemplification becomes the combination of the Priest and Logician. In similar manner, the King, exemplifying Authority, becomes the Government Official and Industrial Autocrat while the factory worker becomes the technician and support/service worker the the Relative-Real. Because we cannot examine all of culture, we will specifically look at a few of the organizing principles of the socio-political power base at selected times in each frame.

The essential unity of the pre/emergent literate society is based on the interrelationship of work. Each person is interdependent and non-specialized so that the shaman may cast blessings, but he also hunts. The jokester may lighten the hunt with humor, but he is also part hunter. In short, no person exists in isolation and the powerbase is cooperative with decisions a matter of the big man keeping consensus. The group has a leader, but he is an ethnarch, a leader of the people because of his personal power, intelligence or charisma. Moses was simply the leader; he did not conquer the Jews; he led by personal influence and divine intervention, not as absolute kingly ruler. Interestingly, Moses was an Inspirator, doubling as big man. His real power is from God, but his secular power resided in the Authoritarian sector. In terms of the matrix, he got his worldly power to the right of where he used it as a religious man.

With full literacy, the "big man" is the leader, ruling as king or emperor and usually setting up kingly imperial institutions to carry on his line as with Xerxes, Alexander, and Caesar. Whether Persian, Greek or Roman, conquerors give way to absolute institutional power. It is important to note conquerors. The head of state was usually the head of the military and needed to keep the military on his side. Again the real power is clockwise from where the user sits, i.e., Caesar was an Authoritarian but got his power from the military which is always in the Physical quadrant.

Thus we see the first clockwise shift in the locus of power. Where desert leader Moses was religious and acted as Leader, in urban environments, the Leader must act with the military for power maintenance or face a coup.

The shift to corporate industrial society is one clockwise move from Authoritarian with its king as head. Corporate power may be created by a "big man" but at center, power rests in the organizational structure and continuity in the Physical. Ford and Rockefeller could have been admirable headmen of tribes, or kings in the previous periods, but they became "industrialists", personally setting up global institutions that became modern corporations - essentially paralleling the functions of governments in previous eras. With the rise of corporations, the personal control of the autocrats gave way to institutional control. Institutional power is exercised by control of information in industrial society (Communicative sector), again a clockwise move from the position of industry in the Physical sector. Information control keeps the assembly line moving, keeps markets in order, keeps advertising and public relations on line, and allows for currency exchange and international development.

To summarize, Moses was religious acting as head; Alexander was head and working as general; and Ford Motor is a corporation controlling information. In each case the cultural shift is clockwise and the power shift is clockwise, located in the next cultural step from where it is used by the given person.

As we are now working in the post-industrial, information, or communicative age, it is interesting to look at how power is being wielded. The corporate giants are not automobiles and oil as in the industrial period but rather information producers and controllers. The largest corporate entities are the Nippon Telephone and Telegraph, AT&T, and the international banks. The primary corporate goal is not more usable horsepower but more usable memory. Supercomputers allow modelling of complex events that used to demand physical execution for realization whether in nuclear physics, economic market interaction, or complex design problems.

Thus, we come full circle. Sitting in the Communicative era, we should find power being derived one step clockwise in the Inspirational once again. Instead of being a religious power as it was in the first expression of the matrix, however, we should find that it is the power of information technology. In fact, it would appear that the locus of power is presently in the Inspirational sector as corporations and governments cooperate to try to develop faster computers with more power. Current government discussion, politically-based as it usually is, at least one step back from the innovators of current culture, would have people believe that the U.S. cannot afford to lose our superiority in computer development as it would signal a shift in power to whichever group won the battle. It sounds strangely like the military in another period, saying we had to keep up with military development or lose our superiority.

The Individual in Matrix Progress

We may have come full circle, but it is hardly the same. Where, in the Mosaic period, the individual for the most part had to follow the larger societal constraints out of the necessity of eating, that is no longer true. The collective nature of tribal life dictated groupness rather than individuality.

Although agrarian life created sufficient food to allow job specialization and the rise of urban civilization in the next period, only the upper classes had leisure for self-development. Rulers from the authoritarian sector lived off the farmers. The ordinary citizen was essentially defined by the job; therefore, Joe the candle-maker became Joe Chandler, and Mike the barrelmaker became Mike Cooper.

Industrialism extended the concept of surplus production, allowing sufficient quantities for a rising middle-class to develop leisure time activities. People could do a job for support and yet not be defined by it. A worker on the assembly line at Ford might define himself, not as a line worker, but as a bowler, a Mason, or a Baptist - what he *is*, not what he *does*. That is a monumental shift in consciousness, and it signals the shift from the industrial to communication sectors of the matrix in the way these people conceive of themselves. It marks the shift from the pragmatic exterior Aristotelian world of doing, back into the interior ideal, Platonic world of being.

With the locus of power in both science and individual life moving from culturally determined definition to self-definition in the information age, conflict is inevitable. With the culture now moving into the ideal, inspirational, intuitive sector, the results can only be speculated on; the gyre keeps moving in the larger sphere.

For the individual, however, choice allows movement within the larger cultural flow to one of the three time cultures previously discussed, i.e., one can move ahead, tread water in one's time, or make a reactionary movement back to "the good old days". Sitting in the Communicative era (power in the Inspirational sector), having completed one turn of the gyre, we find one group progressing toward information science and personal religious inspiration, another group finding its truth in old-time religion, and the third simply passing time looking to get by day to day.

Cultural Progression at One Time

Viewed from another perspective, we can examine cultural transformation in one setting in quite a different fashion. Whereas cultural evolution moved through time in clockwise fashion from the Ideal around to the Communicative, cultural transformation in a given period moves in a counterclockwise rotation from the Ideal around to the Authoritarian. Religious and intellectual visionaries pronounce changes which get amplified through art and the media, applied by technicians and finally realized publicly in the politics of leadership. By the time the politicians realize a change is occurring, that change is fully mature, well-known, and accepted. While this appears very clean, in fact, cultural shift is never quite so delineated as in a graphic representation. With the speeding of cultural change, the lines are increasingly overlapping as different sectors shift at different speed.

In the evolutionary development of the Absolute-Ideal preliterate sector, we see this four stage pattern. We know that early urbanization was made possible by storage of grains, usually under control of temples - the existing power base. The emergence of writing (Communicative) allowed distribution, and supported a political urban government which could in turn support a larger power base. The larger power base expanded the sphere of influence (Physical) in both geographic and political areas. The shift was gradual as people left the country for village life. As villages grew to cities, the critical mass of humanity needed political organization (Authoritarian). Thus, we see counterclockwise movement from Inspiration through to politics in the full development of the Inspirational period.

In similar fashion, the transformation toward fully literate culture in the classical era begins in the Inspirational sector with the intellectual and artistic genius of the Greek philosophers, rhetoricians, mathematicians, writers, and sculptors (Inspiriting). Public art, literary entertainment, and schools rose communicating the new vision (Communicative). Unfortunately, the Greek experiment in political democracy was not allowed to develop fully, becoming dissipated as state resources went to war. The Romans followed, copying the Greek world of inspiration and communication, while greatly expanding Greek technology and production (Physical) in building roads and infrastructure, and finally establishing the short-lived Republic and the enduring Empire in the Authoritarian political sector. The shift during the period is again four steps counterclockwise from the Ideal through the Communicative and Physical to the Authoritarian.

Just as industrialism began to gain momentum in late 18th and early 19th century England, signalling the full fruition of literacy, Romantic visionaries sowed the seeds of the next change, anticipating present day knowledge that the world was becoming more polluted in every definable way. Blake, Wordsworth, and Byron (Inspiriting) all noted the corruption of the earth, society and politics, a view popularized by an emerging press (Communicative). Oppressive, unhealthy working conditions in the mills and mines assured that the workers understood (Physical), but the politicians did not make the connection until labor riots caught their attention (Authoritarian). Again, we have movement from visionary, to media, worker and finally into politics.

The movement to the communicative period of the present day shows a similar progression. In the 19th century, philosophers such as Kierkegaard and Nietzsche show the individual as relative, uncoupled from the absolute in the same manner as inspired artists reflected the breakdown of the absolute by abandoning representative form in painting, sculpture, and traditional melody in music. At the turn of the century, physicists such as Planck, Bohr, Heisenberg and Einstein showed that the physical world was relative, not absolute as Newton had postulated. Slightly later, education shifted from its traditional role and took on the varied attributes of industrialism whether business-efficiency or the socially democratic. With philosophers, artists and scientists setting the stage, education changed the way knowledge was taught, and in the 50s and 60s workers as a whole felt the changes and redefined their way of life. Mainstream politicians still have not understood. The change to the communicative era is only understood in full political terms by the varied ecologic, social, and gender groups on the one hand and by the reactionaries fighting those changes on the other.

Education as a Lagging Entity

Majorities always lag

In looking at education specifically, we find that it is a lagging entity almost by definition because it reflects the majority desires in a given society. The majority never leads innovation, instead following leaders who are usually trying to interpret "current" thought which is no longer current. Thus, educational thought is mediated, often being third-hand, derived from religious, artistic and scientific vision filtered through philosophical and psychological processes and ending with curriculum developers creating something for teachers to use in the classroom.

Where religion and art may lead in cultural transformation, that leadership is usually provided by vision and not by statement. The Romantic Movement of the 19th century is a good case in point in illustrating the overlap of different sectors of the matrix at a given time in contrast to the perception of ideas and events through the matrix over time. With Rationalism and Materialism peaking in the 18th century buoyed by the work of Newton in science and Locke in philosophy during the previous century, the Romantics reacted against absolutist mentality. Times were changing and industrialism was providing a commercial abundance that was unthinkable in a purely agrarian era. The Romantic reaction to increasing industrialism was clearly expressed by Wordsworth and Coleridge in the preface to their 1798 edition, but it remained a vision in the sense that little could be done about it. When Wordsworth berates the materialism of the period with, "The world is too much with us now, getting and spending, we lay waste our powers" he is simply noting that his rural agrarian world is breaking down and that to his mind there are better things for man to be doing than the purely commercial.

At much the same time, philosophy was trying to interpret the changes in the perception of the physical world brought about by Linnaeus, Priestly, Watt, Faraday, Davy and Volta. The way the physical universe could be observed, described, and controlled, changed radically as these men applied the "new" physics of Newton. Where Locke and Hume held the empiricist position of the scientist, Kant, in particular, worked to show how rational thought could be applied to natural chaos. However, the upshot was not to say that reason was everything, as the scientists were saying, but that reason is limited and that we can know only moral truth as all our natural science is a projection of man's own experience and therefore, not absolute. He reflects the demand that rational thought be discussed, but ends in finding the relativeness of the natural world, in contrast to the absoluteness of the moral universe.

Thus, we see great flow within society at one time. The ascendancy of rational materialism in science and the cultural materialism of colonialism in politics are in stark contrast to the artistic and intellectual visionaries who were already moving into the next stage of thought, i.e., beingness rather than havingness.

This time delay especially applies to the world of education where we can see the lagging nature of educational practice in the cultural progressions. In the realm of the real, scientific thought is the leading edge as it has expanded in an increasing sphere since the Renaissance. For the most part, philosophy interpreted the changed world at each turn, while psychology, as a relatively new phenomenon as studied in overt form rather than being a part of philosophy, played little role in interpreting thought until nearly this century. In turn, the study of education developed after psychology, following psychology into being with the pioneering work of Thorndike and Ebbinghaus on varied aspects of then fledgling learning theory. Thorndike's connectionism viewed learning as a trial and error process in which an organism stamped in positive behaviors and stamped out negative ones while Ebbinghaus plotted the original learning curve.

Learning Theory

Learning theory comes from a view of man in relation to the world, i.e. from philosophy through psychology. If philosophically (and inherently, psychologically) man is viewed as born with capabilities which can be augmented or dissipated by disciplined application to a task, then learning theory will say that learning should take place in the ideal school by disciplining children to a task. If, however, man is viewed as being able to be measured in the same way that the physical universe is measured then that will be the basis of learning. In fact, Ebbinghaus demonstrated empirically that when taught nonsense symbols, people will learn "X" amount in a given period of time and will forget "Y" amount in another measured period - the so-called learning curve. He used nonsense syllables because that is the only way to "control" for prior knowledge in the test subjects. Frank Smith notes that schools have been filled with well measured nonsense since then.

Current learning theory is split between the industrial camp with behavioristic measurers following Ebbinghaus, Thorndike, Watson, Skinner and Hebb, and the communicative camp following cognitive psychologists such as Rogers and Bruner.

As noted, changes may be coming more quickly in the modern world than in ages past, but the changes and the response to the changes occur in fundamentally the same patterns now as in the Renaissance. One finds an accepted view of the world which is challenged by new knowledge. The new knowledge spreads, becoming interpreted philosophically, adapted by and for psychology and finally applied in education, furthest step-child of science.

In traditional society, God reigned absolutely in philosophical terms. Since the age of rationalism, science has reigned absolutely. However, with the advent of quantum physics and the theory of relativity, absolutism has given way to probability and relative thinking. Now, point of view and platform for measurement determine the world that can be defined and measured as surely in the social sciences as for quantum physics. With simple assumption gone, clear communication of assumptions was necessary in explaining even the simplest ideas. The world which until the 20th century had had absolute limits was now being viewed as one of process determined by choice of defining principle.

The Process of Choice and the Inevitability of Conflict

The idea of process determined by defining principle is similar to the proposition that, with the rise of surplus production in industrialism, the individual had a choice of self-definition rather than simply being the product of society. The juncture of societal process and individual self-determination brings us to the most difficult aspect of moving into a communicative metaphor of education. When the shift in educational metaphor is laid over the matrix of cultural transformation, several aspects come into clear conflict.

Education from Greece to the 20th century occurred in the formal Authoritarian sector of the matrix. The shift to the Physical sector of the matrix occurred only with the need of industrialism. The shift across the horizontal line dividing the Authoritarian (Absolute-Real) from the Physical (Relative-Real) sectors was accomplished with very little trouble. To be sure, people decried the vocationalism of the business efficiency model and the coddling apparent in the progressive model, but change was swift. From 1893 with the Committee of Ten on Secondary School Studies to the Seven Cardinal Principles of Secondary Education in 1918, the very focus of education changed. Faculty psychology had been discredited by behaviorist experiments, and the new call was for "command of fundamental processes" not a fixed corpus of material leading to becoming an "educated man." In 25 years, education had shifted philosophical orientation, psychological base, and largely physical plant. Where the move from formal to behavioral education, (Authoritarian to Physical in the matrix) caused controversy, both parts remained firmly in the exterior, pragmatic, Aristotelian side of the Matrix. Because both parts retained the external world view of philosophical materialism which had been embedded in American society for two hundred years, the shift was viewed as pragmatic and not questioned by the majority of people who went along with the "leaders". The shift could be justified as social Darwinism in leading America to its proper role in bestriding the world as an industrial colossus.

The current shift from industrial to communicative education takes us from the exterior to the interior sector. The move to the interior, ideal, Platonic side of the matrix cannot be viewed as a minor shift and dismissed by the majority of people. Where, individually, people accepted self-definition as part of themselves in an evolutionary fashion without thought, people in society at-large are still fundamentally guided by philosophical materialism when forced to think. Virtually everyone who has the slightest interest in schools and society knows that there is a fundamental change in process at the moment, but, in searching for an answer, people fall back on their habits of existing thought rather than searching existing information on society to solve for the unknown.   Thus in the schools, we have people applying engineering process methodology to a learning environment which is not concrete and and cannot be explained by conditional analysis. Reductionism has created the marvels of modern scientific life, but it does not work when confronted with the irreducible wholeness of mind.

Just as industrialism gave the common man a self-determining choice in occupation and psychological self-definition within an overall external orientation, post-industrial communication is demanding that the common man work with internally defined process. That is, people are increasingly having to define themselves by who they are and not what they do which demands that the person look inside and have the tools to accomplish self-analysis.

The problem with this is that a "product" of education in 1945 is not adaptable to the speed of change (of process) in 1995.   Product education is necessarily limited to what the product of that moment is. Education has to be on-going in the individual for that individual to remain current. We are not talking about professionals remaining current in their fields of specialization whether nuclear physics, medicine or literary criticism, we are talking about diesel mechanics, architectural drafters, nurses and electronics repairmen. As noted before, where a person used to be educated or trained in a way which was "good enough for his time", that is no longer the case.

In particular, problems arise for individuals making this shift to the internal in their personal lives because there is very little preparation given by schools. The individual is left groping for answers on a personal basis with the archaic thought patterns taught in school, left from another time. Where individuals are left to find their way, schools receive blame for all that is wrong with the changing society. Rather than being perceived as simply a part of cultural transition, schools get blamed for the confused individuals emerging from the educational process.

The Shift

At the height of the industrial period in the Fifties, people lived comfortably dichotomous lives. They worked at one thing, and they were something else in their leisure time; no matter that the two might be in conflict. One could work for the defense department or an industrial polluter and be in charitable organizations with seemingly no personal conflict. Human potential and living to internal fulfillment concerned mystics, poets and visionaries - well out of the mainstream.

However, change had been occurring. Religiously, Buber and de Chardin sought communicative unification of man to man in the seamless pattern of man to God where separation is an impossibility. Gandhi took such individual unification to action, proving in Churchill's words that a "half-naked little fakir" could sunder the British Empire when personal integration meshed with communication to the masses.

In psychology, Perls, Ellis, and Rogers were defying both Behaviorist dogma and the authoritarianism of Freudians with their view of individual cognitive ability dealing with life. Bruner adapted the ideas to learning and said - deal with the individual, not a behavioral class.

Artistically, the Beat poets and rock and roll destroyed the notion that "culture" must come from on high, or at least from Boston or New York. If communication is immediate and instantaneous, place is of no concern. Rather than having a mediated experience, predicated on formalism (Authoritarian sector) as in "high culture", they said, "move directly to feeling" and take in "im-mediate" experience. Ginsburg's "crack of doom on the hydrogen jukebox" moved to the back-beat being laid down by a black man named Berry, coming out of the heartland in St. Louis.

The Matrix, Cultures, and Education

Matrix Personalities and the School

When we apply the matrix personas to education, we have a straightforward method to look at personality types and their interactions. Such differentiation and clarification can also be used in examining role conflicts between the types of personalities typically found in a school. As with any complex social unit, a variety of types are needed in order for proper functioning, even though the types may not understand or even like each other. Without having the four quadrants represented, we lack balance: the current situation. If we examine the matrix, broken down for academic personalities, we can see the possibility for conflict and, at least, the basis for understanding and resolution.

The personas identified in the previous sections fit nicely with educational types both within the schools and the accompanying organizations, i.e., school boards, city and state administrators, unions, colleges of education, and PTAs. In looking at the personalities by sector on the matrix, it is important to keep in mind that any two sides share one characteristic whether both are absolutes, relatives, reals or ideals. Because of this sharing, the truly opposite personalities are on the diagonals, i.e., the   Absolute-Ideal is diagonally opposite the Relative-Real, just as the Absolute-Real is opposite the Relative-Ideal.

As in preceding sections, we will start the discussion in the Inspiriting quadrant. The Inspirational individual as the religious/ intellectual visionary will find his reality in theoretical ideas and value religious or scholarly pursuits rather than the more operational aspects of education whether in administration, maintenance, or teaching. Typically, the Inspirational person will view everyone else in education as being uninterested in theory and an impediment to his work when he thinks of them at all. In turn, he is viewed as not grounded in the reality of the situation by Authoritarians, as being uppity and superior by the Communicators, and is usually ignored or dismissed by the Physicals as much as possible.

On the other hand, the Authoritarian wants to control and will be found in the front office in school, on the school board, or running the union. Here, we are dealing with a decision-maker rather than a valuer; one who is oriented to the exterior rather than interior, a do-er not a be-er. This person does not have the pure truth of the inspirational person, the insight of the communicator or the acceptance of the physical person. Despite these drawbacks, he has chosen to take power and is allowed to do so if only because the other personalities do not want it. Often this person is viewed by the Inspirational and Communicative people as stupid and unbased in his leadership on a personal plane, while at the same time the position behind the person is itself scorned as well. The Authoritarian often views the others as inferior as he is in "control." The interesting part of the Authoritarian position is that the leaders of all of the power units come from the same sector and, therefore, tend to speak the same language.   The union leaders, themselves representing teachers, tend to be Authoritarians, not Communicators, as are the city and state board members.   The head of a union with 100,000 members had better be a leader, able to keep authority clear and working. When such a leader sits down to negotiate with the state superintendent of schools, the only real difference is which person represents which constituency. The administrative power hierarchy in its present form is comfortable to all those concerned with power.

The Physical person is not primarily concerned with thought or feeling, and by being governed by "knownness" with an exterior orientation, will probably be taking care of the school in its physical form. This could well be as a mechanic, repair person, or janitor taking care of the operation of the school, or part of the support staff, whether as an aide or secretary. By sharing the Real with the Authoritarians, the

Physicals act as adjuncts to the given administrative policy, frustrating some of the Inspirators and Communicators who tend to see policy as rather monolithic and not concerned with teaching and scholarship.

The Communicative individual is concerned with values and ideas, but from the point of view of working with and talking about them rather than in innovative or creative thinking per se. The Communicator does not speak with the truth of the Inspirator, but rather in terms that other people can understand and is, therefore, the teacher rather than the scholar. By using truth in a relative way for the convenience of communication, the communicators irritate Inspirators; by criticizing, they irritate the Authoritarians; and by seeking ideas, they clash with the Physicals.

Cultural Conflicts in the Politics of Education

As we have seen so far, there are certain currents in cultural evolution both at one fixed time and also over time. When we examine the movement around and through the matrix and compare it to schools, we are immediately struck by the problem. Although the U.S., as one society in the larger entity of Western culture, largely moved from the Physical to the Communicative quadrant in the 50s and 60s, and derive our present power from the Inspirational (information science), our school systems still remain firmly entrenched in the bureaucracy of the Physical quadrant. The matter is further complicated operationally because leadership resides in the politics of the Authoritarian sector. The Authoritarians, who ultimately control the bureaucracy and who are opposite the communicators on the matrix, try to impose industrial measurement with management and teaching by objectives on the act of learning. This insures that they remain in control even though learning does not of itself submit to measurement directly. Clearly, realignment is necessary.

Figure 7.8

The Matrix and the Schools

	I d e a l	**R e a l**
A b s o l u t e	Educational Theorists Innovators	Administrative Control Political Power
R e l a t i v e	Teachers Current U.S. Society	School Staff The Schools

Movement into the Communicative Quadrant

The shift from the Authoritarian to the Physical sector in 1900 occurred relatively smoothly because both parts are in the Real and orient themselves to the observable and measurable. By keeping the Real world orientation the same, the cultural shift from Absolute to Relative was minimized. Indeed, individuals have always viewed the world with Relative self-interest just as Western culture, and U.S. society in particular, have always been predominantly materialist in outlook.

The current cultural movement into the Communicative represents a huge shift in consciousness: from the operational world of ruling and doing to the ideational world of knowing and being. People make the shift in different ways and at different times; institutions usually take longer and lag more. For example, the factory worker who no longer defines himself by his job, but rather by what he does in his leisure time, has made the shift to the communicative sector on an unconscious level. However, as he works in the factory rather than with ideas, he probably retains a materialist philosophy on the conscious level because he works for one reason: to get a paycheck. Changing types of jobs to become computer operators, for example, might be possible, but the data are not very positive for retraining physical workers into information workers. For example, assembly line auto workers who are given permanent layoffs simply do not do well at computer terminals when retrained. They like the movement, the doing, and comraderie of working the assembly line rather than sitting in isolation, looking at a screen all day. Job retraining seems most successful when the jobs are not too dissimilar, i.e., Physical people can be retrained in Physical jobs fairly successfully, but not very well in Communicative jobs.

The Authoritarians, the people in power, those in the "real world," the "bottom-line kind of guys," the "real go-getters," tend to define themselves with their jobs, not in the old manner of the chandler, cooper, or smith, but rather their success in life relates to their job success. Money, power and prestige come with such success, and the shift is immense in moving from those concrete measures of success to the relative world of ideas and self-definition of personal success. The interior self-definition required in the Communicative sector is anathema to the exterior realist of the Authoritarian sector. The shift from external to internal definition of self is not easily accomplished when the exterior contains the very means of the previous self-definition. The move to the interior is not limited to the job world however.

The Rise of the Feminine

Nowhere is this clearer than in the rise of the feminine, and here, feminine is used to mean the more sensitive side of life - intuitive, fertile, creative, and nurturing. The hardness and lack of sensitivity of traditional maleness mirrors the Real Side of the Matrix. Males have "conquered", "won," or "moved up"- in other words dominated others, but emotional response was not highly prized and in fact rather discouraged as "unmale" in best case, or more usually used derisively as "gay."

With movement into the Ideal side of the Matrix, one sees a rise in the expectations of sensitivity. Males are now supposed to think of their partners and families, not just of themselves. Males are supposed to participate in childbirth, change diapers, take care of the house and be supportive of the spouse and children. They are not supposed to be the breadwinning men of the Fifties who came in and had their wives make a martini while they made themselves comfortable in front of the TV - with the wife also taking care of dinner, the children, and the house.

Just as one saw a developing sensitivity in the Beats and the early cognitive psychologists in the Fifties, throughout the Sixties in popular culture one saw signs of this shift in the rise of the Feminist Movement - and now with the New Age Movement - sensitivity is in full flower - so popular and pervasive that jokes are made of it.

The movie *Tootsie* is illustrative of sex role stereotyping and pokes fun at the coping mechanisms women have had to adopt. To paraphrase Dustin Hoffman, as a male, complaining to his roommate of his ill-treatment as a woman by his soap-opera director: he called me names - Tootsie, Sweetheart, Honey Then he told me what he wanted. I didn't like it, but didn't say anything. I did what I wanted; he yelled at me; I apologized, and that was that.

The coping mechanism is non-directive and non-linear, reflecting the only way a person with no power can deal with those who give direct orders and expect them to be carried out. Just as Gandhi defeated the British with non-violent passive resistance, women have been succeeding for years with little recognition of the approach.

However, with society as a whole moving toward a non-linear, non-hierarchic view, recognition of the feminine is on the rise in a number or areas. Cognitive psychology recognizes the internalness of mind - in contrast to the externalness of behaviorism. Progressive corporations are moving away from hierarchy just as women are becoming powerful in corporations. Workplace sexual stereotypes have had to be dropped as women have assumed many positions previously thought of exclusively as male - firefighters, not just dispatchers; telephone electrical installers, not just operators; corporate officials, not just corporate secretaries; doctors, not just nurses; and pilots, not just young stewardesses in tight-fitting clothes.

That is not to say that all has changed. Change occurs at different rates in different sectors.

Institutional Change and the Schools

Institutions tend to change more slowly and then only when threatened with crisis. In the examples of Ford and Harley-Davidson, to pick two companies which faced crisis in different periods, the threat reshaped the structure of the companies. They did not choose to change because they wanted to, but because existence depended on it. We are viewing the educational establishment looking over the brink into the abyss at the moment.

The first, obvious, and far too easy, educational solution is to say, "let's move the power around to the communicators (teachers), give them more education and make them more professional so they can handle more administration." While being suggested more and more often, that is unfortunately naive because part of the reason the teachers are teachers is because they are "communicative personalities" and they do not want to be in the opposite quadrant dealing with management and decisions. If they wanted to be managers, they would be in the Authoritarian sector and have MBAs instead of being in the Communicative and having teaching certificates. This is not to say that teachers shouldn't have more training and be paid as well as MBAs, but that is altogether another question.

The other naive solution that is being suggested is to adopt the model of progressive corporations which education already did once earlier in the century. Schools adopted the industrial model of bureaucratic hierarchy with the introduction of compulsory mass education, and so people are suggesting that schools adopt the administrative methods of leading corporations today. This misses the point that schools and corporations have different goals.

Having looked earlier at now-emerging models of corporate cooperation, we see a sharing of corporate power for mutual benefit of workers and management - which in corporate terms means increasing the profits. Management "gives up" some of its power to the people producing the goods, whether industrial products such as motorcycles in the case of Harley-Davidson or information products such as software, in return for the producers increasing production and taking greater responsibility for themselves. This sounds like the ideal of workers working for "themselves"; however, the real point is that more is being produced, i.e., the old bottom-line goal remains firmly intact. Again, this is not to say that workers shouldn't work for themselves, but we should not confuse the corporate world with education. Of course, management will give up "power" if it makes more money, that is corporate pragmatism, not social innovation. We also should not confuse superficial rearrangement of items with fundamental restructuring of goals.

Restructuring Education

The idea of changing the superficial look of education while keeping the same goals is at the heart of most educational "innovation." That is, the people in power stay in power while assuaging the various political groups of the constituency, but nothing fundamental changes. Real innovation will occur when the goals and structure of education are changed.

The present discussion will be cursory, pointing the way. It will be taken up in depth in part three.

Goals

At present, the goals of most public schools still reflect the idea that students are empty vessels which need to be filled and the only debate centers around what they will be filled with: facts or skills, with or without values. Of course, the Lockean notion of the tabula rasa completely ignores the findings of cognitive psychology. We know full well that people simply do not learn information; they learn meaning, and meaning is mediated by the individual's cognitive structures. In turn, the cognitive structures are a result of the person's interaction with the world in all its facets - their ways of integrating new information with what they already know. Schools which cannot engage these structures are doomed.

When schools are more concerned with the lines of authority within the bureaucratic hierarchy, or getting through a certain corpus of content material than with the students, is it any wonder that students are apathetic and care little for the schools? Schools which ignore the students are in turn ignored or, worse, subverted.

Just as cognitive structures change with the addition of meaningful new information, educational goals must change to reflect the new awareness of learning. Rather than viewing students as empty vessels which need to be filled, we might better view them as interactive beings who seek meaning in the world and need to know the ways in which to find that meaning.

Clearly, the industrial hierarchy of present school systems is anachronistic. At its best, the present system was merely a convenient means for controlling compulsory mass education with its huge numbers. At its worst, it fits students into preset slots, ignoring the individual needs of the student.

Structurally, the system is set up to provide information and control to the top of the hierarchy, not for the top of the hierarchy to see that the needs of the bottom are met, i.e., the students and teachers. As mentioned, flattening the hierarchical power chart and making the teachers into administrators will not work. In like manner, making the administrators understand the necessary autonomy of the teaching process is not likely either.

Restructuring, in which the parties redefine their roles, demands that all the involved parties make concessions. Rather than having administrators "over" teachers, we must see administrators "next" to teachers, providing the necessary facilitation of education. Whereas teachers are the key in educating students, they need clean rooms provided by janitors, curriculum aids provided by school system developers, media help provided by the school, and a principal to coordinate these needs. In each case however, the teacher and class must be the focal point; help must directed by the teacher and come in as needed to provide the most beneficial environment for student learning. Just as the doctor and lawyer have office managers to run day to day operations, teachers must have administration as help.

The reformation of education in the restructuring of both goals and hierarchy will emerge from the current antagonism, malaise, and distrust. It will not be imposed from the top, but rather grow in organic fashion from the bottom as teachers and parents finally decide action must be taken: Backwards to the Basics will give way to Just Say Know.

Part II

APPLYING
THE
MATRIX
TO
Schools

School
in
Present Time

CHAPTER 8

Educational Demise - The Rise of Productivity and Accountability or Backwards to the Basics

The idea of communication as the basis of education demands that the interior and ideal become valued over the pragmatic and exterior. This shift forms the basis for our current educational conflict: industrial measurement is being imposed on a system for which it was not designed. Present day industry is changing because people are not machines; when people are valued, when their opinions are solicited and acted upon, when there is meaning in what they do, they work more productively. The orientation of industry is so pragmatic that it is switching to communication in both machine design and production as well as in worker relations as a way to keep productivity up. Education, on the other hand, being an immense bureaucracy with no identifiably pragmatic bent other than to be self-sustaining, is not so easily adaptable. Productivity in industry is easily accounted for in output per employee. Quality, while not so directly measured, can be assessed by numerous indirect methods, the simplest being, "Are the customers satisfied? Do they come back?" Educational productivity cannot be measured, and no one even bothers to ask about satisfaction.

In traditional education, quality was assured by the reputation of the teacher or school. From the time of Socrates' school to the Harvard and Yale of the turn of the 20th century, quality meant name brand product. Aristotle's appeal of ethos determined the good in education with absolute accountability: one either followed the prescribed form or left school, whether it be grammar school, high school or college.

With the technical specification needed for industrialism, the good in education came to be determined by pragmatic action, not reputation of good solely, allowing a geographic spread of institutions and knowledge. Land grant and private institutions sprang up to meet the new need. Engineers could come from Carnegie Tech, Colorado School of Mines, or Purdue, and agronomists from Penn State, Michigan State or Texas A&M and know they had good training. People chose their field from among many and then pursued their choice single-mindedly to the exclusion of other knowledge. The broader aim of liberal education had perhaps been lost, but a booming America seemed happy.

The transition into a communicative form of education seemingly demands a similar flattening of educative process. By flattening, we mean the shift from the vertical societal structure of elite, traditional education as it gave way to broad-based mass compulsory industrial education. That, in turn, seems to be giving way to completely open access with an emphasis on education as a lifelong pursuit as deemed necessary by the individual. From the shopping mall aspect of modern high schools, to the continuing education components of universities, education is increasingly by choice - not demand.

Even in this atmosphere of individual decision, reactionary Authoritarians are trying to go back to the "good old days," while substituting the new prescription of productivity and accountability for the absolute right and wrong of traditional prescriptivism. The reductionist analytical approach which ensures productivity in projects such as the space shuttle is inappropriately applied to education which is a cumulative, synthetic, creative endeavor, not subject to the simplistic quantitative measures of industrial productivity.

Some people may argue that educational productivity can be measured by standardized or competency based tests, just as quality in industrial and military training is assured. The response is equally simple: productivity as measured by standardized or competency based tests can be only a tiny fraction of what is even overtly desired to be taught in school (let alone what is) and that they only test one level - the students. With so many propositions suggested in that last statement, let's enumerate and then elucidate:

1. Standardized tests are limited in scope. We should work for more than limited education. Competency-based tests (often noted as minimal competence) are even more restricted by testing only stated objectives.

2. If the elementary school curriculum is considered, subject matter is only a part of the day - socialization, for example, is virtually as important - what then is going to be tested at that level and why?

3. In high school, three different tracks of subjects are commonplace. How can a standardized test possibly be fair under such circumstances? Or - to use testing terminology - how can it be either reliable or valid?

4. With state mandated curriculum competencies, how can nationally standardized tests hope to test what is specified?

5. At all levels, standardized tests show bias according to sex, ethnicity, native language, and geographic location.

6. What is productivity?

7. Why are students evaluated by standardized tests when teachers and administrators are evaluated by written reports?

8. Productivity seems linked to accountability - always from the top down.

While many other possibilities come to mind, these eight are sufficient to discuss the problems of industrial measurement in a communicative age. The point here is not to cite testing as the primary evil in schools; it is only a reflection of the operative industrial metaphor. As long as people are considered output machines which need to be monitored and measured, then testing will have hegemony. Because people seem to think education is reducible to quantitative measurement, the best that can be hoped for is one set of information chosen by a person in a high place with an accompanying standardized test which will measure a representative sample of the total set.

Such reductionist simplicity may have classified a portion of the natural world and given the ability to fly to the moon, no mean feats, but it has also given us pollution and nuclear arms which threaten our very existence, all without giving us a clue as to how people learn, what a mind is, what is the meaning of life, and what the human race needs to do to survive. By applying a reductionist mentality to school, we seek to apply teacher-proof, fail-safe mechanisms to the school in the same way that engineers apply them to the space program. Without being morbid, the space shuttle Challenger disaster was only an accident in the sense that it occurred when it did, failure had to be expected at some point as with any mechanical device.

Reductionism as the basis of the scientific method breaks items down beautifully (analysis), but it does not build items up (synthesis) or have a way to work with creativity or meaning. Aristotle and Linnaeus, in classifying a portion the natural world, only sought to arrange a good classification, not tell what it meant. Biochemists can reduce any life form to its molecular structure, but not build it backward so it works, *or* tell what it means. Biochemists are presently in the same position as structural linguists were in the 1940s. The linguists could analyze a language thoroughly enough that every sound in the language was accounted for and yet say that language was habit - not expression of meaning, i.e., they described; they did not explain.

When we apply reductionism to the schools, we get the present system - disembodied information being thrown at students and then carefully measured, all with a sense of purposelessness on the parts of both teachers and students. The majority of politicians stand to the side shouting, "more and harder," each trying to out-grandstand the others to an ignorant populace, sounding like the ugly American who when confronted with a non-English speaking person raises his voice in the thought that volume will compensate for lack of comprehension.

Problems with Testing

Standardized Tests are Limited

On that note, let us look at the first criticism: Standardized tests are limited in scope. We should work for more than limited education. Competency based tests (often noted as minimal competence) are even more restricted because they attempt to measure only from explicitly stated objectives.

Standardized tests by nature must have a particular subject matter to test, such as content material from the classroom or a psychological profile, to take just two possibilities. "Standardized" simply means that the given exam has been tested against a known population and has been found to be reliable and valid to within accepted limits. That is to say that it has been tested against a specified group of people possessing known qualities; that the test does in fact test what it is supposed to test (validity); and that it will work every time with similar results within a given margin of error (reliability). The population distribution will be the familiar bell curve of a few good students at one end, most in the large swell in the middle and some less able students at the other end. Given these strictures, such tests must be limited, especially because the development cost is so great that material must be applicable to a wide variety of groups. The last statement seems to be a violation of norming but is not as practiced. If one takes a stratified random sample (assuring inclusion of all representative parts of a given population) of all high school students, one will measure (or sample) a correct percentage of each ethnic group, each geographic group as well as age and sex group for the entire group of students. Insure fairness? Not likely. Not unless your group matches the entire population of the norming group and not necessarily for any individual.

If, for example, we take a typical reading test normed against all high school students in the U.S., and we give it to students in Albuquerque, New Mexico, the higher percentage of Hispanic and Indian students almost assures that the mean for the city will be lower than the national average. If, however, we move 65 miles up the Rio Grande Valley to Los Alamos, home of the lab that created the A-bomb, and home to the highest per capita ratio of Ph.D.s in the country, the reading mean will almost certainly exceed the national mean. This statement is not about genetics, but rather assumed culture behind the construction of the test. If one grows up Anglo and takes an Anglo reading test, shared assumptions on language and culture allow the test to be fair. If, however, one grows up Hispanic and takes an Anglo reading test, then the test may be as much about how well Anglo culture is understood as about how much is known about reading. And yet the test may fit all national test criteria for being valid and reliable.

The same comment can be made about any academic school reading test which is used for testing a group such as vocational students. Academic culture has its own language and norms which may not be shared by the special population of a vocational school. This is a serious problem for vocational schools as they often base admittance on a test which has little or nothing to say about the ability of students to read vocational material. When ethnicity and vocational training are combined the margin of error is compounded substantially and unfairly.

Competency-based Testing

When examining standardized test results, limitations must be noted, but with competency based testing, the limitations are even more severe, and the chance for error greatly increased. Competency-based curricula and testing are founded on the premise that the students being targeted should achieve a given level or competence. Sometimes this is stated as a minimal competence. The problem with such structure is that it is suited to training and not education. It does indeed say what desired knowledge a person will possess and be able to manipulate in a given manner. However, would you want your children to know only what could be written down by a group of people at the state capitol? Such limitation of knowledge is not suited to the open-ended goal of education which presumably assists someone in dealing with the world in a meaningful way. It is far more useful, for instance, for teaching someone to be able to repair or install an engine part. The limitations of training are custom-made for competency testing where the competency is usually demonstrated as a performance level as in military training or industrial assembly. Ultimately, performance competencies determine whether a robotic machine can perform the task even more efficiently than a trained worker. In school, it is very difficult to write a competency for appreciation of poetry or music because those activities do not reduce to behavioral terms with any fidelity. Testing such a competency is even more elusive.

While the establishment of minimal competencies sounds laudable when compared to having no standards, in fact, minimal competence usually assures just that: minimal. Rather than focusing on the potential of learning, the classroom aim becomes achieving the minimal, especially when teachers are often rated on how many students do or do not reach the minimal score on the test. Assurance of mediocrity seems less than desirable in such a light.

Finally, the point one never hears discussed is that tests, whether competency based or standardized, reflect a few correct answers but are usually scored by what the student does not know. Tests do not work with the sum total of what a student knows, as though that could possibly be broached. They measure what the student does not know, against a criterion which may or may not be explicit, and the information for achievement may or may not have been taught, and to a norm to which the given student may or may not conform. And yet, we have people calling for expanded testing.

The current move toward 'qualitative' testing is an example of trying to placate a few strident voices while keeping the present system intact as a bureaucracy. Although qualitative testing may sound less offensive in its political correctness, the basic underlying premise remains the same as before.

Elementary School Tests

If the elementary school curriculum is considered, subject matter is only a part of the day - socialization, for example, is virtually as important, especially in the early grades. What then is going to be tested and why? Standardized tests in elementary school look at the content material such as reading and arithmetic, but by everyone's admission social aspects have great importance in the curricula. Getting along with others, listening to the teacher, and following directions always receive importance in parent-teacher conferences and report cards yet they are not tested. Why? The most obvious reason is that it is practically impossible to create a standardized test of such behavior in any meaningful way, especially one which could be administered with suitable ease. The other factor is that people broadly agree on what is suitable. Ordinarily, acceptable behavior is considered to be not causing too much trouble, paying at least some heed to the teacher, and mostly doing what one is told. The teacher recognizes this pattern just as do the parents and children and almost everyone agrees.

Why, if we trust teachers to report on how a child acts in class, whether the child seems normal, or whether he or she is making social progress, do we not trust teachers on the so much more easily statable issues of whether the child is progressing in reading or arithmetic? We trust them in the social aspects of education, but not in the areas in which they receive most of their training. The clearest implication of such a schizophrenic reaction is to state that such complete trust would give teachers true autonomy in their classes - a position the educational hierarchy is not willing to grant. It is the exact position that must be achieved if teachers are to deal with students as individuals and not as a normative sample of childhood.

High School Tests

In contrast to elementary school, high school commonly has three different tracks of subjects. How can a standardized test possibly be fair under such circumstances? Or to use testing terminology - how can it be either reliable or valid? Clearly, if there are three tracks, a standardized test will be valid for only one group, presuming that at least one group matches the standard population used for norming. A standardized academic math test, used for prediction of success in college, will be normed for the general academic track where students can go to a non-selective college; it is not for the vocational students on one hand, or the advanced placement students on the other. For either of the latter, the test will not be strictly valid. If the test is not valid, it cannot be reliable. Therefore, it may be valid for one group while the other two groups have their test scores recorded as though the test was worthwhile even if it was a travesty.

In short, anytime tracking isolates a non-random sample of students, the chances are good that test invalidity will occur if the test is administered to all tracks. Certainly, reliability is impossible to guarantee.

State Mandated Competencies

With state mandated curriculum competencies, how can a standardized test hope to test what is specified? It cannot. When California approves an English Only Amendment and New Mexico is officially bilingual, the state competencies will be different and reflect state attitudes. It would be very difficult to construct a Reading, Language Arts, or Social Studies standardized test that could incorporate competencies of both states when one is overtly seeking assimilation and the other promotes multiculturalism. Such state diversity, let alone the diversity reflected by local school boards, call into question the usefulness of practically any standardized test.

Test Bias

At all levels, standardized tests show bias according to sex, ethnicity, native language, and geographic location. Ethnic and native language bias have already been discussed and are readily apparent. Additionally, sex and geographic location appear time after time as test biases. A New England Anglo male will typically outscore all others whether female or minority from the same area or a male from another area. In contrast, a minority female from the South or Southwest will underscore all other groups on nationally standardized tests. Furthermore, age will affect testing greatly if it varies from, or even within, the norming sample. For example, on college admissions aptitude tests, seniors typically outscore juniors. This can easily be explained by more developmental maturity, more test experience, greater subject matter knowledge, more motivation or all of the above. If individual 'aptitude' changes so consistently over a year, such tests must be achievement tests measuring education and maturity - not individual aptitude as is claimed.

In response to the public outcry as well as several court cases about testing discrimination, the College Board and Educational Testing Service among others signed an agreement in 1989 to try to eliminate these biases. Such a frank admission means that women, and minorities were discriminated against until the outcry became too great to ignore. By making an admission and saying they will correct the problem, they are following the Authoritarian Principle of assuaging angry power groups by political means while retaining their own power in much the same form as before the outcry. Alternatives exist.

Productivity

What is productivity?

What is productivity? Politicians seem to be the only ones who know what educational productivity is. From reading the newspaper, one surmises that productivity is figured as were the body counts in the Vietnam War. Just as body counts were based on bomb tonnage dropped on the Vietnamese, educational productivity seems to be based on how many students are enrolled, not on whether anyone learns anything. Between educational administrators who are really politicians in disguise in the Authoritarian sector and the openly declared politicians, discussion rages around FTEs (full-time equivalent students). Because monies are allocated by governmental jurisdictions based on student enrollment, the body count is important in order to keep operations running at full funding.

Productivity seems to revolve around the number of students in school and the number who graduate. There is a tenuous assumption that in the intervening period of time desired learning has actually taken place. Tests are a very easy way to justify the assertion that something productive has occurred. One does not know what the student has learned as that is not possible to know; one can at best sample the facts that something on which time was spent at school was discovered on a test. The simplest way to have a high graduation rate is to assure that the standards or minimal competencies are so low that no one could be flunked out. Then one can say we have a 100% graduation rate, put on a big smile, and shake hands in self-congratulation.

If, in fact, productivity means integrating knowledge into one's life, then that cannot be measured. One must accept the word of the students and have faith.

Different Evaluation within the Educational Hierarchy

Why are students evaluated by standardized tests when teachers and administrators are evaluated by written reports? Seemingly, we evaluate students by the use of standardized tests but not teachers and administrators. Yes, there are certification tests for teachers and administrators, but those tests are not what determines promotion, tenure and advancement. We will not even talk about teacher minimal competency tests; the idea of a minimally competent teacher is not a pleasant thought.

Although tests often determine student advancement as well as what is considered to be "learned," teachers and administrators have written reports based on observation by superiors. Presumably these observations have stated criteria, but the process remains that of one individual observing another and judging his or her ability. Curiously, what is acceptable for administrators viewing teachers is not acceptable for teachers viewing students. An administrator can say a teacher is not acceptable simply by observing him or her, but if a teacher were to say, "That student is unacceptable by my observation" the administrators would demand "objective" proof, i.e. something external as a validation of the teacher's views because in administration eyes *teachers cannot be trusted.*

Anyone who has spent time in the classroom as a teacher knows that just by looking at the class it is clear who understands and who is confused. Students are not a rare breed of human being; when they do not understand, they look confused, bored, distracted or demonstrate a host of other behaviors all of which say to the teacher, "I am not with you." The teacher who is not able to understand such signals should not be in front of the class. And yet, teacher observations must be validated externally, not accepted at face value as valid.

Productivity Equals Accountability?

In the political terms in which education is discussed, productivity seems linked to accountability - always from the top down. When people speak of educational productivity, it is always viewed that the students are the product and that the performance of the product can be squeezed from the top down just as Henry Ford squeezed his workers by increasing assembly line speed. In the common view, students are accountable to teachers who are accountable to principals and on up the line to superintendent of instruction and the state board of education. Why is it that no one takes the view that the state board (and everyone in between) is responsible to the teachers and students?

Why does it sound so preposterous to imagine a member of the state board of education coming to a school, attending a faculty meeting at Washington Elementary or Roosevelt High, and asking, "What do you need?" Suppress your giggles because that is precisely what should be happening - and as we looked at industry, that is what is happening in the best run companies. The managers of Harley - Davidson know what is going on with production workers and work with, not over, the assembly people. Clearly our educational system is confused when a motorcycle manufacturer is more socially and organizationally advanced than our schools.

Communicative education demands that hierarchy be dismantled and be replaced by non-vertical relationship in which students are the most important item. They are, afterall, the only reason for schools. Just as surely, teachers are the most important school officials as they are the ones who work directly with the students on a daily and yearly basis. All others connected with schools are distinctly secondary figures and should be treated as such. The janitor who keeps the school clean and warm is more directly important to students than members of the state board of education.

Viewing the Limits

Clearly, the eight points are not comprehensive in criticizing industrial education, but they are sufficient to illustrate the shortcomings of viewing education as an industrial commodity to be constructed in mechanical fashion. Leveling criticism is very easy in such a case, and in that sense, it is more productive to look at what is needed rather than what is already in existence. The real point of the eight criticisms is to show that industrial education is concerned with limits.

Limits specify how poor something can be and still qualify, not how good it can be. Whether one discusses the qualifications of a worker on the assembly line, the quality of an SG oil rated by the American Petroleum Institute, or the training of a technician, the discussion is not of the optimal or the potential, but rather of the minimal acceptable level. As long as we ask for minimal education, I am sure we will have it. I think we deserve better.

CHAPTER 9

Communicative Education or Just Say Know

Communicative education must be meaning driven. Without meaning, facts are simply random information - like white noise on a tv - not knowledge. The present backwards-to-the-basics people react to the idea of communicative education (from the few who try to practice it) just as behaviorist linguists reacted to the transformational-generative grammar of Chomsky by saying, that it is mentalist conception which lacks rigor... only speculation with no grounding in fact. In other words if it can't be measured quantitatively, it doesn't exist.

The Language Model

The comparison of language study with overall educational endeavor is instructive as language study has reflected both the theoretical and applied sides of educational controversies, often leading the way. The link between language, thought, and philosophical expression would seem to explain the connection.

At the turn of the century, language teaching was prescriptive. The school master told the student what correct usage was and the student copied the precepts given. This method had been accepted practice since

Aristotle laid down the types of arguments that could be used and under what circumstances. In foreign language teaching, the grammar translation method dominated, with the written text constituting reality, whether in a dead language such as Latin, or a living one such as French.

In the Thirties, behaviorist linguists came to the forefront led by Bloomfield (1933, p. 33) who stated, "The materialistic (or better, mechanistic) theory supposes that the variability of human conduct including speech is due only to the fact that the human body is a very complex system. Human actions...are part of cause-and-effect sequences exactly like those which we observe, say in the study of physics or chemistry." The effort to make linguistics an exact science along the lines of physics and chemistry put language study in the same position as the sciences describing action and reaction, and classifying the linguistic world. Politzer noted (1972, p. 6), "Structural descriptive linguistics...was primarily the manifestation of scientific positivism: the goal of linguistic science was the gathering and accurate description of observable facts." Thus, the descriptivists formed mind-numbing "rules" of English as spoken (as only actual spoken language behavior was reality, not what was written or what schools taught) and ethnolinguists wrote down the patterns of the previously unwritten Indian languages. The idea of habits and patterns dominated discussions of language.

The advent of the Second World War brought a great need for people to speak another language and the behaviorists got a chance to put language patterns to pedagogic work. As summarized by Fries (1958, v), "learning a foreign language consists...in developing a new set of habits." Lado added (1964, p. xv), "to learn a new language one must establish orally the patterns of the language as subconscious habit." They showed that language could be taught as sentence patterning, but with the number of hours needed for the audio-lingual method, virtually any other method would have worked as well.

What was missing was any discussion of meaning. For these people language was nothing but pattern, a habit to be acquired.

In 1957, Chomsky wrote *Syntactic Structures,* saying, that language had two levels: a deep level where the core propositions of meaning resided and a surface level which was the actual expression of the deeper level. Thus, language is meaning driven, not pattern driven - the meaning determines the form rather than the meaning being fitted into the form. As he later noted (1965, p. 4), "The problem for the linguist, as well as for the child learning the language, is to determine from the data of performance the underlying system of rules that has been mastered by the speaker-hearer and that he puts into actual performance.

Hence, in a technical sense, linguistic theory is mentalistic since it is concerned with discovering a mental reality underlying actual behavior." When he specifies "performance" he is using that in a technical sense of what the person actually said in contrast to the competence level which is the sum total of the person's knowledge of the language. Thus, a person's competence is always ahead of his performance as expression never hits the ideal. This helps to explain why children can, seemingly innately, understand more than they can produce, even if they cannot formulate the rules of language overtly.

The innateness argument for language acquisition comes about because children are not taught language: they acquire it by meaningful use. Afterall if linguists cannot describe a language fully, how can the average parent? and yet virtually everyone acquires complete language in four years with no teaching. As Politzer noted about children's learning a language (1972, p. 84), "Since it has not been described, it follows that it could not have been acquired by overt teaching. [this attitude] emphasizes that the learner, rather than the teacher, is the important factor in the learning process."

The impact of Chomsky's work was, in essence, that previous views of language were inadequate to explain the immense variety and creativity of language itself and the ability of the learners to master such a complex system in a couple of years with no formal instruction. He had moved beyond the prescriptive and descriptive into explanatory theory which reached in directions far beyond his purely theoretical linguistics, among them reading, rhetoric and language teaching.

Where structural linguists were interested in grammatical description, devoid of meaning, and behavioral psychologists were interested only in the observable actions of a person, not the underlying reasons, the generative grammarians investigated the process by which grammar formed a given surface structure, just as cognitive psychologists looked for the process behind a person's behavior. This teleologic difference illustrates the shift from the Physical sector to the Communicative.

Wider Implications of Meaning-Driven Language Systems

When Chomsky's ideas of deep level/surface level and competence/performance are integrated into a language teaching approach, the amalgam must be meaning-driven and context sensitive, subject to social and psychological variables. In English as a Foreign Language (EFL), theorists immediately saw applications of the transformational principles such as the competence/performance duality which was useful with the goal always being a more complete competence. Gategno's Silent Way, Curran's Community Language

Learning, and Asher's Total Physical Response arose in EFL; Frank Smith and the Goodmans led psycholinguistics; and rhetoric moved from Aristotelian product orientation to the process orientation of Pike, Toulmin and others. In each case, the view was of dynamic language which people needed for communication, not simply a subject to be taught. Additionally, the emphasis is on the learner learning, not the teacher teaching, or the corpus of content material.

Caleb Gategno felt that learners needed time to assimilate new information before having to produce a response (allowing time for integration into competence before performance - the exact opposite of the behaviorist pattern practice). His "Silent Way" method had the teacher give students a sample of language which was then silently manipulated by the teacher using colored rods as substitutes for the words or language parts while the students reformed the sample phrase. For example, in teaching the question inversion form, "There is a pencil on the desk - Is there a pencil on the desk?", the use of the rods allows students to see the relationships of the inversion. Then when the students could perform the material, they could manipulate the rods to ask or answer questions with other students while substituting their own words.

In a similar fashion, Curran felt that students must have control of what was learned if they were going to be fully engaged. A teacher for him was a facilitator helping students learn what they needed - thus the name Community Language Learning because the students had to agree on what was needed. Essentially, students would say what they needed to learn about in their native language, and the teacher would supply the necessary context, usage, and grammar to express the need. The teacher was present to help, but not to direct the class which had to generate its own direction, empowering the students.

Asher's Total Physical Response grew out of the discoveries in brain hemisphericity. The difference in the apprehension of subject material between the left and right sides of the brain and the different means of encoding that subject material in the brain led Asher to try to use a means of teaching which used the special abilities of both sides of the brain. The method demands that language learners use both analytic and holistic means of processing information.

The emphasis in all three of these EFL methods is on the learner learning, not on the teacher or subject matter. In like manner, the psycholinguists looked at the way people learn, that is, how new information is integrated with old to produce entirely new structures.

Psycholinguistics is broadly the intersection of linguistics and psychology and is an often misused term. Kenneth and Yetta Goodman and Frank Smith are often viewed as founders. The Goodmans initially examined the cultural differences between the reading errors of black and white children, discovering that background knowledge of the white culture appeared most significant in the reading of white school books. Smith noted that reading is not primarily a visual process, but rather a mental process, determined by knowledge of language, knowledge of the subject matter, and knowledge of the world in general. Without the combination of the three processes, integration of new knowledge with old knowledge is difficult.

Finally, in rhetoric, the major change has been in the internalization of process as opposed to the very external product sought by Aristotelians. The classic ideal of heuristics, or discovery, was to find the best argument to persuade your opponent to come over to your position. Modern rhetoric's goal is not so much to persuade as to identify, to find a heuristic which gives personal identification and discovery to an event. Pike's tagmemic rhetoric supplied a heuristic useful for examining virtually any event in objective or personal terms. Burke's Pentad, while overtly for drama, can be more broadly applied. Langer, Toulmin, and Ricoeur, philosophers as much as rhetoricians, also see language as a means of discovery.

Applying Communicative Language Education to General Education

The shift to communicative education means eliminating much of the hierarchical framework as it now exists, and substituting a multidimensional network around the student. The present school system is predicated on a past tense technology. The older buildings resemble factories (the newer schools resemble shopping mall) with rows of classes and rows of students in the classes. Students "progress" through the school as so many widgets being inspected in timely fashion. When they are finished, ironically "commenced," do they have the tools to understand the world? Usually not with their industrial/ semi-vocational education. Do they have true vocational skills? No, they were probably in the large middle track of "could go to non-selective college", where they could take or not take almost any mishmash of courses with no focus - not in vocational training or advanced placement college courses. Has there been any real purpose to their education beyond keeping them off the street, off the unemployment roles, and registered for the student body count? Not really. Do they understand. Yes.

The precepts of Curran's Community Learning, Smith's non-visual principles of reading, and Pike's heuristic demand that individuals be connected in their activity, be able to relate what they are doing to why they are doing it, and therefore, care about their activity - in short, to have a purpose. Without a purpose, there can be no education, which is virtually our position right now. Traditional education teaches cultural values; industrial education teaches productive skills; communicative education teaches relationship in the universe.

Values are as embedded in traditional teaching as skills are in industrial teaching. Such inherent parts of the systems cannot be questioned without questioning the entire system for it shakes the assumptions of what is good and right. Eliminating values in traditional education voids the entire notion just as does eliminating skills from industrial teaching.

Equally awkward is the current eclectic notion of combining traditional values or cultural facts with skills education and thinking that all will be right. One will simply have a bastard child which answers neither side and infuriates both. The current battle in education rages between the conservatives speaking of values (traditional, classical, religious, or moral), and industrial educators speaking of skills (reading, math, and thinking) with a few people on the side saying, "let's move on." No one seems to question why we have school at all - despite the fragmentation of agreement over what schools should teach.

Values in Education

Traditional values never have to be discussed when they have hegemony over a system: everyone knows what the accepted values are and lives them rather than talking about them. One can be sure that when values have to be discussed that they are not traditional. Current participants in educational debate would have us believe that we could go back to the simplicity of 19th century America if we just embraced "traditional values." Maybe they would like to chop wood to keep warm, bathe in a cold bucket of water, and fight cholera, tuberculosis, and influenza as well. The values of hard work and discipline were lived because there was little choice: work hard or die.

The current writers who would enforce classical values by seeking "the good" in a neo-Platonic fashion might well keep in mind that Plato said in *The Republic* that education must always be spontaneous and never forced. State of the art in his time, Plato still sought change and improvement in education. His parable of the cave in *The Republic* used available imagery - fire in a cave vs. the sun. Today, he might well use the common man in his livingroom cave shadowed by the luminous gray glow of the television tube contrasted by lasers providing a god-like beam of fire in the night sky.

The traditional, religious, moral or classical outcry for values is simply a quest for power in which the anointed decree, "what I believe should be enforced for everyone because God is on my side and I am right." We heard similar statements from the Inquisition, Hitler, and the Ayatollah. The paranoia of these moralists is exceeded only by their ignorant hubris. Enough of this nonsense.

Skills in Education

Books have been written praising or excoriating skills. There is no need here to recap the whole argument. Students certainly need skills in order to read, do arithmetic, or to think, but the present emphasis is disembodied. Where people such as Hirsch criticize skills teaching as empty of facts and want to teach facts with skills, Frank Smith raises the fundamental question which Hirsch takes as an assumption: that facts equal knowledge. If you know 5000 items of culture, then you will be cultured. Smith points out that facts do not equal knowledge and that meaning is the essential ingredient in learning anything.

It is obvious at present that skills teaching is not working - simply from the uproar over the failure of the schools. Unfortunately, skills teaching is a very easy target for both traditional critics such as Hirsch as well as values critics such as Bloom and Schlafly. Skills teaching is only a natural expression of industrial education, which believes in measurable activities, not the over-powering evil some paint it to be (skill is measurable in a way knowledge is not).

Skills are needed for reading, math, and thinking, but several questions arise: whether skills can be taught in isolation (without content, context, or integration), whether skills come before or after understanding of the whole, and whether they need to be taught explicitly at all. The first problem in discussing skills comes from confused usage of the term. A skill is a subcomponent of an activity. Thus, when people refer to whole actions as skills such as reading skill, the usage is not correct for the present discussion. Yes, one should be skillful, or adept, in reading, and if you have gotten this far in this book, one could presume your skill, but that does not use skill in proper educational context.

When skills in reading are discussed, reading educators mean, ocular motility, recognition of features, letters, clusters and words, supplying the missing letter or word, context clue recognition, or answering a host of "comprehension" questions. For math, skills are basic numeracy, recognition of operative signs, and, depending on definition, control of the basic processes of arithmetic, (sometimes called skills in their own right: addition, subtraction, multiplication and division).

Thinking skills, so much in vogue now, is rather more vague than the previous two areas. Depending on definition, thinking skills can be: use of logic (rather a classical definition), application of values to a personal situation (moralist definition), or a disembodied study of definition, description, classification, analysis, synthesis etc., ad nauseum (freshman composition presaged).

It is interesting to note that skills are only mentioned in regard to activities which lend themselves to measurement. Proponents of skill based education do not emphasize appreciation or valuing - all components of the affective domain. Thus, areas such as art, music and non-competitive sport suffer. Sports seem to be important only insofar as scores are kept with the idea of winning, of being number one. The only time people pay attention to music seems to be with a prize-winning band (done on their own time with a director more interested in quality than dollars) while art seldom gets a nod even with gifted student artists.

Taking a closer look at skills taught in isolation, the problems arise precisely because the skill is not the activity. Teaching the feature, letter and cluster as parts of reading ignores the point of reading, i.e., to receive meaning. I can "read" Arabic if one defines reading as decoding the letters. However, my vocabulary for textual purposes is so severely limited that I can get through the letters and then may or may not know the word at the end of applying my decoding skills. If I don't know the word, my effort is wasted unless I have an Arabic speaker next to me to tell me the meaning. In that case, I learn a new word, in addition to practicing my decoding skills, but it must be noted that the skills did not give me meaning, the speaker did. If I don't have an Arabic speaker next to me, then I don't understand the word, and my vocabulary isn't strong enough to use a dictionary. Thus, my skills may be perfectly polished and yet completely useless. This seems absurd as presented, but it happens everyday in school reading classes.

Similar ignorance is perpetuated in math in much the same way with the mechanical repetition of rows of additions and subtractions on worksheets, but little application of those skills for the real life needs of students. Worksheets are easy if the student can take care of needs in the store, but if the student can take care of needs in a store the worksheets are not needed.

Thinking skills is the latest buzzword for educators interested in further reductionist application of nonsense. Having reduced reading and math to nonsense parts, they attempt to take an even more abstract set of conceptions and break them apart. A typical two year old can classify very well, using both definition and description with absolutely no training in thinking skills: four legs, fur, a tail and going arf arf is known to be different from four legs, fur, a tail and going meow. Doggie and kitty have meaning to the inquisitive mind of a two year old - dessicated discussions of definition, description, and classification have little meaning whether in elementary school or English 101.

The issue of teaching skills before or after understanding should be clear from the previous discussion. Skills cannot give understanding, and once understanding occurs, then working on isolated skills is ridiculous compared to working with the whole to gain further meaning.

The Challenge: Redefining the Purpose of Education

Where traditional education taught a corpus of material imbued with societal values of good and bad, and industrial education placed a value on productive skills, communicative education values the individual in the world making choices. Traditionally, the individual was subsumed by the entirety of the tribe or society. With industrialism, the individual became part of a class, or corporate entity. In communicative society, individuals are left in existential isolation or communication, depending on their choice.

CHAPTER 10

Redefining Schools

When people think of school many images arise: the cozy warm-hearted, one room, prairie school house, the urban high school resembling a textile factory, the new suburban shopping mall schools, perhaps the smell of the sawdust cleaning compound used by generations of janitors, or the smell of gym class, maybe the one good or truly horrible teacher, the kids - both friends and enemies, and groups to which one could belong or not. Rarely, in thinking back on school do we think of educational policy, administrative decision making or the development of the curriculum with which we wrestled, let alone what the teachers really did or what our role might have been or should have been.

Yet, at this juncture, these issues are facing society as a whole in a most self-conscious manner and must be dealt with on an individual basis by children, parents, and educators. Society has moved from traditional shared, assumed values to prizing marketable industrial skills to communicative individual decision-making: the role of the individual and school has changed. From going to school because it was good, to going to become a productive citizen, school has become a means to develop relationship between the individual and the world as defined by that individual. While such a statement sounds naively simplistic, it forms the basis for educational direction into the future.

Relationship sounds amorphous and, to our hardened industrialized ears, rather soft. Not as macho as the "dog eat dog world" or "survival of the fittest" credos of the industrial age. Necessarily, teaching relationship does not revolve around the teaching of traditional values or industrial skills, though both could conceivably be involved, but rather the moving back to comprehensive education in which integration of knowledge rather than dis-integration is demanded. Integration demands relationship of parts and cooperation between parts rather than competition between the varied elements. Comprehensive cooperation changes the very core of the school.

Initial schooling must provide a comprehensive base for learning to which the person can always come back as needed. Values, skills, and facts of themselves do not provide such a base. Values certainly affect learning positively or negatively, but they do not cause learning. Skills are demonstrable after learning has taken place, but do not cause learning. Facts often are taken as learning simply because we confuse information with knowledge. However, meaning which is accessible to the individual allows learning to take place. A person can learn only what is understandable to that person at that time. We have to build on that base, not cram skills or facts at children and tell them that they had better learn the information because they are going to be tested on it. A school environment which provides children understandable information i.e., knowledge in a way that allows them to comprehend, shows them how to learn.

When values, facts and skills are integrated, one usually finds meaning. However, all too often, schools try to teach one of the above excluding the others. If one begins from the basis of meaning, i.e., information put into a context which relates to the child and lets the child relate to the larger world, then, there will be value as the child puts the information into his or her own schemata, the facts will relate to the needs or desires of the child, and the skill will be understood within a context.

The Need for Relationship and Cooperation

The need for relationship and comprehensive cooperation comes from a number of areas both individual and societal: the convergent nature of jobs because of information control, the complexity of modern projects, and the fundamental issue of man as a social being.

Convergent Jobs

The convergent nature of jobs demands that people learn certain kinds of information as a prerequisite to being able to work. Isolated skills are an anachronism of the industrial world. When architectural drafters, diesel mechanics, and medical technicians all find themselves using computers to control the processes in which they are involved, one has to ask what is necessary for those people to know? The question really has several levels. Apart from the simple manipulation of the machine which can be learned in a day or two, the larger questions remain: if change has come so quickly in the last 20 years, what is ahead that people should know in order to work - and the far larger question of how do the people see themselves in the process?

If education as vocation, as it has been taught in industrial society, is not good for the life of an individual, then how must it be viewed as continuing? Certainly we've seen the inadequacy of models positing education as a final product or a simple collection of skills or facts, yet, continuing education at present is a pastiche of needs and desires presented on an ad hoc basis through colleges, universities, community colleges, high schools, churches and companies. In answering the questions about lifelong learning, we must make a distinction between initial schooling and continued education.

Complexity of Projects

It used to be that individuals invented items. Bell and Edison are representative: one man in a laboratory, thinking, tinkering, directing a couple technicians and finally succeeding. Now, Nobel prizes in technical areas largely go to groups of people rather than individuals. No one "invented" the television, the atomic reactor, the nuclear bomb or the computer. Vast research labs and government funding allowed groups of people to cooperate, sharing information for a larger goal.

Increasingly, the pattern is toward cooperative effort because of the complexity of work. Where Pasteur discovered microbes, and Jenner invented the anthrax vaccine largely as individuals, Salk gets credit for polio vaccine, even though he was as much administrator as doctor, directing government funding and large lab. In like manner, Oppenheimer, "the father of the bomb," was a brilliant physicist, but the bomb came about through his administration of thousands of people, not by his individual mentation.

Man is Social

Finally, our schools teach students to work in isolation and prize the "independent worker" or "self-starter," even though, at center, man is social. The American myth of the rugged individual stands in a most silly juxtaposition with the cooperation that allowed the individual to survive on the trip west. Our projection of the man of strength conquering the frontier omits the support by wife and family, omits the cooperation of the wagon trains, omits the social interaction of a barn raising; in short it omits everything that allowed one scrawny ill-fed guy to live on the frontier.

At the most basic, we evolved because we cooperated. We did not succeed because of speed or strength; we succeeded because we thought and organized. While an individual may have to do some things in life alone, when one considers that work and family are both predicated on amicable social relation, perhaps school should reflect that need.

The most fundamental aspects of family are based on social cooperation. Having children and a place to live takes social effort. Cleaning the house, taking out the garbage, earning money, agreeing on a budget, in short, keeping a place going does not depend on the rugged individual, but rather on cooperation and that means talking in a mutually understandable manner. That is how we learned to talk in the first place and is the basis for the rest of our survival and existence.

In like manner, when a person has a question on the job, the question can usually be answered by a manual or a fellow employee. In doing research on workplace literacy, I found that people talked if they could and used books only for information that is not easily memorized, usually technical. Managers and supervisors became suspicious if newly hired individuals did not ask questions because entry-level people were not expected to know the job completely. Furthermore, it was the types and quality of the questions which largely determined the early recommendations and progress within a company for a new person.

Why, given the social reality of being human, do we insist that students in school work alone? Why do we test students alone? Real life "tests" are of the person working with others on the job and at home. It seems that the individual is only in true isolation in the eyes of the business efficiency experts who geared up assembly lines at the turn of the century and began measuring students as if they were so many pounds of cold rolled steel.

The test for the success of computers in school will likely be decided by how they are used: for drill or interaction. As drill agents, they are unparalleled. A computer can generate an infinite number of arithmetic problems or spelling problems for children to solve - literally the never-ending drill-book of our early school nightmares. Without any work from the teacher, this infinite number of problems is corrected and tabulated, ready for entry in the electronic gradebook. Used in this fashion, the computer becomes more mind-numbingly boring than any paperback workbook.

As interactive devices, computers can present simulations which neither the teacher nor books can provide, teaching reading, math or thinking skills with innovative intensity. Anyone who doubts the intensity of such interaction has never tried to wrest control of a Nintendo game from a child.

The parallels between the family, work, and school are striking. The increasing institutionalization of American life with concomitant specialization and depersonalization has followed much the same pattern though at different times in the century. Traditional life revolved around known values whether in the family, work or school. The husband, wife, and children all knew their places in the family. Work meant the physical labor of keeping the house for females and farm or shop labor for the male - in both cases the expectations were clear. Such knowledge of place occurred equally at school with only about 10 percent of students graduating from high school even in 1920.

With rising industrialism, and particularly with the need for workers in World War II, women had the choice of working outside the house, but at the price of day care for the children. With two parents working, there was more money, but less time together. Instead of simply having a father who was gone, now both father and mother were gone. Just as mom and dad were working at more specialized industrial jobs than their parents, so the children had specialized people to take care of them whether in day care centers or increasingly, at schools which have become surrogates, providing latch-key programs. Realistically, if the parents work 8-5, they leave the house between 7:00 and 7:30 and get home at 5:30 or 6:00. That leaves two to three hours for parents and children to have dinner, do homework, and get to know each other. Is it a wonder that family life is different in present day America? It is as dis-integrated as is the industrial workplace, i.e., each member lives individually, and, for the majority of waking hours, has nothing to do with other family members.

As in other areas in the present day, some people are choosing, not to follow the industrial pattern, but rather to choose to spend more time with family even though it means there may be less money. People are discovering that quality of life is not predicated solely on income, but rather on being able to use income well.

Response of the Schools

Schools will become more socially responsive as we move further into the communicative era. As people realize that many of the limits imposed on education were simply part of the industrial worldview and serve no purpose, they will be dropped. For example there is no pedagogic reason for keeping children in the same "grade" other than that they are more easily administered as a single group. Thus for years, children have moved through school, being divided into grades and into tracks within those grades as though they were sides of beef labeled "prime" and "choice". Just because meat on a hook in a slaughter house has moved down the carving line and received stamps of approval in good industrial fashion for years is no reason that children must follow the same unequal pattern.

Inequality, Non-Inequality, and Limits

Anyone who has ever been around children or observed people in general knows that each person is different. Some students are better than others in math or English or carpentry or football. This is not mysterious. Every kid comes to the realization that he or she has strengths or weaknesses and that some people are bigger, better-looking, or smarter and others smaller, not as good looking, or less analytically intelligent. This is natural; why do we try to impose unnatural industrial limits on children when such limits are not apt for children and not useful either. Mario Pei comments (1966,4), "the phrase 'all men are created equal' holds true in only two fields, religion and the law...Inequality, rather than equality, seems to be the law of nature." We must assure equal opportunity in our schools while realizing that some individuals will benefit more than others from whatever is offered.

On the other hand, the efforts since the Sixties to legislate non-inequality among all students is as limited in view as those who would impose arbitrary limits based on age, sex or ethnicity. Inequality is simply a fact of life and should be so acknowledged. Anyone who has ever participated in sports, or even watched them, knows that some people are better than others. Why is it that we have such a hard time acknowledging that some individuals are more 'intelligent' than others? Especially when 'intelligence' is such a subjective term. Are we going to use the 'analytic' intelligence of the Stanford-Binet? or a more progressive idea such as Sternberg's which examines analytic, social and creative intelligences as separate entities? Or Gardner's seven intelligences? Is it perhaps our trust in the observable versus realizing and understanding the not directly observable? There is no disputing a record whether in running, jumping, shooting baskets, or kicking field goals; why then should we question that such and such a person is not as analytically intelligent as someone else. This selective denial of inequality would appear to be a holdover from the Real side of the matrix where the observable is dominant. Let's acknowledge inequality as natural, see to it that no arbitrary limits are imposed, and then move on to more fruitful areas such as the full development of our children's potential.

Removing the Limits

Traditionally, students learned together, older helping younger whether in social areas or content material. The one room school house is predicated on such a cooperative effort. The idea of age-level grades is only a product limit of industrial education. Other limits which must be examined are the fixed curriculum, the structure of schools in administrative, temporal, and locative terms, and the uniform means of instruction.

When these issues have been addressed then we will be making progress toward communicative education.

CHAPTER 11

Rhetoric, Reading, and Culture

Having looked at some of the problems of education in a changed world, we should look at the educational basis for reformation. Where communication meant survival of the species originally, changes in communication have marked the other turning points in human cultural evolution. Basic writing in the Middle East allowed recording of information and growth of civilization. Self-conscious writing in Greece allowed analysis and development of specialized branches of knowledge. The printing press in Europe began mass literacy, the Renaissance and Reformation. Now, electronic communication allows analysis of greater breadth and depth than is possible by any single person and allows that analysis to be transmitted anywhere in the world instantly. Each development brought about changes in the pattern of thought and the way that thought could be expressed. Each changed rhetoric and the schools as well - both being reflections of the larger cultures.

Rhetoric as Educational Basis

Certainly, rhetoric can provide the mechanism for education - as originally constituted by the Greeks or as being rewritten in the present day. The current negative image of rhetoric has not always been the norm, but it has been a recurring theme. When there is a need for real language use, rhetoric flourishes and is well-thought of as the basis of education.

Perhaps the greatest change in the history of rhetoric, and one which has reverberated to the present, was the change in 1546 when Peter Ramus split rhetoric and logic. In the mid-16th century, with the rise of scientific thinking and increasing mass literacy, logic was the driving force of exploration and explanation. Where rhetoric had always had five parts in the classical period (discovery, arrangement, style, delivery and memorization), Ramus put invention and arrangement with logic, leaving rhetoric with only style and delivery, ignoring memorization completely. It is fitting then that logic received the "important" parts of rhetoric when one views the needs of writing: logical, coherent, linear thought.

Classical rhetoric was oral in base and only as an afterthought was it applied to writing. Ramus, on the other hand, redefined rhetoric roughly one hundred years after the invention of the printing press. Mass printing and growing literacy gave new meaning to language use in religious, scientific and political terms. The linear argumentation of print differs dramatically from the presentation skills of an orator. At the same time, the decline of Latin and the rise of European vernacular languages gave impetus to widespread education in their literate use.

With printing, there was no need for the oral aspects of memorization and little use for the performance aspect of style and delivery. This left rhetoric gutted until modern times when discourse analysts began investigating the relation of language function and discovery mechanisms with arrangement and delivery systems. With electronic discovery, delivery and processing of information, the linear structure of writing was called into question and the study of language became vital once more.

To this end, we see the rise of cognitive and developmental psychology, artificial intelligence, and electronic communication devices pushing the examination of language and communication from new perspectives. The understanding of psychological and developmental universals as well as the changes inspired by global communication demand reinterpretation of the world as we know or construct it for ourselves. From the same spring of inspiration, the communicative school must arise; therefore, we must look at rhetoric in more detail as the basis of the school.

Rhetoric and Cultural Pattern of Thought

"Rhetoric, ... is not universal ... , but varies from culture to culture and even from time to time within a given culture." (Kaplan, 1972).

Rhetoric then is not a fixed entity in the sense of a textbook, but is constantly changing as the patterns of language use change. While Aristotle is usually thought of in a static textbook sense, his definition of rhetoric as "all the available means...of persuasion" indicates that as means change so will rhetoric. The scope of this variation can be tremendous because of the latitude given to rhetoric, "Almost anything related to the act of saying something to someone--in speech or in writing--can conceivably fall within the domain of rhetoric as a field of study: phonetics, grammar, the process of cognition, language acquisition, perception, penmanship, social relations, persuasive strategies, stylistics, logic, and so on" (Young, Becker, Pike, 1970).

Within this broad purview, Kaplan shows how a variety of languages develop paragraphs with different organizational thought patterns. English is linear, usually going directly from A to B with a main topic and supporting details before moving to a new topic. The Semites (usually Arabic for Kaplan, Hebrew having been muddied by European influence) develop paragraphs by moving back and forth across a topic showing both sides with parallel development. Chinese encircle a topic from the outside in in a vortex pattern while Romance and Russian speakers can allow extra thoughts to be added to a paragraph.

For example, a Spanish speaker looks at non-linear paragraph development in Spanish and calls it "style", saying that English is boring in its linearity. English teachers when responding to Spanish-style papers in their English classes mark in red pen "off the topic" or "vague and diffuse" even though the sentences may be perfectly grammatical. Language is clearly more than words or grammar.

Lackstrom, Selinker, and Trimble (1973) go well beyond Kaplan by asserting that in technical rhetoric the grammatical choice available to a writer (or reader) affects both the surface syntax and the internal reference system of a piece of discourse. Selinker, Todd-Trimble and Trimble (1976) note that foreign students often cannot understand a technical paragraph even when they understand all the words in each sentence and all the sentences that make up the paragraph. Finally, it must be noted that this phenomena is not limited to foreign students, but applies equally to less able native readers of English as well (Jordan, 1985).

When English teachers say, "use a topic sentence and support it with details in writing a paragraph," that same subordinate structure is mirrored in the sentence-level grammar. The preferred sentence form taught in school is the subordinate sentence, consisting of a main idea and a subordinate idea. In oral narration, children will say something along the lines of, "I got out of school, and I went to the park, and we played baseball, and then we went to the ice cream placea and

...and...and." The English teacher notes that, when written, this is a "run-on" sentence. The teacher looks for proper subordination along the lines of, "After finishing school, I went to the park where I played baseball, followed by a trip to the ice cream parlor..."

Dominant/subordinate sentences have not always been the rule in English. In fact, parallel sentence development has been the rule in "good" English throughout its history, taking the Greco-Roman model of rhetoric, despite the paucity of coordinate conjunctions in English. In contrast to English on the syntactic level, Greek and Latin were case languages (English is word order) which allowed great latitude in the order and arrangement of words as each carried its own case marker. When the classical rhetorical system was imposed on English, and English words lack case markers, it was forced to develop alternate means of using parallelism, primarily punctuation and relative clause structure to compensate for our inadequate coordinate system.

When we combine the ideas of English having main idea/supporting detail paragraph development and subordinate sentence structure, we find that the grammar and rhetoric of English are finally fairly synchronous. Within the idea that languages evolve in culture, we find that English is *the* industrial language -- a use predicated on hierarchy and lines of subordination (of authority, production, and distribution). Our rhetoric and grammar are mirroring our culture.

General and Specific Language

Unfortunately, the entire issue is not quite so simple as presented in the last paragraphs. When we examine occupational English, we find anything but synchrony in the language used, let alone what is "general." When we speak of "general" English, we are really specifying a set of language with which all people of a given group are familiar; however, what is "general" is not agreed upon except in use. Thus, if we examine language and gender from a sexist view, women generally know the vocabulary and processes of a kitchen while men generally know the tools and processes of the workshop. What is general knowledge for one group is special knowledge for the other. As a little test of your knowledge of a foreign language, try to think of the words for a frying pan, colander, and mixing bowl in the one circumstance, and nut, gasket, and screwdriver in the other. Essentially, we have these same gaps in English in areas that we do not know, and it is only our proficiency in "other" English which allows us to understand information in new areas. Let's look at how this idea plays out in several occupations and by extension into how and what we teach in the schools.

Occupational rhetorical analysis finds that, essentially, form follows function. Thus, where English demands a linearity of development in paragraph thought development, there can be a variety of means in expressing such linearity in work culture. To take two extremes, diesel mechanics and law, both have paragraphs keeping to one idea, but diesel does it with subordinate structure and discrete units of information, expressed in troubleshooting form as in, "If the motor turns without starting, then go to page 53." Law on the other hand uses coordinate structure and cumulative information as in a typical contract, "The first party shall be responsible for X and Y, but not A or B, unless 1 and 2 apply, in which case, Z and D will be in force until such time as..." The two forms stand at opposite ends of the syntactic and rhetorical spectrum, and yet both are "good English."

To be more precise, if the information is discrete, that is, can be accessed without regard to other bits of information, then the most logical organization will be vertical and subordinate with many possible independent entrance points depending on what condition is placed on the information. This conditional (If..., then...) form demands a subordinate sentence structure to go with the vertical rhetorical structure. However, if the information is cumulative in nature, rather than discrete, that is, what has gone before will influence the present information, then the organization will be horizontal, rather than vertical, and characterized by coordinate sentence structure rather than subordinate.

Summarized in general terms, occupational areas which function in discrete units for a given piece of reading are characterized by subordinate sentence structure and hierarchical organization while occupational areas which function in related units for a given piece of reading are characterized by coordinate sentence structure and cumulative organization.

While this sounds mysterious, it is derived from the same precepts which guided Kaplan's work in native language culture determining rhetorical pattern. When one looks at how native culture shapes the way in which people develop thoughts, and one realizes that people live spend the majority of waking hours at work, it is easy to say that work culture must affect patterns even within the constraints imposed by the native culture.

Discrete, Subordinate, Hierarchical Organization

The typical diesel manual is a good example of hierarchical organization, though almost any written unit dealing with mechanical repair or operation would suffice. The organization of the book, of the paragraph, and of the sentence type follows the pattern which appears to develop from the function which is discrete, i.e., the only connection between the starter motor and the brakes is that they are mounted in the same vehicle and may be bound in the same repair manual.

Diesel mechanics (and mechanics as a whole) is organized from the top down in a hierarchical classification and is characterized by subordinate sentence structure to support the "If..., then" type of thought development. The whole is made up of parts, but the parts, being discrete, only have relation through the whole. If one part were omitted, it would not necessarily change the other parts.

The manuals used in diesel mechanics have a very discrete organizational pattern. Just as the systems of a truck are discrete and not linked, so the parts of a manual are not linked. The isolation of each system from the others allows repair to proceed in a logical sequence, organized by a typical trouble-shooting procedure: "If the engine does not turn, go to page ... Check primary electrical system.", "If the engine turns, but does not start, go to page ... check ignition system," "If the engine starts, then dies quickly, turn to page ... check fuel system." Each sentence is subordinate, placing a condition on the reader that takes him to a separate part of the manual where the noted system will be further analyzed in the same manner -- rather than continuing the discussion within the same section or unit.

Furthermore, in diesel manuals, the pattern is hierarchically larger-to-smaller in each unit--whatever the unit size whether complete manual, sub-system, chapter, or sub-chapter. Manuals begin with an overall physical, functional, and operational description of the unit and proceed to subdivide, with each subunit following the same pattern of top-down, larger-to-smaller classification.

Unified, Coordinate, Cumulative Organization

At the other extreme is the legal language encountered by lawyers and people in law offices (and peripherally in many other occupations as well) which is characterized by a horizontal rhetorical structure and coordinate sentence structure. Again, this grows out of the function. A legal document, a trust or contract for example, demands to be dealt with as a unified passage in which the various parts contribute to a whole. The invalidation of a single part can invalidate the whole.

In law, a definition must say what a thing is as well as what it is not, and there is as much litigation about what a thing is as about what it is not. The positive definition stands in coordinate relation to the negative definition, e.g., "The company will be responsible for ... and ... and ..., but it will not be responsible for ... and ... or ... unless...."

To accomplish this need, the rhetorical form is organized horizontally (as in the lists of whereases in a contract where each is equal to the others), and the sentence structure uses coordination rather than subordination.

Expansion to Other Occupational Areas

Rarely is an occupation limited to just one type of structure. Just as several types of paragraph development, for example, cause and effect, and comparison and contrast, may occur simultaneously, so might types of organization and sentence structure overlap.

For example, in the health fields, one sees both types of reading. If a nurse reads a patient chart or history, the information must be cumulative as it is following a temporal sequence leading to the present. On the other hand, following protocols, or instructions for a mechanical device, will probably be characterized by discrete information.

In like manner, the electronics industry is characterized by maintenance on one side and research and development on the other. One of the characteristics of research and development (R&D) work is the recording of all pertinent information: material, procedure, and result. Both positive and negative results are recorded because both are important, especially in light of any variations of material and procedure involved. This is necessary not only for the ability to replicate the experiment but also for establishing the date and procedure for patents and proprietary rights. Maintenance and repair troubleshooting, on the other hand, has a known linear sequence proceeding in a top-down fashion until the piece is serviced.

Reading in R&D must be cumulative in nature as previous variations in material and procedure must be taken into account. Then, in recording results, note must be taken in what happened as an end product of the protocol followed. On the other hand, reading in troubleshooting is discrete, concerned only with the part under consideration while recording of information is limited to material fixed or replaced. Necessarily, reading in an R&D setting must be more involved than in troubleshooting as the researcher must be able to follow linear procedure as well as the troubleshooter, but must additionally be able to go beyond, dealing with results and at least a tentative discussion of why the results occurred.

Most occupations have at least a little cross-over of types and many use both frequently. Diesel mechanics encounter legal style language in warranties and insurance work while legal secretaries find discrete forms of reading in following office protocols.

Obvious patterns such as those discussed are of little help in aiding comprehension in a direct fashion, but they help a person understand the organization of the material. A road map does not shorten a driving trip in itself, but by helping to organize the trip efficiently, it can help the driver immensely. Cognitive schemas do not guarantee comprehension, but they let a person anticipate and organize information as it arrives. Several other aspects of specialized job reading must be considered, however, before we get back to general academic reading.

Job Reading is Qualitatively Different

The first consideration is that occupational reading is a cognitive skill, usually demonstrated on the job in performance terms by problem solving. Two areas implicit in such a statement involve the interaction of reading and reference skills, and the problem of distinguishing between vocabulary and concept.

Because reading is not just decoding, but involves an interaction between the reader and the text to determine meaning, the background knowledge a reader brings to the task is important. Equally important on the job is the knowledge that not everything is known, and, therefore, reference skills will be needed to fill in gaps in knowledge. The gaps in knowledge are especially acute in technical fields where there is a great deal of very specific, detailed information which cannot possibly be remembered. A diesel mechanic cannot remember bolt sizes, torque specifications, and clearance tolerances for a whole range of trucks, but he must know not only where that information is, but how to read it and when and how to use it. The same applies equally to electronics technicians troubleshooting circuit boards, nurses checking drug interactions and dosage levels, or draftsmen checking a drawing against building covenants. In each case, the worker must realize his or her lack of knowledge, know the type of manual which will contain the information, know how to read the manual and then apply the information to the given problem.

Employers repeatedly note that they are suspicious if a new employee never has questions, and that they can judge how well the person is doing by the types of questions that are asked. In many cases, reading is not directly an issue for employers, but rather a catch-all for an employee's inability to use information. A new employee may "read" adequately, but if he does not use manuals adequately, his reading skill is worthless. Clarity in the distinction between reading and reference skills is necessary in discussing job performance.

Vocabulary versus Concept

Another specific observation is the difference between vocabulary and concept. Employers note that new workers many times seemed to know the words of the field but lacked a thorough understanding of the concepts behind the words. Electronics entry-level workers can define in academic terms an "ohm" as a unit of resistance and state aspects of Ohm's Law, but in work habits may not be able to use the concept, creating inadvertent short circuits, or misreading text or schematics. A drafting supervisor may note that a person becomes a drafter only when they can "see" the room or building as a finished product by looking at the drawing. It is not enough to be proficient in drawing parts, if one cannot see the parts in relation to the whole. Otherwise, one might make three separate perfect drawings showing room layout, electrical layout and heating and air-conditioning, never realizing that the heating duct protruded a foot into the room at the seven foot level.

Thus, words defined in academic terms during training attain a conceptual reality on the job, quite apart from their denotative value. It is not enough for a mechanic to view torque as rotational force; he must also see (understand, feel, "know") that, in application, too much torque breaks a unit while too little torque allows the unit to come loose.

To summarize, reading is subsumed by the larger entity of cognitive skills and is put into operation to solve problems. As the information comes into operation in the worker's life, pure denotative value is transformed within a larger conceptual framework into a new reality.

General Reading, Knowledge, and Conceptual Framework

The previous discussion has been a way of coming to the central point of the entire book: that knowledge must attain a conceptual reality in education. Anything less is just words, facts and nonsense.

Reading is not an isolated skill; it is an interaction of the reader and the text in the discovery of meaning. With the knowledge that reading provides the communicative means for gaining the other subject matter knowledge of the curriculum, we should look at it more closely as a basis in the reformed school.

Psycholinguistic research has shown that the more a person knows of a subject, the less is demanded from the printed page. Smith (1971) notes that reading is not primarily a visual process. It is the interaction of the text with the knowledge that the reader has of the language, the subject matter, and of the world. What has been termed the psycholinguistic guessing-game occurs as we read. When we read, we constantly try to anticipate what is going to occur next on the page. A good reader with some knowledge of the subject matter can guess what is coming with little hesitation. When that same good reader has less knowledge of the subject matter, he must slow down and look for more information to be supplied by the text. If the text has enough information, and the reader has sufficient time, then good comprehension will again occur. However, if the text makes assumptions and does not provide enough information, then even a good reader will not comprehend the text. In like manner, if a reader does not have sufficient knowledge of the language, even a complete text will not allow comprehension because the reader does not have facility with the rhetoric, the syntactic constructs, or the vocabulary of the language itself. Clearly, facts of subject matter, and facts of the general world are not sufficient in themselves to ensure understanding, nor is knowledge of language, rather it is the interaction of all three components.

Just as the factual knowledge of an architectural drafter is not sufficient until he can "see" the whole of the drawing, so the idea of teaching cultural knowledge to unite the culture will fall short until one has the entirety of the cultural knowledge in integrated fashion as knowledge - not a group of facts. We need acquisition, not overt learning, otherwise, one finds the veneer of learning caricatured in *Pygmalion*. One becomes knowledgeable (literate, in current jargon) in one's culture by the very process of attaining that knowledge - though reading, social interaction, and work, and not by the memorization of mere facts, adoption of an accent and adapting a pose - whether that culture is one's native culture or an acquired culture such as being a diesel mechanic, architectural drafter, or literary critic. This is the basis of the transformation of information to knowledge. What's more, not a single test is required for the acquisition of a culture.

Typically, the focus in elementary school is on decoding and in high school on reading the text in isolation. Rarely does one see real integration of text into the students' lives. Students may gain a factual reality of the text but find such information to be meaningless in personal terms. Many teachers, especially in high school, would be happy to have students who could understand the material at a factual level because they are fighting for their personal survival and integrity on a daily basis. We don't need to be too critical of those teachers, but simply point out where we might want to go in education with our changes.

This criticism comes from both personal and professional experience. In college, I had one of the top scholars in the study of Wordsworth. He would come to class to pass on his erudition by reading notes of the past thirty years in which he showed us references to Plato, *The Iliad,* or Shakespeare for a given assignment of Wordsworth's poetry. When I spoke to several people about how completely irrelevant class was, i.e., he could have copied the notes and given them to us a a whole, I was told that he knew so much about Wordsworth that, "he didn't have time in his class for the stupid observations of students." Some of my observations might have been stupid, some not, but what happened was that we had facts, passed the tests, and promptly forgot the facts - and because we had no personal connection to the poetry of Wordsworth almost nothing remained except shadows and intimations.

Information which is meaningless is not knowledge, it is just facts. When facts are understood in a denotative fashion and then integrated into the life of a student to form a conceptual reality, then the student is able to comprehend, to "see" knowledge as a drafter is able to "see" a room from a two dimensional drawing. Then and only then does knowledge live - it jumps right out and hooks the student.

Extension of Rhetoric and Reading into Teaching and Learning

Language and education share a great deal in the means of acquisition and examination. One of the problems of looking at the study of language by people who are not language scholars is that they find a complete void of subject matter on one hand, and the complete recursiveness of language study in using itself to study itself on the other hand. The combination of a vacuum paired with metalanguage bothers people who like material in neat, clean, isolated boxes whether that person is a mathematician, engineer or school administrator. One can study math using general language and move from arithmetic to higher functions in a progression that makes apparent sense to normal people. One needs to add and subtract before doing algebra, and one needs algebra before undertaking calculus. In contrast, when one studies language, one is presented with a whole, a complete operating system, intact and functioning which one is already using from the very first utterance when beginning to talk about language. It is as though the first discussion of arithmetic needed the knowledge of all mathematics.

The study of language has traditionally been sequential, but never consistent as such a statement might suggest. The Greeks and later the Romans decided on a bottom up sequencing in which children studied grammar first and then progressed to rhetoric. Later, with a certain amount reductionism, people spoke their vernacular and studied Latin as the proper model, using it as a template, appropriate or not. In industrial America, people continued reducing the language components to the point where students study reading, language arts and literature as though they were unconnected entities. Proficiency in decoding is mistaken for reading because meaning has been gutted from the classroom by basal readers. Against this absurdity has arisen the whole-language movement where children in elementary school work with real books which have real meaning instead of the artificiality of basal readers. At the high school and college levels however, we still continue to teach composition as though grammar equated the language of writing, as witnessed by our grading on correct grammar. Grammar is a component, but only that - there is, obviously, far more.

If mathematics teachers were as confused as English writing teachers, they would be teaching arithmetic at the same time they were teaching algebra and trigonometry and applying the whole to the physics of movement in calculus - and then wondering why the students had no idea what was going on. The analogy applied to language shows us teaching the linguistic grammar of morphology and syntax, the rhetoric of tone, persona, and audience as they relate to paragraph development and document form, and then asking students to make it both interesting and full of personal meaning. And we wonder why they are confused?

My point in criticizing language teachers for applying reductionist techniques and then praising math teachers for the same action is that we have had "scientific" methodology foisted on us, and we applied it willy-nilly with no thought as to what was appropriate. Where scientific reduction is the basis of western science, it is a severely limited model when talking about language use. Descriptive linguistics reduced language to its smallest, physical, behavioral component parts, but along the way they left out meaning. One cannot discuss one part of language use without considering the other parts, or one risks invalidating the whole. Language in use is a cumulative whole, not a series of discrete entities put together progressively. Mathematics, though cumulative, is progressive; that is, it is an artificial construct invented by man in order to solve a variety of problems. Arithmetic is necessary for geometry and algebra, and these two areas logically extend into trigonometry and calculus. In contrast, morphology, syntax, semantics and rhetoric are all equally necessary to express meaning, and one does not necessarily lead to another in any instructional progression.

The Redefining - The Communicative Model

When speaking of communicative education and organic growth of schools, students, and knowledge, I am purposely mixing my metaphors to form a synthesis. Where, on the surface, information theory and biology seem to share little, they are models of looking at the world and formed the basis for Bertalanffy's expression of general system theory.

Recapping the first chapter, oral cultures teach their culture wholly and broadly but do not expand into discovery methods. Literacy, with conditional analysis, brought the ability to reduce larger units to their constituent parts at the price of examining only a very narrow field. From either position, the other seems an unlikely model to adopt for education. However, twentieth century America did adopt the latter which suits the hard sciences well, but does little for the humanities except fragment them from their essential unity. Fortunately, our choice is not limited to whole versus fragmented education.

Rather than simply adopting one model and trying to fit all subjects into that as modern America has, we must look for what is appropriate to varied subjects and methods of learning and teaching. The very idea of a "single" model comes from the sort of binary, troubleshooting, engineering, thought pattern that limits us to the dualism of "If this, ...then that" rather than being able to see that there are, or can be, several ways which are appropriate.

Bounded Thought Unchained

Eastern thought has always featured multiple pathways. In contrast, Western thought, bounded as it has been by the absolutes of Semitic religion, Plato's forms, and Aristotle's logic, has consistently been dualistic up until the 20th century when a number of events occurred. The first, quantum theory was so disturbing to thinkers that we still hear Einstein's lament that he couldn't believe God played craps with the universe. In like manner, when the mathematician Gödel proved that a closed system was an impossibility, he essentially ended Western philosophy as it had been practiced for 2000 years, i.e., searching for a single, definable, sustainable, closed system of thought. A third reason, the most recent, and certainly the most verifiable by the average person, who is not able to delve into quantum and advanced set theory, is what is permitted by the computer. Not only do computers not operate on the same linear principles as industrial machines, they do not do it on several different levels simultaneously.

Non-linearity of Computer Thought

The real beauty of a computer in use is the sheer computational capacity. Even the simplest home computers allow the user to perform complex equations and spreadsheets which by hand would take days of computation.   One only need look at pictures of the computation facilities used by the Manhattan project: room on room of women with adding machines, to appreciate focused computation. The ability to analyze large numbers of facts in terms of large numbers of conditions gives us a new power for examining the universe, using breadth of information and and depth of analysis.

The most obvious result has been the exponential expansion in use and knowledge of information. From complex projects such as the navigation of space vehicles to economics modeling and engineering design applications, computers allow previously impossible tasks. Simply stated, flying to the moon needs more information faster than can be supplied by hand.

A less obvious result of the power of computers is the newly-emergent study of chaos. When scientists look, for example, at the seemingly chaotic discontinuity of fluid dynamics as fluids rotate in a cylinder, linear equations cannot predict when or why the discontinuities will occur.   On the other hand, non-linear problem-solving by computers can occur because the computer can search for multivariate options until it finds a suitable match for the limits of a defined observable phenomena. Not only is the study of chaos interesting in and of itself, it has provided a break in the idea of Western thought that reductionism is the one and only way to progress. Chaos forces non-linear concepts to the forefront of philosophical thought and cultural evolution just as quantum mechanics did 80 years earlier.

The other side of computers being non-linear is that there are a variety of ways to program a computer, even within the same language. The engineering mentality says, "There is one best way to do a chore." Computer programming says, "Forget that notion - there are different ways to do almost any task." The speed of computers is such that for all practical purposes a program can be written any number of ways and still be "right." The notion of "right" does not apply in any normal sense, however, because the only matter of import is - does the computer do the task for which it was programmed? Ten different programmers can write ten different programs in the same language for the same function - all of which are "right", i.e. they work. For a typically linear student who has been brought up to think that there is one answer and one way to do something, the idea that there are many "right" answers comes as a surprise.

Thus, the limited notion of linear education, of one way to teach, one way to learn, and one model for the schools, is hardly appropriate in a changed and changing world. Science is no longer linear in Newtonian fashion; why should the schools be frozen in patterns which are no longer appropriate, rather than working to reflect the current reality or the possibility and potential of the future? The speed, depth, breadth, expandability, and decentralization of computers and their ability to form encompassing networks show the way for a school model with linear, non-linear, and comprehensive patterns of thought all accepted: bringing Aristotle's "all the available means..." to bear in school and life.

Part III

REFORMING
THE
SCHOOLS

School
in a
Creative Future

CHAPTER 12

The Communicative School

Knowledge and Regression in Modern Life

When Aristotle says that a rhetor should be able to use "all the available means of persuasion in any given case" he neatly sums up the foundation for the communicative school - that an educated person should be able to discover and use pertinent knowledge in any given situation to maximum effect. The ability to use knowledge depends on being able to get and then understand information as it comes to us at an increasing pace. The understanding of information, let alone the use, is not being equitably distributed at present, however.

The "available means" in current society are indeed broad and deep and increasing rapidly. The very amount of information has created a dichotomy in current life where the well-informed have a great advantage over the less well informed. In industry, education may determine who is hired, but it is becoming equally apparent that survival is going to people with access to information and the ability to turn that into useful knowledge. We see examples of this all over, but two examples will suffice to make the point: AIDS and drugs.

Where AIDS came to public notice in the U.S. as a disease among middle and upper-middle class highly-aware urban homosexuals, it has now become a disease of Black and Hispanic drug users. Not only have the public awareness campaigns cut the AIDS infection rate among urban homosexuals, they have changed the entire sexual behavior of the group as witnessed by the drop in other sexually transmitted diseases. However, as the rate has dropped for the Gay population, it has been rising in less media-aware drug-users.

Drug usage has followed the same pattern. Against a backdrop of heroin users which has remained relatively constant over the last twenty years, the usage of other drugs has varied greatly. In the late Sixties, marijuana and hallucinogens achieved popularity with middle class adolescents and college students. As this population aged, alcohol joined the drug list as witnessed by the huge increase in liquor sales, but more importantly, in crept cocaine. From the political explosions of the Sixties to the Me-ness of the Seventies to the Yuppies of the Eighties, this was not a shy generation, and cocaine, with its psychological and physical boost, was the perfect drug for such ego. However, just as free sex in the Sixties had not solved anything - one just had to talk when it was over instead of before - cocaine could only keep a body going so long before a price was exacted. Informed users realized the dangers and began to back away. However, as yuppie drug use was peaking, a new technology made a cocaine concentrate available at a much lower price which opened a whole new clientele. Crack was cheap enough that it could be bought with lunch money. Cocaine went from the business office to the streets which have been a free-fire battle zone since.

In the cases of AIDS and cocaine, what started as white upper-middle class intense frivolity has become a lower class scourge for people of color. The advantaged play, and when it gets dangerous, and they become aware that it is dangerous, they change their behavior. The disadvantaged continue the behavior unaware because they are largely out of the mediums of communication which could inform them and the programs which could help.

We could cite birth control and diet as two more issues which fit the pattern. To bring all these issues to the same level is not fair or quite appropriate, nor is the over-simplification of attributing change purely to availability of information; however, the regressive aspect of modern life is inescapable and must be dealt with in any attempt to reform the schools. Schools must not only give information, they must give the means to use information as knowledge, and, absolutely as importantly in this instance, they must give people a sense of empowerment such that they see a reason to use the information for their well-being.

Ethnicity, the School, and Evolving Culture

Current debate on immigration centers on what we should do with the current low growth stage of the population with greater declines predicted in the future. However, before we invite the poor, the tired, and the hungry to our country, we had better reassess our willingness to help them become productive citizens or give them fair warning that they can become part of a subclass in the U.S. just as they were in their native land.

We can divide immigrants into two groups, skilled/professional and unskilled. Iranian, Pakistani, and Latin doctors, Dutch and British nurses, and German or Scandinavian engineers are welcomed and fit in quickly. Nicaraguan, Salvadoran and Laotian refugee/peasant farmers, Hmong refugee/tribesmen, and Mexican farmworkers are not welcomed and are accepted only for their physical work. While there is nothing wrong with physical work, there has to be hope as well. When we accept refugees, especially when we have caused them to become refugees as with the Hmong, it would seem that we have a responsibility to help them.

The cutbacks in federal entitlement programs during the Reagan years will certainly go down as one of the most cynical moves in U.S. history. Educating a productive workforce is cheaper than welfare down the line in purely economic terms while in social terms, a gainfully employed populace is both happier and more stable. Cutting is not only cynical, but stupid.

The difference in acceptance and assimilation of the two groups of immigrants comes because they enter different parts of the matrix. The professionals enter the matrix in the U.S. in the communicative sector, already in tune with expectations of the culture. The refugees/peasants from Southeast Asia and Latin America enter the matrix in the physical sector, but little equipped to join the mainstream, even if they so desire. They are not accustomed to any of the current (outer box) parts of the matrix. They do not know the politics of the Authoritarian sector, the religious or intellectual tradition of the Inspirational, or the educational/media framework of the Communicative sector. To varying degrees, they know the physical demands of work in the Physical sector. I note varying degrees because a farmer in Latin America or Southeast Asia does not recognize farming here as the same entity. They recognize picking lettuce in California, but not Western ranching, Midwestern grain farming, or Southern cotton and peanut farming. In like manner, they know something of sweatshop sewing, but not much of assembly line clothing manufacturing. And this is only for relatively advanced groups.

The Hmong, tribesmen from the Vietnamese highlands who helped our Special Forces got evacuated to avoid extermination by the North Vietnamese. As a roughly neolithic hunting and gathering tribe, they made a quick transition during the war from bows and spears to M-16 assault rifles and grenades. Now they find themselves living with electricity and Safeways instead of fires and hunting. Language is not the only issue in working with the Hmong, and this simply points up in exaggerated form the problem with any immigrant: acculturation and enculturation. The Hmong refugees had to move from the center of the Matrix with the hunters and gatherers to the outside of the present day. To a lesser degree other Asian and Latin refugees only have to move one or two levels in the Matrix as opposed to three for the Hmong.

English Language - Culture

English is the dominant language in the world for several reasons, both intrinsic and extrinsic. In external terms, the decline of the British Empire occurred coincidentally with the rise of the U.S. Thus, the dominant world power for two historical periods spoke the same language and shared many cultural attributes which has never occurred before in history.

A far more powerful reason however is the inclusiveness of English as a language. English borrows from other languages prodigiously, allows variant dialects, and reflects change in ways other languages have not allowed or accepted. Where the other European languages have their governing body such as the academie francaise, English grows and changes according to people's need. Of course, all languages except the dead ones change and evolve, but English revels in change. The academie francaise cannot stop the evolution of French but they can retard the changes, keep the changes to "accepted" Gaullic forms, and, by far most importantly, keep the people aware that there is only one way to speak French and that bastardization is not allowed. Anyone who has traveled to Africa and Asia is well-acquainted with the former French colonies speaking "real" understandable French in contrast to the former English colonies speaking awful English and mixing English into pidgins and creoles. With a Latin lexicon on a Teutonic grammar, English started with a mixed heritage and has continued to expand with help from all corners of the British Empire.

Another curiosity of English is that one can speak English without thinking about being English or American, or participating in English or American culture which is not true of other languages. One cannot speak French or Spanish without reference to the culture, yet culturelessness is the norm in English as a world language. When a

KLM plane lands in Geneva neither Dutch nor French is spoken, but English - and the people speaking don't have to think of London or New York because they are just doing business, and English is the lingua franca. The next stage for the development of English is already set as it has become the medium of communication on the Internet.

Language and Bilingual Education

Where English as the world language for business, accepts change readily, and adapts to local use and need, the people who speak it may not. For whatever reason, Americans appear to resent the new immigrants as much as their grandparents resented the last wave of immigrants at the turn of the century. In fact, the same xenophobic comments are being made now that were made then about our being an Anglo-Saxon English speaking society, and that foreigners will pollute and dilute the purity of thought and not be good citizens. If we look at the Polacks, Swedes, Italians, Jews, and Slovaks who came at the turn of the century, they did not do too much damage. In fact, they powered enormous growth and enlivened the entire country, bringing an awareness of a world beyond our shores, and enriching English as a language once again. The fears that a fascist, monarchist, or communist Eastern European or insular Italian or Jewish population would not adapt and become part of a greater America proved unfounded. They learned to vote and worked to provide a better tomorrow for their children just as the English, Irish, Dutch and German immigrants had earlier. Why, given the opportunity, should the current Latin and Asian refugees prove different?

Refugees around the world and at different times look remarkably the same. Dirty and ragged, the sunken cheeks from poor food, the haunted eyes of persecution, the look is the same whether on Ellis Island at the turn of the century, or in a Thai, Central American or Palestinian refugee camp.

The problem for education is related to the problem discussed earlier of the place on the matrix that the immigrant/refugee enters the system, i.e., physical or communicative in the present day or farther inside the matrix, representing a different cultural time period. Rather apparently there are different problems for a literate Spanish speaker compared to an illiterate, or someone who has a concept of the symbolic representation of an alphabet compared to someone who comes from a neolithic, oral culture.

To aid the transition, bilingual education was established to allow children to continue to learn in their native language while they learned English. Gradually, the student makes a transition to English instruction exclusively, without having lost a grade or more likely several grades, learning English before pursuing the other subjects. This system arose because, historically, students had simply dropped out if they spent two years learning English and then were put at a grade level two years behind their age with the accompanying comments of being a foreign dummy and too old for the grade.

In the previous period of immigration, students faced the same ridicule, dropped out, got a physical job, and made a go of life without education.   That is no longer true.   When we cut funds for compensatory education, we are not saving money by not spending it on some "foreigners," we are insuring that we will be spending more when those students cannot get a job and cannot support a family. Then, instead of paying to help one student for a limited amount of time, who then becomes a productive citizen, we are paying for a whole family on welfare indefinitely.

Certainly, the problem is more difficult with unschooled students who are illiterate, or have no concept of alphabetized language. The tendency has been to dismiss such people and try to get their children as they come along. This approach seems somewhat myopic. We cannot ignore someone just because they are on the bottom. Triage may be appropriate for medicine in a war; it is not appropriate for education in peacetime.

Ethnicity and Competition

As measurers, America has few peers, but what we choose to measure says volumes about us as well. If we look at various ethnic groups in the schools, we find competition and measurement but in different areas depending on cultural outlook.

Stereotypes are always dangerous, and nowhere more so than in discussing ethnicity and the schools; however, bias and discrimination appear universal. In the ten years of the 1970s, I spent the majority in Africa and the Middle East. I have seen Whites treat Blacks and Blacks treat Whites like dirt in the U.S. and Europe. I've seen Blacks treat other Blacks like dirt in Africa . I've seen Blacks treat Arabs like dirt in Africa, and Arabs treat Blacks like dirt in Arabia. I can say with certainty that discrimination and racism do not know national or ethnic boundaries, and the best we can do is to look at those two issues directly and try to work for a more equitable world. The world is better in confronting these two scourges now than it used to be, *at least we are aware,* but we have little room to congratulate ourselves.

Westerners, and typically white America, look at the individual as being most important, perhaps cooperating with society, but just as likely to be a maverick. We look to the natural ability of the leader, rather than the acquired social/political skill of leading. To this end, our tests reflect the bias - aptitude tests to show where we are strong and should concentrate our efforts.

On the other hand, Asians as a whole see the individual subsumed into the larger entity of society, and therefore, individuals should labor to become better in all areas, whatever their ability. The focus on effort and achievement stands in contrast to Westerners who stand aside, waiting for natural ability to rise to the task.

Latins and Blacks tend to see themselves in between these ends of the continuum. They are neither so isolated as the typical Anglo-American nor so group connected as Asians.

One result of looking at individual ability as a natural phenomena is that elites are then natural, rather than produced. In the groupness of Asians, elitism is no less prevalent, but stems from group superiority rather than the natural superiority of the individual. White Americans get their exaltation from watching other individual Americans win; Asians get their superiority from the group's achievements. American business seems to think that it is best because of a natural superiority and others should recognize this and buy; Asians work harder, work longer, and tailor their product to the audience to whom they are selling. In article after article, Japanese businessmen wonder why we have lost our "collective will" to compete. I wonder if that is perhaps a projection on their part; we have always been a collection of individuals who sometimes got together on a project, we have never really been individuals in the collective in their sense. We do know which group is prospering in the current world market, however.

In school, the same sort of effort is paying off for Asians in this country to the degree that they have now filed discrimination suits against top universities because of the disproportionate numbers who are qualified and yet not getting admitted. This is not unlike the accusations made by Jews against gentile institutions for many years. When people work harder, work together, and start to achieve because of effort, Anglo-America seems to have a problem and feel a paranoid insecurity toward that group.

Blacks, long excluded from the chance for good education, have made strong academic advances according to the 1988 National Assessment of Educational Progress (NAEP) report. Given some success to build on, greater success should come in the future if previous group patterns hold.

On the only playing field that was level, that is, the playing field, blacks have long held a strong position, despite the discrimination of professional sports. When bigots make overall accusations of laziness or lack of competitive spirit, there is a blind eye with regard to sports where they drop back and say, "it's natural ability", i.e., lazy bones vs. natural animal instinct. If it weren't so serious an issue, that Anglo position would be laughable.

The unfortunate aspect of this is that when a community sees its ticket to success based on physical attributes, the statistics are sad - most Blacks are no more able to compete at a professional level in basketball, football or baseball than most Whites, Hispanics, or Asians. Almost all of each group fail to make the professional level and, if there is no education behind them, then other failures are bound to follow that first one.

Blacks don't need another white Ph.D., even one who tried and failed to make it beyond N.F.L. rookie camp, to tell them about sports and school. However, if the amount of work, talent and ambition were focused in other directions than sports, Blacks could create another Malian Empire right here in America.

Uniting the Factions in the Communicative School

Whether one examines the philosophical, temporal, or ethnic divisions in the U.S., it is clear that we have lost the "Common Good" so well expressed in the Melting Pot image of assimilation. We have not replaced the image with one in which the majority can agree such as the linguistic/cultural toleration in Switzerland. In a pluralistic society, there must be an agreed upon center which is currently not present in the schools or society at large. We are so clearly caught in our own dualistic philosophic tradition that we have trouble seeing and holding onto multiple images.

The three periods identified in the metaphors of education have clear views of what sort of animal man truly is. The traditional view of education, derived from the faculty psychology and philosophical materialism of Locke, sees man as an economic being, trying to control natural, chaotic, irrational impulses for greater gain. Here, man must dominate nature. The business-efficiency group extended the materialism of Locke into the 20th century. In contrast, the Progressive view of education led by Rousseau and Dewey saw man as a perfect, natural being, corrupted by social forces and who must learn naturally to regain a certain perfection in society. Here, man is part of the revered, spiritual force of the world who has become separated.

Communicative education demands a shift in view reflecting relationship with the world: neither domination nor reverence, but an ecologic symbiosis. Lockean exploitation and Rousseauian reaction are both inappropriate. We cannot be blind anymore to the Lockean imperative of materialism: we know the world is finite. With regard to Rousseau, we know that we create society, and thus, if society corrupts children, then they are corrupted by us. Neither the world nor society is separate from us and our needs; therefore, we need to found the school within the freedom of connected balance: an *equiliberation.*

The exploitation allowed in a Lockean view of the world pushed the Rational view to its extreme in the domination of the world by the British Empire. While the "natural rights" of the White gained domination over the world of the Black, Brown, Yellow and Red, people seemed to forget that just as surely as the master binds the slave, the master is bound by the action. The hubris of the Victorian English was exceeded only by the fragility of the base of their Empire.

The British were as blindly, destructive in their actions as an alcoholic who continues to drink with the aid of a spouse, taking both parties down. The dependency of this relationship continues until the slave or the spouse says, "stop," and then the master or alcoholic has to take responsibility and either change or fall. Whichever result, by becoming responsible and ending the dysfunctional tie, liberation is gained for both parties no matter how long or painful. It has taken Britain most of this century to redefine itself from the crash of the Empire, just as the former colonies are struggling to find the meaning of independence.

Rousseau's view of a naive, Pollyannaish benevolent nature corrupted by society simply flips the design upside down, projecting human desires on inanimate Nature. Rather than dominating Nature, the desire to be dominated by a Nature with certain human characteristics puts mankind in the same position as in Locke's design, just on the other side of the equation, caught in our own projection.

Problems arise because both views take an isolated vertical view of man rather than a connected view. Man is dominating or dominated, never balanced, never free.

The Matrix and Balance: Equiliberation

Both Locke and Rousseau exist in the Absolute half of the Matrix: Locke clearly on the Real side of the Matrix, in the Authoritarian sector, and Rousseau on the Ideal side, in the Inspiriting sector. Clearly, neither is sufficient. We need the whole in order to function because society is built of all four sectors. The real issue is the exclusion that such limited worldviews impose on their believers. In each case, man, society and culture *must* be on one side or the other in dialectic opposition to the other side. However, rather than providing a powerful tension of opposing views which could animate further understanding and progress when synthesized, the two sought absolute domination as was typical of their periods. Thus, society was left hanging with half a view, and the belief by each side that it was right, and the other side, therefore, had to be wrong.

In contrast, the Matrix provides a four way descriptive and explanatory view of mankind which can also be used pedagogically to keep balance. In this sense, it is not unlike other mandalas of balance such as the Taoist yin-yang. My term equiliberation is meant to suggest that with balance comes freedom on a cultural, societal, organizational, and education basis.

Reforming School

Where the traditional school was dedicated to a limited subject matter and the values of society, and the industrial school was dedicated to industrial skills and enculturation to work, the communicative school must shift to recognize people - not arbitrary content or skills. Increasingly, the focus of schools will have to be personal identification. Identification here is used as a complementary term to equiliberation used on the personal level. The individual must be able to see "all the available means..." in order to make the informed decisions which shape his or her life - literally, to be able to identify the choices and see the ramifications of each possibility.

Thus, when reforming the schools, we should not look at simply changing the curricular emphasis in the way that the business efficiency group and Progressives did just after the turn of the century. Rather, schools must be changed in terms of community involvement, attitude, development, physical formation, curriculum, testing, and instruction. Many of these are related and all stem from the principles so far stated. Change will likely come in piecemeal fashion for the simple reason that we have a decentralized system at the national level, and different states and local school boards will adopt some ideas before or instead of others.

Community Involvement

When people speak of community involvement in the present system, the issue usually revolves around trying to defuse a tense situation caused by racial, ethnic or religious issues. There are nominal

Parent-Teacher Associations with meetings, but little action is expected to come from such a group with regard to educational policy.

Where is the parent concern over what is taught and where responsibility for education lies? To be sure one hears a great deal from a small group of religious people and grumblings from the political right or left, but the ordinary person has virtually no contact with schools, the school board, and policy making. This is not to suggest that the schools and school policy be turned over to parents who have neither the time nor training to run them; however, policy needs to be balanced to local needs - not those dictated exclusively from the state or national legislatures.

We will see this change in educational involvement just as people have become involved in their health. People used to be passive on-lookers in their own health and simply go to the doctor when they got sick and say, "Fix me, doc." That has given way to people understanding that diet and exercise can change the quality of life, and that they have a personal responsibility for their own health. In like manner, education for adults has shifted greatly already. People are continuing education whether for career advancement, career change, or personal enhancement, and people are taking personal responsibility. The next shift will be to the lower schools.

In addition to helping themselves by caring for their own health, people wrought a change in the way medicine is practiced. Doctors used to be exclusively white males who felt themselves to be God. Now 40-50% of medical students are female, and a fairly representative sampling of minorities can be found as well. Additionally, physician's assistants and nurse practitioners have taken over many of the jobs previously done exclusively by MDs.

Interestingly, medicine is one cultural step behind education organizationally and so provides a good example, especially in contrast to the advanced organization of some of the communicative companies previously examined. At the turn of the century, the teacher was the arbiter of good in the class, and the school revolved around what the teacher thought and taught, just as doctors had absolute power right up to the Sixties. The teacher and the doctor were in the Authoritarian sector of the Matrix. Just after the turn of the century, education got caught in bureaucracy which educators told each other would make for more "efficiency." In the Seventies and Eighties, medicine got HMOs which would make for "more efficient" practice. Instead, doctors found, as had teachers 50 years earlier, that they simply had one more level of bureaucracy, less freedom, less respect, and more people wanting to dictate what could be done, when, why, to whom and for how much. They are now facing the frustration that has been building in teachers, resulting in teachers forming support groups, finding outlet in alternative schools, and working to change schools on the grass roots level. One suspects many doctors are already exploring alternatives although their rigid education as Authoritarians makes such a creative exercise painful.

The majority of a family practice doctor's time does not need a graduate degree. When an M.D. looks at 45 sore throats and snotty noses on a typical February day, he is practicing assembly-line medicine and doesn't need seven years of special training. In like manner, a large percentage of a teacher's time is not spent in teaching, but in administering the bureaucracy. There are better activities for a professional.

The rest of a family practitioner's time demands no substitute for intensive education and training; art, technique and experience become mutually complementary and lives are saved or lost. Less dramatically, but no less importantly, a master teacher keeps a class learning as if by magic with no discipline problems and with the students engrossed in their activity. Respect for professionals cannot simply be given; it has to be deserved, but at the same time, we cannot function individually, or as a group, without having that respect.

Respect and Local Involvement

Personal involvement tends to breed at least a self-interested respect in a project. If one is to continue to remain involved in an activity, there has to be a degree of satisfaction that gives a feeling of respect. As people become more involved in education, then they will come to understand and work with the host of variables which are constantly in play at any level. Informed decisions can be made from involved interest, but only if a sense of personal involvement can be sustained. At present, most individuals feel at a distant remove from the city school board, let alone the state board of education. Parents take an interest in their own children, but rarely say anything of import through a conduit such as the PTA.

The present system is set up to keep power centralized at the state level, however much talk is made about local control. The state sets teacher qualifications, sets curricular competencies, and controls by distributing state and federal funds. They do not want individuals and communities to be involved as that will lessen the central authority.

What are the areas in which local people can exert an influence? Within the context we have developed, the obvious areas would be having teachers work with parents and administration for a mutually agreed upon curriculum and attitude toward learning. For this to occur, we need truly professional autonomous teachers, a curriculum flexible enough to consider local needs, schools and classes small enough that individual input matters, and an administration which views itself as present to help children learn, and not simply to be self-sustaining.

Contrary to the elitist notions of some recent writers, I think the "common" person in the street has a lot more sense than some give credit for. Just looking at the 1992 and 1994 elections, many states split their voice sending a Democratic President and a Republican Congress to Washington. Unthinking mobs go in one direction; people thought about the choices and sent a mixture. Jefferson would be proud of the people, if not the candidates and campaigns.

The areas of curriculum and attitude toward learning should be related. Not only should the community be able to ask for electives within the curriculum, but also ask for establishment of a conducive atmosphere for learning. This choice may seem arbitrary, but the current idea of school being the place to teach facts hasn't always been the case. Traditional education was concerned with a concept of "being educated." The unspoken facet of being educated was being "well-educated" and therefore "good" as though one was "better" because of being educated. Such a value colored all of education just as mastering a set of skills colored industrial education (which seemed crude and utilitarian to the traditionalist). As the next shift occurs, teaching the principles of relationship appears mushy next to the hard-edge of behavioral objectives in industrial education. Integral to the notion of teaching relationship to students is the notion that students must be able to relate to the world of school as a first step.

The idea of local input on curricular decisions is based on the fact that people who have a voice in a decision usually care more than those who are have no voice. Give people a stake in their community, and they will work more actively. Strip people of power as in many cities, and they give up - give up on themselves, on their communities, and certainly on the schools.

Curricular Shading

If we take seeing relationship as a guiding principle in education, how does it affect the current discussion? From the schema theory of learning which says that one learns new information by integrating it with previous information, we really should be able to teach almost anything from anything else. Lest that sound too vague, we should look at some examples.

The reductionist mentality presently at work in the schools says that children should have separate literature, language arts, reading, history, math and science classes as if those are mutually exclusive areas. First off, separating language arts and reading is preposterous as though reading exists outside of language in all its guises (phonology, syntax, semantics, rhetoric, pragmatics) let alone separating reading from literature. Then, if we look at history, why does schoolbook history mean politics and war (neither of which do people ever study again - other than if they become specialists)? The literature and science people should get together and demand a little representation in history. Students never study the history of ideas, even though politics and wars are derived from the concepts a given period. The history of science, technology, literature, art, and, music rarely rate so much as a footnote. Certainly, Pasteur, Darwin and the Impressionists are more important to the world than looking at the Carpetbaggers of the same period. Students learn of the French and Indian War of 1763 as though it was the dominant conflict of the world rather than a brushfire in the worldwide conflict between two imperial powers. At a more advanced level, one cannot hope to understand Wordsworth, Byron, and Beethoven unless one has a grasp of the Rationalism which went before them and the concurrent impact of the ideas of liberty and rights.

When one looks at the limits placed on the corpus of the curriculum in present schools, the suggestion to have community involvement is not so far-fetched. For instance, materials which are appropriate for a student in downtown Chicago may not be appropriate for students in downstate Illinois. This does not mean that the students learn a "different" science (as though such an entity exists) but one must approach the content and students from a different perspective and the local communities should have a say in demanding that appropriate materials and methods be used. In a multi-ethnic city such as Chicago, people see the effects of genetics in everyday life with the surrounding community. A kid from central Illinois sees a village with virtually all Germans or Bohemians or whatever group settled there, but they are acutely aware of genetics in the pigs, cows, and corn which they have to tend. Genetics does not care if the discussion revolves around people or pigs; however, in current teaching, students find rarefied discussions of Brother Mendel and his pea plants so boring that they ignore the entire message, whether in Chicago or Peoria.

When one uses such regional knowledge as a means to tap a student's prior experience in order to explain and expand knowledge in new directions, one can then show the generalizations that allow people, pigs, and peas to be compared. Individually, good teachers have been doing this forever, but only recently has science teaching even been aware of approaching the teaching of science by using cultural knowledge. For instance, a high school science course using Native

American folk knowledge met with great success in New Mexico and Arizona not only on the cultural aspect of students feeling more at home in approaching science, but in the equally important aspect of their increased knowledge of western science. This is extremely important for the simple reason that if the Indian students feel too awkward with Anglo ways, they simply disappear and their "formal" education is over. Studying science is worse than useless if it drives students away from school entirely.

Local influence should be a ballast against a great deal of irrelevancy which occurs in school.

The School as Physical Phenomenon

Schools are a beautiful physical representation of what we are as a society at a given time. The one room school house reflected the decentralized agrarian "everyone helps everyone else" existence of traditional life. As many children as could walk to school came, others received what their parents could give them, and some received no education whatsoever. School had to end in time for spring planting and not resume until fall harvest was completed. One teacher taught all the subjects, using older pupils to help teach the younger ones. This was not necessarily the desired form of school, given the variety of forms which occurred in the large cities, but it was a dictate of necessity.

Industrialization brought compulsory mass education, with students forced into schools which had all the look of textile factories. The masses came and went together as though performing a shift change at the plant every 45 minutes in high school or twice a day in lower grades.

There is no reason for either of these designs in a communicative age. Neither the climatic time pressure of yearly farm cycles nor the physical concentration of educational commodities is a necessary, let alone a sufficient reason to continue with either model. In an era when both time and space are irrelevant in terms of previous human experience, we must be very careful on the limits we impose. We must remember that limits are a hallmark of industrial education, and reformation demands redefinition, but what are some of the constraints and possibilities?

Miniaturization

One of the major thrusts of modern life has been toward miniaturization by the added value of information. Transportation is a good example. Until recently, each advance was bigger and all advances have been faster. Walking gave way to domesticated animals and then carts and wagons while on water, rafts led to row and tow boats and sails. With industrialization, steam engines brought the largest vehicles ever made for both railroads and steam ships. Airplanes downsized travel, increasing speed by a factor of ten while rockets mark both a downsizing and another exponential increase in speed. Though one may argue that a rocket carries very little, in fact one rocket can carry several satellites which can transmit more information electronically that all the planes of the world filled with airmail or trucks and trains filled with ground mail.

Education, always a laggard in the world of thought, is still in the era of bigger is better. We continue to build high schools for several thousand students and universities with 35-40,000 students even though we know that educationally, bigger is not better. Personal attention has always been the hallmark of quality, and it so remains.

Miniaturization of Schools

If added information tends to allow reduction in physical size, why should schools be built to the same size as they have been for for half a century? The most obvious reason is that the extant hierarchy is built to administer units of that size. Many other reasons can be summoned, however. For instance, if one side of town gets a radically different kind of school, calls of discrimination will immediately emanate no matter which group has the "new" school (partly because the community probably had no say in schools in the first place, and partly because of the sense of forced equality as to what is needed). Another issue to unequally sized schools is that athletic competition would become skewed with the larger schools dominating - of course this assumes winning is the goal rather than "physical education.". (This is also a major flaw of a voucher system as high school coaches would recruit junior high students just as college coaches recruit high school students now. With vouchers one could imagine one gigantic athletic school which would represent the city, all others doing something else). A third negative reason would come from administrators and the idea of body count as a way to secure funds and prestige (of course this assumes an unregenerate administration).

Now, if we look at the "best" schools in the country what do we find? - this is subjective and defines "best" as those private schools which have the money to do anything they desire academically and choose to remain small, giving personal attention. Of course, others looking at the same schools might note that they all have test scores exceeding the average by a great deal no matter what level - from elementary school to college. We find high schools with 400 - 600 students (roughly, what most elementary schools have) and an 12 to 1 student to teacher ratio, and universities which rarely have more than 12,000 students, and colleges of roughly 2,500 students (the size of many public high schools). Present day large public schools are built within the industrial paradigm which says that a larger size gives economy of scale. In contrast, this is not true of decentralized communicative design.

Thus, the first suggestion about miniaturization of the schools centers on reducing the size of schools in an absolute sense. A high school student cannot feel as connected to a school which has 3000 students as one which has 500. The sense of connection is immense when a student literally knows every other student in the school and every person on the faculty and administration knows every student and most of the families. Personal connection, forming a team leads to responsibility because everyone knows that one's weight must be pulled, in contrast to the present day anonymity which breeds the "someone else can do it" attitude.

The other facet of the "best" schools is a reduction in class size. So many studies have shown the advantage of smaller classes that there is no disputing the effect. Even slight reductions have marked effects - even if one cannot quite approach twelve students to a class - the closer the better. Of course, this doubles the number of teachers.

With more smaller schools, we can let a number of schools specialize, in the way that magnet schools presently do in the larger cities. However, rather than concentrate power in a few large places, we can spread the schools out for greater access to the community. When there is only one arts or engineering magnet high school in a large city, only a few students can participate because of transportation problems, but take the one mega-school and create five small schools in five areas, and everyone can have access.

The major criticism against having smaller schools, other than economies of scale, is that variety of coursework would be limited. We must keep in mind though that one of the principles of communicative education would be comprehensiveness - not specialization. Where curricular room would be made for local community needs and personal electives, the main focus would be on using core disciplines for the individual to understand the world. In other words, we would simplify the curriculum - refocusing to do fewer tracks, and fewer total courses, but do it more comprehensively.

Classes could not be taught in isolation as in industrial education. They must be able to show relation of knowledge. English classes could not progress, pretending that reading and language are separate entities, or that literature and the technical languages of math and science have no relation. Math could not simply exist in limbo as though it had nothing to do with science and philosophy. Sciences have both a history and a social implication - they are not unto themselves.

In the present system students can graduate from high school with 3 years of English, 2 or 3 of math and one year of science and assorted other electives. Why shouldn't students have four years of each of these disciplines? If we assume, for the moment, a seven hour day as in the present school day, English, math, science, history/social studies use four hours a day, and a community based course takes one, still leaving two hours for personal interest electives.

One might argue that teachers couldn't tailor their courses to fit such a generalized comprehensive framework or wouldn't want to. To a degree that is true, but only as the system and teachers are now. Teachers have been trained to keep to their little boxes of facts and not try to integrate knowledge because "biology teachers teach biology and history teachers teach history, and I won't teach yours and you won't teach mine." When biologists look at the ramifications of Darwin or Pasteur, they see social history in action, just as they see history of ideas in events leading to discoveries by those two men. Knowledge is isolated or integrated purely on the definitions surrounding it. Knowledge in teaching is isolated or comprehensive based on the guiding principle of the system.

Of course, it will take more time and more money to educate a teacher who has studied enough history *and* biology to be able to integrate ideas and express them to a multicultural class in clear English so that all students will have a chance to learn. However, we provide comprehensive training to other professionals - why not to teachers

Paying for Quality Education

Now the question arises of how to pay for such a system, and, without going too deeply into urban economics, a city willing to make such a commitment to quality would find companies wanting to locate there as a draw for their employees to get educated teachers for children. Forswearing the idea of raising taxes which would probably get voted down by a myopic populace, the shift would need to come from extant monies whether local or higher government.

As a country, however, we need to make a decision as to whether we are going to educate enough people to keep our economy functioning. We are running a shortfall of people to take on critical tasks. We do not educate enough engineers to keep industry functioning, let alone expanding. Of the roughly 12,000 graduate engineers who graduate each year, 5,000 are foreign. Even if we kept all of the foreign students, we would have a shortfall of 6000 jobs based on current projections, according to Mildred Dresselhaus of M.I.T. Instead of remaining here, of course, many will go back home to develop their native countries. Something is wrong when we cannot get enough students to study science and engineering. 20 percent of high school sophomores express a serious interest in science, but they don't pursue science - are we turning off our own children by our science teaching methods? Surely, an MBA or law degree is not that much more attractive or easier, but it does pay more.

The issue raised, which is bothering an increasing number of people is whether or not we can keep ignoring our human resources domestically while developing weapons systems. We are, in turn, critical and envious of Japan for the focus which they apply to both education and industry. A country of few natural resources, they produce engineers and scientists for technology, and an educated workforce for production. Their workers produce more than ours, and their children outscore ours. They have virtually no defense budget and use those resources for self-development. Perhaps the time has come for us to reconsider our options.

While doubling teacher salaries and doubling the number of teachers adds to the payroll, it is a small price for a new beginning. We must reallocate to progress. Reallocation does not mean ending military defense; however, if the government used the same congressional committees and allocation process to education that they did to the defense budget, we might find our resources going to education - in the name of national defense. Rather apparently, it simply depends on how one defines national defense.

We could come much closer to meeting expenses if we applied thoughts from an earlier chapter showing that education is an on-going affair, and integrated education with the larger culture. Our schools duplicate many of the services that the city provides for the public as a whole. Why not integrate these resources? Swimming pools, softball, football, and soccer fields, basketball courts, libraries, convention facilities, audio-visual and the computer services of the school system are only a few of the overlapping areas where schools could share expenses or generate profits for the city. When one pro-rates these sorts of expenses, teacher salaries look less forbidding.

Integrating Schools into the Community

Not only is money reallocated in such a system, so is the sentiment that school is separate from other aspects of life. One starts to eliminate the perception that school is for kids and that when one graduates, one is finished learning and bearing responsibility for learning.

Rather than duplicating the books needed for public libraries and school libraries along with all the support services for both, why not integrate them? Not only would the money savings be great (to be applied to higher teacher salaries) but people could see their schools as part of the community and students could see libraries as a place where people come to read and learn for their personal pleasure or business information. In other words, both schools and the community benefit from the change in perception.

In similar fashion, cities maintain football, softball, and soccer fields in schools and parks. Why not combine fields eliminating those not necessary? "Better service, less cost", or "America, this ball's for you."

Instruction and Instructional Flexibility

When we have more, smaller schools, classes of 15 and well-paid teachers who work with parents, the local community and the school administration, classroom instruction will change as well. Not only will knowledge be integrated between subjects at a given time it will be integrated over time as well.

There is little reason for classes to occur as they do in linear sequence with regard to instructional hour after instructional hour during a day, or grade after grade in a school. Ease of administration may be the major concern in the school, but it is not best for education. Nothing inherent in the subject matter dictates that classes have to be 45 minutes long. If students studied in intense blocks of several hours rather than six or seven subjects a day a far greater flexibility could be gained. Such a block design would also facilitate students moving with their ability level, rather than with their age level.

In the current curriculum design, information is parceled out as so-many 35 or 45 minute units per grade. Little thought is paid to the fact that in a 45 minute period, a good teacher is lucky to have more than 25-30 minutes of actual instruction. How can one present evolutionary theory, the slave trade in the revolutionary period, or discuss a literary work in a 30 minute block? In lab courses, the problem is especially acute in setting up and breaking down equipment.

Working with a two hour block allows the teacher a great deal more time to develop the ideas at hand. One would still lose 15 minutes for administrative details and settling the class, but it would be a much lesser percentage of the time available. Under such a system, students could take the usual yearlong course in one semester, and would then take new courses the next semester. Therefore, students would receive the same amount of instruction for the year as a whole but have much greater intensity.

This flexibility would allow greater student participation at grade level rather than age level. When one makes a case for students being kept with students their own age, the argument is usually in terms of maturational issues, and the social norms expected for age groups. This issue really centers about whether schools are for socialization or learning (not that those are completely separate). When we keep a very bright student with others his own age rather than letting him or her progress in naturally acquisitive learning patterns, we risk frustrating that person into noncompliance with the system. In like manner, when a less-able student is forced to compete with students with whom he or she is not really able to work, that frustration can make for a drop-out. It seems that both patterns run counter to proper socialization and, certainly, counter to learning, but it is easy to administer.

If, on the other hand, we let students study and learn to their own level, switching grades up to twice a year under the block study program, then bright, average, and slow students would all be accommodated. Students would socialize with their own friends regardless of whatever grade they were in because the whole school would be in flux as is the society. When people in the present system talk about having a student skip a grade or repeat a grade, the consequences are great because the school is set up in such a linear fashion that students literally lose all their friends. When the whole school is adaptive to student need, friends remain and subject matter is appropriate to student need and interest. Students who were good in one subject and poor in another would not be forced to slow down in one or be pushed uncomfortably in the other. The result balances student need with the available teachers, promoting real communication in education.

CHAPTER 13

Communicative Administration

When we speak of communicative administration are we really dealing with an oxymoron? Certainly in present schools we are. What we need is a transformation, not elimination. Much as intellectuals and religious leaders from the Absolute-Ideal and communicators from the Relative-Ideal resent imposed administration, a certain amount of direction is needed in order to get things done. The problem is that the administrators in any situation quickly seem to view themselves as the reason for being rather than seeing themselves as the people who help get things done.

As people from the Authoritarian sector, administrators simply assume control, and, unless checked, really do take control. Because of the reluctance of people from the Ideal side of the matrix to take control, power usually remains firmly in the Authoritarian.

Transformation of Power

As has been extensively noted, people in power do not usually of their own volition give up that power. The real issue in transformation of power then is how to take a vertical structure and change it into a connected network where the administrators of the Authoritarian sector are not "over" the teachers of the Communicative: not in school level, not in status, and not in pay. The most obvious block at the present time is that administrators earn considerably more than teachers in the public schools and would not accept a pay or status cut to be put on the same level as the teachers. That sentiment is backward. Because teachers do the actual productive work of the schools, i.e., teach students (lest one forgets - that is the only reason to have schools) teachers should be paid and regarded as the producers.

Given the changes in teachers and teacher training outlined in the section on teaching, teachers should start at the same pay levels as other professionals: doctors, lawyers, and accountants. For equity, a graduated salary scale should put equals at the same pay whether teachers or administrators.

Aside from the issue of pay, which always denotes status in the present system, who will make the decisions? Isn't that what an administration is for? In the current system, the answer is yes. However, administration does not mean decision-making, it means taking care of needs: literally, ministering. Decisions will have to be made on a consensus basis. The two functions have to be separated if the communicative school is going to achieve its goal.

Administering Needs

Most of administration is mundane, not unlike many other activities. Actual administration in the schools usually breaks down into the routine areas of classroom needs, physical plant, and personnel. Someone has to make sure that teachers and students have books, chalk, light, clean rooms, paper, and required auxiliary equipment. In like manner, the classrooms have to be clean, well-lighted, and a comfortable temperature. Although this sounds obvious and easy, the principal who can keep these basics functioning has far fewer problems with both teachers and students than one who doesn't.

Next time you walk into a school you may want to make some observations and use your senses actively. Does it smell? If so, of what? Cleaning compound? Lunch? or rotting fruit and stinky shoes in student lockers? How dark or how inviting are the halls? Does it have plain brick walls or does it use student talent for decoration? Are student decorations uniform having come out of a teacher's manual or are they student created, showing variety? Are the halls and, more importantly, are the bathrooms clean? If students are frustrated, they destroy the bathrooms first, littering or setting fires in the trash containers, putting heavy fireworks down the plumbing, or dislodging and dropping the windows out. The bathroom has the only privacy for students in a place where they are observed all day. They vent their feelings in the bathroom if they cannot do it in a more constructive way in class.

The greatest changes in administration in re-formed schools will not occur on this physical level although the effects may be noticed. Someone will still have to oversee the day-to-dayness of the school whatever the structure of the personnel.

Policy Formation and Administration

The real changes will be in personnel and policy formation. With an equalization in pay and status of both teaching and administrative personnel, decisions will come about by consensus with both teachers and administration having to relearn the issue. Consensus decision-making means rethinking decision-making process for Americans because we typically look for one person to make the decision and take credit/responsibility. For all our democratic system and talk about representation, we still expect one person to be responsible rather than all of us being a part of a decision. Truman's, "The buck stops here" may be the most visible sign of this view, but we see it everyday in the schools. We have to change this process to see that all of us are responsible. The school will function in a more integrated fashion when teachers and administration share the decisions rather than the front office making decisions, and the teachers putting rude comments on their teacher room bulletin boards. Joint decisions ensure joint responsibility in carrying out those decisions and making the policies succeed.

The demands for this restructuring come from several different areas. The most obvious issue at present stems from teacher dissatisfaction, but that is not surprising given the circumstances. Underpaid, overworked, with little to no say in how the schools are run, it is a wonder we have as many dedicated teachers as we have.

If we simply adapted the most current corporate management techniques, we would find that the producers, the workers, are being given a say in corporate policy. While this is viewed as "smart" in the corporate world (because production is going up), education is looking backward and trying to apply even more stringent controls from the top down in order to gain accountability and increased production as corporations did thirty years ago.

When Americans examine Japanese companies, one factor keeps emerging - consensus. They form a consensus on a government policy and then follow it through - as in the domination of semiconductor production. Within the corporations themselves consensus decision-making is the rule. Americans, with their linearity, want decisions immediately and get frustrated when told "we" are talking about it. Americans want to know who is responsible, who to talk to, and can hardly believe that no "one" is responsible.

Management consultants tell us that we shouldn't try to emulate the Japanese on consensus decision-making as it is a cultural phenomenon. Well, of course it is a cultural phenomenon as though any human actions are outside of culture. They learned one way, and we learned another; are we too stupid to learn something new? I give us more credit than that.

What is far more interesting than whether Japanese business strategy is applicable to the U.S. or not, is the pattern that emerges from the Matrix. Remember that each leader acts with power and decisions made in the next clockwise quadrant. Moses was in the Inspiriting sector and acted as leader, making decisions in the Authoritarian sector. In like manner, Authoritarians such as Caesar and Ford ruled with power and decisions made in the Physical quadrant (geography and military for Caesar, commodities and workers for Ford). Then, corporations took over from the Authoritarians with control of information in the Communicative sector (engineering process). Now, from our perspective, sitting in the Communicative quadrant, we should be getting our power and decision-making from the Inspiriting. It is clear that power is increasingly coming from that quadrant: for the majority, the power arrives in the guise of information science with microelectronics applications; however, for a growing minority the power is coming from the religious part of the Inspiriting sector.

For decision-making strategy, we must look at the structure of the Inspiriting where the dominant characteristic is that of wholes. One finds whole forms whether in the religious or intellectual arena. Wholeness and consensus was the order of rule in hunting and gathering society. Similarly, Moses spent much of his time trying to gain consensus among his tribe as it wandered the desert as he had no army to enforce his will. We might wonder at the direction wholes can take as the present age emerges.

Emerging patterns of decision-making will not be based on the wholes of hunting and gathering society or the Biblical pattern of leadership by ethnarch, rather the wholes of one 'global village.'. When we look at the pattern on the Matrix and combine that with emerging corporate patterns, and contrast both with the failure of the present hierarchical system with regard to education, we can see a change coming. With consensus, the school can move forward with unification rather than each group fighting for its own segment - to the detriment of students.

Where the faculty will have an equal say with the administration in forming school policy, they will also have an equal responsibility in making sure that the policy is not only equitable, but executed. Rather than the present system, where administrators are over teachers, both sides should view the strengths that they bring to the process. Teachers know the students and the curricular material; administrators know the money and politics; the issue becomes finding the best way to meld the different facets. Only by having equals at a table can an equitable policy be set. If, as in the present set-up, there is an implied superiority and inferiority, then not only is free discussion discouraged, but the policy is weighted to those in power no matter how much lip-service is paid to "openly expressed views."

This policy is in keeping with the balance of power outlined in a previous chapter where it was noted that parents, teachers, and administration should all share in curricular decisions. To the degree that policy decisions affect the atmosphere and attitude of the school, parents should be part of the process at this level as well. However, just as parents are important in helping set broad guidelines in curriculum, but not formulating the details, that being left to professionals, we find the same reasoning applying here. Parents should be able to choose the school which fits the needs of their children and then work with the program to carry it to fruition - not simply tell the schools how they should work.

To draw an analogy, at present, parents choose a doctor with whom they feel comfortable and with whom they can work for their children's health - but they don't tell him how to practice the details of his profession. Parents should have a choice of education for their children and be able with our smaller, more numerous schools to find one which has a compatible philosophy and then work fully with teachers and administration, trusting both to be professional in their execution of the established defined good.

In this manner, one side does not "win" the schools: varied schools serve a varied community. The schools of a city are not prisoner of either the state board of education or any one community within a city. The core subjects provide sufficient unity for all students to have an common reference framework for understanding while the community and personal electives allow interests to be pursued.

Achieving the Transition

Changing the status quo in education seems, at times, a monumental task. The bureaucracy is so large and so entrenched and so connected to the rest of the power system of government that it seems impossible to move. It can be done.

There are two key areas which must be altered to achieve the transition: restructuring the political framework within which educational administration operates and redefining the roles of administrators, teachers, and parents. In a larger sense, these problems are really two parts of the same issue: where is the power in the system.

The present power elites, whether in federal, state, or local government, operate in a hierarchical manner, no matter whether they are Anglo, Black, or Hispanic, male or female. Those who join the elite from a minority quickly find themselves transformed. I was amused to find that Indians from the Zuni Pueblo in New Mexico have a term for the Indians who join the federal government's Bureau of Indian Affairs (BIA): Washington Redskins.

When people from outside the established educational power group tell that group what to do, it patronizes the individual and sends him on his way out. Minorities have long been treated in this manner, and now many white males are seeing this first hand with affirmative action placing racial or gender hiring restrictions on employers. Whatever the race or sex, complaints tend to be dismissed summarily, being decided solely on the current atmosphere.

The idea of stripping the power of administrators and sharing it with teachers and members of a community seems blasphemy to those who are currently powerful. How can those who don't know, try to take power? Such an attitude is not unlike what has been experienced by Blacks, Hispanics and women who all were patronized for years by bureaucrats saying, "not now, wait until you know more." Women and minorities finally said, "Stop doing that, we aren't going to take it." Redefinition is still taking place, and people are healthier for it, male and female of all races.

The restructuring of the political framework is the primary change necessary; the rest is derived from that shift in focus. Why should the people charged with the guidance of our educational institutions be state political appointees. At the federal level, we see parallel idiocy when we note that Department of Education officials do not have to have anymore qualification than State Department officials: the better the campaign contribution, the better the position. Similar patterns emerge at the state level when we look at the boards of regents appointed by our distinguished governors. Car dealers, beer distributors, and insurance agents become regents and have a direct hand in running our large state research universities. Such people would scoff at a university professor coming into their dealerships and telling them how to run the business, but they think that they can come into the university and know what to do, with no education or experience in the field.

At the local level, city school boards are usually elected, but on what qualifications? As often as not they get elected to represent one group or another, whether that group is racial or social - rather than looking toward education as the means to open minds and opportunities.

Strategies of Change

Against this three tiered array of ignorance, politics and narrowness of scope, progressive local administrators and teachers have worked for years in a female fashion. The macho male tells the little woman what needs to be done and how it should be done and that now he has important things to do or he'd do this job too - and the woman says yes and yes and yes and then does it her own way. The local progressives know that confrontation will not work in the face of power so they simply fulfill the minimums required and then move on to real education, just as women have for years understood confrontation to be a losing battle and therefore, formed their own strategy.

There comes a time, however, when women said we really don't have to be second-rate, we can do it ourselves. Just as with the civil rights movement, grassroots feeling spread. One person in a bus; one person in a lunchcounter just saying no, "I won't move." and others joined in forming a chorus. As the shift in government continues toward local autonomy and issue voting, school change will occur.

Redefinition of Roles in Local Administration

Where the larger aspect of change occurs in the political arena, we cannot ignore the problem of redefinition of roles at the local level, whether in the relation of the school board and superintendent to the schools themselves or the principals to their own schools. As noted, administration's job is to provide for the necessities of teaching and learning and in so doing to be at the same pay and status level as the teachers. If so limited, then there will many bruised egos at the apparent demotion in power.

Change will come with pain as those who produce, the teachers, get rewarded and administrators have to change their position in both relative and real terms. Administrative rule by fiat, that perk of the Authoritarian sector, will be replaced by mutual accountability with teachers.

CHAPTER 14

Curricular   Content

Content Defined

The content taught in the schools remains the loudest and most controversial aspect of the current educational debate, though it is not the most important. This most likely occurs because it is easy for people to identify the "what" of content in contrast to the not so readily apparent philosophy of the system or the psychology of teaching methodology. People can see and touch the "reality" of books and other physical materials where they need to "understand" philosophy and psychology in order to analyze the educational foundations of the school. Once again, people fall back to the Real side of the Matrix.

Will students be coerced into the classics and great books? Or will they be coerced into skills and manipulation without traditional "irrelevant content"? Can there be a balance between the two? Do we need a third entity? Can American freedom of choice be applied to the decision?   At what point is the teaching of "cultural" values an imposition of the beliefs of one set of individuals on the beliefs of another set of individuals rather than a statement of assumed cultural knowledge? In an age, when virtually any fact can be gained in seconds on a computer terminal, what is the purpose of learning facts? Are facts learned for tests? or for an understanding of the world in which we

live? In *The House of Intellect* Jacques Barzun wrote an eloquent
passage on facts and exams which applies to all students although in
this case he is referring to doctoral exams.

> After a suitable number of lectures and one or two seminars, in
> which students read papers haltingly in front of their
> uninterested peers, the comprehensive ... examination suddenly
> looms, demanding of the candidate a breadth and depth of
> knowledge equal to the sum of the same in the heads of his
> half-dozen examiners. In most subjects, few attempts are made
> to educe principles from ever larger masses of facts and to
> relegate detail to handbooks.   The sum total of many
> specialties is required of the student, no matter how many
> years of his adult life are swallowed up in the preparation.
> Many give up. The rest go in for cramming, which after the
> strain of vomition leaves a man reflecting that there was one
> week in his life when he knew a great deal.
> (p.131)

What he said of doctoral students of the Fifties applies equally to
students today. Questions abound and can help illuminate the role of
content in the communicative school. As a rule, most books on
education select a few of these questions, set up a straw man against
which to joust and claim victory when, in fact, they have merely
defined a narrow frame of reference in which to examine the problem.
As a counterpoint to the way the questions are usually framed, we must
note that, as a basis, communicative education must be meaning driven
with the students possessing a feeling that there is some purpose to
their being in school.

Areas of Knowledge in Content

Through the ages, knowledge has been viewed in three primary
categories: logical, social, or physical. Whether one sees knowledge
from an Aristotelian perspective or a modern teaching-by-objectives
view, the idea of three categories holds with little modification:
Aristotle's three persuasive rhetorical proofs (logos, pathos, ethos) or
the modern taxonomies of the educational domains (cognitive, affective
and psychomotor).

In present day mass schooling, we seem to lack conviction in our
curricular eclecticism, changing our emphasis every few years between
logos (business-efficiency) and pathos (progressive) in teaching and
learning, with a dash of ethos thrown in by moralists every now and
then. The Greeks had a distinct advantage over us as they knew what
they wanted from their education. They did not try to be all things to

all people.   Aristotle taught logical persuasion; Plato taught the passionate search for truth; and the Spartans taught warrior culture. In trying to teach everyone everything, we seem to have lost focus in what we teach, and in many cases even what we can teach. That is why in describing the reformed school, emphasis is placed on teaching fewer courses, but with a more comprehensive approach.

Regaining Content Focus

The major question in regaining the focus of content teaching is to ask whether we can be everything to everyone? Quite apparently, we cannot, if the present schools, or the debate between the varied cultures of America are any indication.

First, for simplicity's sake, we should discuss those courses which do not vary according to a particular cultural point of view. Math is math, and 2+2=4 whether white or brown, atheist or fundamentalist, traditionalist or progressive. In like manner, chemistry, physics and physical education can be disposed of, as can be the modern languages, acknowledging that in some areas Spanish, Chinese, and Japanese carry a political agenda. That ends the culturally non-controversial subjects. Needless to say, within all of these courses, there is and should be debate on how best to present the materials in instruction and what underlying pedagogical assumptions are made by the curriculum developer and teacher. Rather than examine the possible courses taught in school and then seeing where different groups affect them, let's go back to the cultures themselves and contrast how they look at content in the current school arrangement. The metaphors of education and cultural position in the Matrix should inform the discussion.

Traditional Approaches to Content - The Authoritarian

Broadly we have two cultures vying for dominance under the rubric "traditional:" the religious right and the academic neo-conservatives. Each has its own program for change, though each would deny that premise, and say they were simply opting for the correct choice as shown through the ages, adding that current education is an aberration from their time-proven agenda.   In fact, current education is an aberration, in the sense of a break from the last two thousand years. Equally, it is a search. Having broken the pattern, one cannot simply turn around and go back, even if that were desirable. However, as Authoritarians, they see their approach as the way to get back to order - where power was in the "right" place, and the world spun according to their rules. It is little wonder that they are upset.

The religious right has an agenda of change which includes classical languages, biology, English, and all of the social sciences. Ancient languages are having a rebirth sparked in large part by fundamentalists wanting to learn Greek and Latin to read the Bible in the original tongue. With similar bias, biology has become controversial in recent years with fundamentalists insisting that creationism be taught if evolution is taught. They also seem to think that many of the books in English class are corrupt because of language or ethical grounds, or, in general, for supporting "secular humanism." Thus, we find that *Catcher in the Rye*, and *The Adventures of Huckleberry Finn* should not be taught for lack of moral tone. In like manner, history and social studies come under fire for any serious discussion of political issues such as majority rule/minority rights, affirmative action, or women's rights. Health education, including sex education and substance abuse awareness, are viewed as something that simply shouldn't be talked about. To paraphrase Phyllis Schlafly and the Eagle Forum - kids just shouldn't touch anything covered by a bathing suit. Such an enlightened view on sex is matched by the "just say no" attitude toward drug abuse. Don't explain, don't treat children as normally curious human beings, just say repression.

Those academic conservatives who envision an educational system which holds past knowledge as an immutable sacred gift to be passed to future generations are no less restrictive than the previous group. Instead of putting absolute belief in God, they simply put their absolute trust in abstract intellectualism. Rather than God, Jesus, and the Apostles, one finds "Intellectualism," with supporters pointing to Plato and 5000 associated items comprising the isolated fortress of the educated mind. The neo-classicists might note that static fortifications proved less than secure for the Trojans, and simplistically naive in the Maginot Line and Kuwait.

In an age of communication, one cannot simply erect walls and pretend nothing will change whether from religious or intellectual persuasion. Laser-guided smart bombs and digital satellite mapping show the foolishness of hiding in a bunker in a present day war, just as expanding knowledge in an inter-related multicultural world shows the foolishness of trying to define current lines of learning by what was successful one hundred or two thousand years ago.

Industrial Approaches to Content

The original industrial groups: business-efficiency and progressives had distinct views of content in education. Briefly, the business people looked at what industry needed and asked for that to be taught in schools. Thus, we saw the rise of commercial and vocational courses such as accounting, management, metal and wood shop. Content was lodged in the realm of pragmatism and utilitarianism and the focus was on the material - not how the students could best learn. The Progressives saw content as a way to promote their agenda of social democracy and acculturation to the newly emerging industrial world and thus, we got courses on family and home for the first time. In contrast to the subject matter centered courses of the business efficiency people, the Progressives stressed student centered curriculum.

Presently, the back to the basics people apply the utilitarian approach of the business group but in a completely different circumstance. They want to apply the precepts of 1918 to the 1990s. What was practical in 1918 is not necessarily practical now and just because it was good enough for my father is not a good reason that it is good enough for my son, in other words they really are not practical as the business efficiency group certainly was. They are simply looking backward with no grounding for their thought. They would eliminate sex and drug education on the grounds that schools are not in business to teach such frills. In their conservatism, they would also eliminate most of the arts as well, leaving a Spartan education for a non-spartan culture.

In contrast, the open classroom movement of the Sixties and Seventies tried to focus on letting the student learn in a self-paced environment according to the student's need at the time - a nice Progressive thought. However, to insert a non-structured environment into a structured system is to invite disaster and the movement went down in flames as a result. Such ideals cannot be applied piecemeal in a mass education system. Where A.S. Neill and his education without compulsion made the private school Summerhill a success, he had control from the beginning of a student's school life and children grew up in a non-structured environment. When a child has open classrooms K-12, with no tests or expectations, then that system can work. It is not a likely occurrence in the near future in public education.

Role of Content in Communicative Schools

The first item that must be acknowledged about the content taught in school is that it is always culturally and politically based. If we envision, as did the traditionalists, school as a transmitter of a corpus of "culture," then it makes sense that we teach the content of that corpus, and if people get job skills along the way that is okay but not primary. If we see school as a place to learn vocational skills, then the content becomes quantifiable with measurable behaviors while the other information learned along the way is irrelevant - so long as the measured skills are learned. However, if we see school as the learning of relationship with the world, then both informational content and the ability to manipulate it are important.

Because present schooling really does not answer any of these statements, we might look at the logical, if absurd, extension of these current positions into the schools. If we take the first viewpoint, that students should learn cultural facts as a means of learning culture, then rather than instituting a "Great Books" program in college, why not start in Kindergarten? Students could learn 5000 cultural facts in order to leave elementary school and another 5000 or so to leave high school. Then they could display a passing familiarity with many thousand points of light before arriving at college where they could get a good 19th century education and become true gentlemen.

On the other hand, the rampant vocationalism of so-called "professional" schools belies the notion of education at all. If all one knows on graduating is engineering fluid dynamics, the biochemical process of enzyme metabolism, or ten variations of costing expenses on a corporate ledger, then again education has not taken place. There is nothing so very difficult about differential pressure, enzyme metabolism, or finding a cost position that a 15 year old couldn't do just as well as a 22 or 30 year old. Why not track elementary students into the specialties? We could get 5-15 more years out of our ignorant engineers, doctors, and accountants. Since they are ignorant of the impact of wider ideas in ethics, ecology, and economics anyway under the present system, why not accelerate it to the logical conclusion?

However, if we view education to be the discovery of relationship with the world, we can have freedom of choice within a range so that individuals become broadly "educated" *and* have depth at the same time. Such comprehensiveness has been practiced at liberal arts colleges for some time with "area requirements," ensuring that math majors had English, sociology and philosophy, and English majors had science and physical education. Extending the same idea into high school and elementary school can ensure a breadth missing in present schools; however, the execution of the idea would need to work in quite different ways.

High Schools

High schools are presently divided into tracks according to "academic promise" with advanced placement students at the top and vocational educational students at the bottom, if they choose to remain in school at all past age 16. One or two levels exist in between for the majority of students who can go to non-selective state colleges if they so choose.

The money and entitlement programs go for the top and bottom minorities with the large middle forgotten because of a lack of special interest voice. Instead of a track system as presently practiced where the top students become mini-college students going into the specialist tracking of industrial education, taking only courses in their chosen specialty, the public would be better served if they studied a broad range because when those individuals become "professionals" they would know something beyond their specialty. In like manner, the students in vocational education would be better served if they took a complete range of coursework enabling them to learn enough to be able to change and adapt to the change in the future, rather than being left jobless and untrainable after ten years in a vocation which no longer needs him or her. The specialization demanded by the industrial hierarchy is not the comprehensiveness needed in a communicative world. Seeing connections and understanding relationships is the key to remaining able to function with change. In short, the little experts of the fast track are as limited in their education as those taking job skills courses.

Every high school student should have to take English, math, a range of the sciences, social sciences, and the arts and humanities, as well as physical education. Far from having all these courses taught from the perspective of becoming expert, the need is for connection. To say at present that most people never will need algebra is begging the question, most people have no idea when algebra can be used, so of course, they don't need it. They didn't need it when they took it, never saw why they should take it, other than a requirement, and still don't know - and no one ever explained why it was a useful subject.

If a course isn't based on learning that is meaningful, then it is precisely meaningless. Why is philosophy a useful subject? Very few people have ever earned a living with philosophy. But both philosophy and algebra allow students to see relationships, ways of facing and testing the unknown, ways of creating order out of seemingly random events. The usual approach to teaching both of these subjects is to emphasize that they are important to know for themselves, not for what they give to the totality of education. Thus, one struggles with Kantian imperatives and existential nothingness, striving to become a mini-expert rather than a person able to view the world from a number of perspectives, knowing why one's own view has value while being able to see the strengths and weaknesses of another's view. In similar fashion, students wrestle with the quadratic equations of algebra, plotting functions and solving for an X that is mysterious as to how it can be used or why all the sweat is worthwhile, rather than seeing algebra as the basis of many forms of measurement in architecture and engineering and the statistical regressions for all the social sciences.

In similar fashion, rarely does physical education concern itself with education in the physical domain. Rather it is an hour of competitive sports in which gifted athletes pulverize the less-able just as gifted math students pummel the less-able in algebra class. No one ever wanted to be the last boy or girl left in line as teams were picked and the "top jocks" shrugged and laughed, "Okay, I guess I gotta take John and you're gonna get the real loser. Hee Hee." Where physical education could teach students about physiology, metabolism, movement, weight and stress management, it becomes a sorting mechanism for coaches to see which students could help the school win the "Big Game."

Elementary Schools

At the elementary level, people argue that students should have one teacher rather than moving from class to class as do their older counterparts. And yet, art, music, computers and gym are all taught by specialists, in separate rooms, representing a sizable portion of the elementary week. Given that these activities are not deleterious, and most agree that the students like these classes more than their regular ones, we might look at some of the reasons why. In each case, students are exploring the world in individually meaningful ways and, to some degree, controlling their environment. Whether the action is the power of controlling the computer screen, motion in gym, sound in music, or color in art, students find personal meaning. In contrast, reading class with Dick and Jane has little meaning, and, for the "slow" students, phonics drills have even less meaning. Repetitive rows of addition and subtraction problems on mimeographed homework sheets are not learning: they are drudgery. If a student can do the sheet, there is no need to waste time doing it, and if they can't, such idiot sheets are not going to help them learn.

If the "content" classes of reading and arithmetic in elementary school had the individual meaning and, therefore, the involvement of the computer, art, music, and gym classes, the extant content could be taught in less time, allowing greater exploration. People say that this is not the purpose of elementary school, that students shouldn't be pushed, but how can one push an inquisitive child? Nothing is more eager to learn than a child who is interested - ask any parent.

Summary

In both elementary and high school, content must be unified to a coherent whole. Clearly, when literature comprises the areas of reading, language study, social history, or aesthetic theory, and the sciences of biology, physics or chemistry can be theory, technology, history, philosophy, or social implication, depending on emphasis, what we need is not specialization, but the integration of knowledge.

The most extraordinary teacher of whom I have had the pleasure to be a student, and standing in sharp contrast to the first grade teacher who told me not to ask about a word that was 75 pages ahead of the class, my fifth grade teacher expected his students to ask questions and explore for themselves. Charles Meyers, in 1959, a teacher in Ypsilanti, Michigan got his usual round of criticism for expecting students to learn something. As a fifth grade teacher, he taught his students about atomic energy down to the relative stability of U-238 versus the instability of U-234, U-235 and plutonium and why the latter were useful in making bombs as a result. Students also learned the human body, including names and functions of all the major organs, arteries, veins and nerves in isolation, and in situ with anatomical dummies. In like manner, he brought in automobile parts and students learned engines from the carburetor and intake manifold, through the pistons, cylinders and on out the exhaust with time on all the peripheral systems and the very process of intake, compression, combustion, exhaust of internal combustion. More than the excitement of having a teacher who expected students to learn, was the excitement he brought in looking at the similarities in the world. Greater volatility in fuels means greater power whether nuclear instability or octane rating of gasoline. The heart is a pump circulating blood to keep the body alive; the oil pump keeps oil circulating to keep the engine lubed, alive, and in motion. Air and fuel move through an engine, and air and food move through the human.

Meyers taught comprehensively. We didn't have boundaries between reading and science - we read science, and we read about the people and history of science. Music meant that he told us about his marimba sitting in the corner of the class, radio waves, and we discussed acoustics and compared marimba notes with a set of drums, and then he played, and we sang. Music, science and reading were all just part of the fifth grade explosion. He refused to be boxed and teach as though subjects had separate realities. Even as a fifth grader, I knew that this was education - many years later and having a Ph.D., I appreciate it even more, though not so innocently.

Critics - some other teachers who felt intimidated, people in schools of education (he was never given a student teacher), and school board members - said Meyers expected too much of children, but no one ever asked us as students. Not only were there no discipline problems, students couldn't wait to play with valves and pistons and plastic livers and spleens and atomic models made of marbles glued together with electron orbits of string which had been wound around balloons and glued to form a circle. He worked with us, not over us; he acknowledged us, and we acknowledged him. When, 35 years later, this student can still remember the valve from the left ventricle is roughly parallel to the exhaust valve when the heart and a car cylinder are compared, he was not overestimating what fifth graders could learn.

Meyers was not limited to teaching minimums. He thought the world was exciting and gave his students a view of dynamic process. In so doing, he gave them a chance to try to figure out things with accompanying successes and failures. Failure in his class was not humiliating as in other classes; it became realizing why we hadn't made connections. For example, he brought auto parts into the class and had students try to figure what they were in operational and functional terms. Rather than doing this in the confines of a programmed 45 minute period, he let the parts sit around the class and encouraged students hold them, play with them, to explore, and find out on their own or working with other students what the parts were or did. One could go to libraries and look at books, ask service station mechanics, or quiz parents. The most difficult auto part and one of my greatest frustrations in fifth grade was when he brought in a gasoline gauge measuring float which sits in the gas tank and moves up and down with the level of gasoline (not unlike a toilet tank float) telling the driver whether the tank is full or empty. In trying to find out what the gas gauge float was, we learned many other parts before he gave in and told us what the float was. Had he had to teach a specific set of objectives, he couldn't have allowed the discovery that provided the magic spark for learning. Such discovery doesn't follow a neat timetable.

Just as specified objectives in lesson plans done weeks in advance limit discovery possibilities, administrators are hard pressed to account for the variety of knowledge taught in a class by the Mr. Meyers of the world - measurable minimums are not so important as possible maximums. However, the greatest stumbling block to overcome in having more such classes is having autonomous teachers who can integrate a wide array of knowledge.

CHAPTER 15

Teachers

When teachers set their own guidelines for teaching, they will be professional. At present, they are hired hands, not unlike farmworkers. "Two National Merit Scholars and all I get is a @#*^+# 'Good job, John letter,'" "We be pickin' de lettuce for bio today boss," "Eh patron, I peek two bushel of A student, I getta raise, no?" Teachers get just about as much respect as farmworkers. If it isn't students, then it's parents, principals, industry, city school boards or the state demanding something from them.

Doctors, lawyers, accountants and engineers set their own guidelines for practice and would scorn state authorities who pretended to meddle with that practice. Why should state authorities know anything more about teaching than they do about medicine or law? Children spend seven hours a day at school, but may spend half an hour a year with a doctor. Yet that half hour can cost as much as the school taxes for the year for the child. Isn't something out of balance?

Should Teachers Be Considered Professionals?

On the other hand, do teachers deserve to be be treated as professionals? It rather depends on one's perspective. At present, some certainly do and some certainly do not. The question is still out for the profession as a whole. In that they allow themselves to be treated as they do and to receive little respect and pay - no they do not deserve to be called professionals. Doormats is more appropriate. Should they be called professionals? Talk is cheap and teachers hear more of it than they need. More than any other group, teachers should *be* professional.

The difference between being called professional and being professional is great. Professionals are autonomous; they set their own standards, create their own entrance tests, and police their own ranks; they pass a standard course of study for a B.A. or B.S. degree and then spend time in post-baccalaureate study, only after which may they be tested in their proficiency; they undergo intern/probationary status in the profession; and they define their profession as a benefit to society and yet do not see why that should mean they are poor. Teachers do not have any of these characteristics

Teachers are not autonomous. They take orders from practically everyone and can give orders only to students. Teachers do not set their own standards, make their own certification tests, or police their own peers. Outsiders do all of these tasks - even though those who make the tests and set the standards have never had to be a classroom teacher. Teachers in many states can major in education, taking as few as 50 hours of subject matter courses; thus they graduate with, at best, a limited understanding of the inter-relationship of knowledge that makes us what we are - in no way can many claim to be well-trained, let alone educated, in the broad sense of the word. New teachers graduate from college and move from being a student to being a teacher without support, let alone an internship or probationary period of limited and supervised work to assure professionalism in the classroom. On the other hand, teachers accept all of these sub-professional standards along with the argument that they don't deserve as much money as other professionals because they are public servants.

The Case for Teachers

I do not want to seem hard on teachers. They take enough abuse without me adding to their woes, but current teachers do reflect what society wants of education. As long as the public has little respect for education, teachers will be treated as they are despite their ability, dexterity, and endurance. Teachers have to be skillful in many areas, changing hats throughout the day. They must know a subject area as a professional, be an instructor, test-maker and evaluation specialist in the classroom, be a diplomat in dealing with parents, be a negotiator in dealing with the administration, be a cop and judge on the playground, and a psychologist and social worker rolled into one - and all for $17,500 according to the NEA in 1987. Makes you wonder why anyone would enter teaching.

In addition, the popular conception that teachers work essentially "part-time" is a great myth. School teachers typically work 8-3:30 with one preparation period allowed during the day. One period is not sufficient to prepare materials, let alone presentation and activities for the rest of the classes. That means that after school, the teacher has to do class preparation, grade student papers, fill out reports to the administration, do long-term planning, and attend the requisite number of committee meetings, and after school and evening activities. Sounds like a part-time job to me.

Correcting the Imbalances

Saying that teachers are over-worked, underpaid, and don't get no respect is to state the obvious. The way to correct the imbalances, however, is more complicated than just saying, "change teacher education" - though that would be a positive start. The deluge of educational reports indicates that people are worried about the level of teachers as they emerge from schools of education, but those same people who are worried, want better teachers for less money, i.e. more productivity as viewed from an industrial perspective.

If we, as a society, really want professional teachers, we can have them; we know how to make them, and how to describe them. They will be better prepared, will serve internships to prove and improve themselves, will test and certify themselves, will be autonomous, and will certainly cost more money. They will also be brighter, more demanding of support, and less tolerant of the abuse which teachers regularly suffer today. In other words, they will demand the professional respect that teachers today only wish for. I rather suspect that America wants something less; it always has. The question is why? and more importantly, will the changes presently going on affect public opinion?

Respect for Education

Traditionally, America has had no love affair with education and the educated - aspects of the Ideal side of the Matrix. Everyone has paid lip-service to the brilliance of the Founding Fathers, but when it comes time to make a choice, America has always gone for the man of action or commerce, not the man of thought. Our artists and writers stand out as much in contrast to their primitive surroundings as for their artistic brilliance. Melville and Twain were men of action who wrote well just as Remington sculpted and drew the West.

Jefferson may have lived in the Inspiriting quadrant of the Absolute-Ideal, but America as a whole was firmly bound in the Real. The calls for George Washington to become King came from the Authoritarian sector of the Absolute-Real. People generally know more of the personal history of the uncouth, musket and knife-toting Physical Davy Crockett, Daniel Boone, and Jim Bowie than of the men who shaped the Constitution.

Are times really achangin' or is the Matrix simply a nice device where it fits? The winds are blowin', but as of yet, it seems more like a dust storm than a spring zephyr wafting change gently to us. If change really is coming to America, it would appear to be coming directly from that spring of pragmatism: business, and not from any academic institution.

A good example comes from that bastion of the Physical: Texas - where H. Ross Perot took on the old boys of education and had'em roped and branded before they understood he was serious. As Founder and President of Electronic Data Services, Perot understood the practical value of education in providing people for his information company. He was taking the pragmatic approach of the business-efficiency group at the turn of the century - simply that America needed more educated bodies. Electronic information services may up the educational ante from the industrial education of the earlier period, but the principle remains the same.

Perot was asked to head a commission on education for the state of Texas and thus, went to work. Of all the sacrilege in football-crazed Texas, Perot had the nerve to say if players couldn't pass their courses, they couldn't participate in extracurricular activities. His proposal affected not only football but also cheerleaders, band members, debate teams, and all others in extracurricular activities - not that debate members have ever worried about 'passing' their courses. He also wanted to have a variety of standards applied to teaching and schools which met with varied success, but the real issue for us is that pressure is coming from the only area that the U.S. has ever respected: business.

Increasingly, we find business leaders becoming involved in education whether from the directly corporate side in setting up their own programs or working with public entities. This is not altruism, but fear. They need a more educated workforce than ever, and they are not getting it. The bodies needed earlier in the century could be trained, now people must be educated because they will probably have at least two different jobs before they retire. The general education needed for such work flexibility precludes the narrowness of training.

Will things change? Yes, it would appear so right now. And amusingly enough, education will get dragged along by business, pushed by the very Philistines they decry. With business in the communicative sector, education will follow just as they did previously, always the laggard.

The irony that respect for teachers may not be derived from the intellectual academics but rather from business is not being lost on universities even now. Teachers will finally get respect as members of the business of teaching.

Teacher Education

By standard measures (always a dubious yardstick), people in education are inferior to almost everyone else in the university. On average, they have lower high school grades, lower college grades, test lower on college entrance exams and graduate school exams, and get paid less on graduation.

One can say that the bright students enroll in challenging courses of study which will reward them for their effort whether that is course is business, pre-law, or pre-med; or one could trot out that basest of all accusations, "people who can do, do - those who can't, teach" but both miss the mark. Of course, one can never underestimate the power of greed; it is pervasive, but there is more.

As usually practiced, business, law, and medicine are exercises in simple, direct problem solving, requiring application rather than deep thought, fitting the typical pattern of utilitarianism over idealism. MBAs examine management techniques, financial projections, and market economics; lawyers write wills, contracts, mergers, and defend people; doctors look at sore throats, skin rashes, and cut out gall bladders. Rarely does theory impinge on the bottom line of these professions.

To be sure, business, law, and medicine all have their theoretical sides and, curiously, given the axiom mocking teachers, it is only the best in each of these professions who teach. One finds financial practitioners such as Galbraith and Feldman retiring from the public to teach, while surgeons such as DeBakey cut and teach. Demonstrably, those who do - teach, and those who teach - do, in the professions.

Personality and Profession

Several notions appear when discussing the personalities of teachers. The first is that they are "nice", and the other is that they are "people persons" - statements which add up to saying that teachers can put up with enormous amounts of grief without self-destructing. On the flip side, they are not terribly analytical or ambitious. Given the constraints of current education, analytical, ambitious, controlling or agitated persons simply cannot last. Spending six hours with 30 seventh graders is more than most people can tolerate. When the other job constraints are applied on top of the sheer nervous energy of such a class, an analytical or ambitious person says, "there has to be a better way, and I'll do it or leave."

MBAs, lawyers, and doctors are not usually described as "nice", "placid" or "people persons" while analytic, ambitious and controlling are apt adjectives. Thirty seventh graders would reduce each of these professionals to babble in weeks just as 70 hour weeks of financial spreadsheets, 45 different patients a day, or 12 hour days in isolation in a law library would destroy most teachers.

Two Explanatory Models

The point of this discussion centers on the characteristics of teachers compared to other professions. Right or wrong, business, medical, and law school entrance is predicated on grades and test scores. They take courses designed to eliminate a certain number of students and other courses where they face sabotage by their peers. Finally, after taking all the requisite courses, and often spending thousands of dollars on test preparation courses, these pre-whatever students go on to professional school. A killer attitude is needed as much as intelligence.

Teachers on the other hand are, by and large, left to select themselves out of the program on the basis of not being able to put up with all the nit-picky bureaucracy and genuine stress of teaching. With the constant and growing need for teachers, no one is actively discouraged.

Sternberg's Intelligence

A useful way of looking at the two groups is Sternberg's tripartite theory of intelligence in which he posits analytic, creative and social intelligence, noting that standard intelligence tests only measure analytic ability. When one looks at the strong (roughly .70) correlation of intelligence tests and the standardized aptitude tests, it is clear which of Sternberg's intelligences is being measured. This is not surprising since such testing is a direct result of the mental measurement movement, an off-shoot of the business efficiency group, which was concerned with measuring analytic ability for business purposes.

Trying to measure creativity has always been elusive. The major factors surrounding creativity are not difficult to identify, but measuring them is rather like trying to measure learning. People measure facts and call it learning when it is at very best a sampling of information, saying nothing about how it can be used or how it affects a person. When one measures aspects of the creative factors in a personality, there is not great assurance that one is actually measuring creativity.

Measuring social intelligence had not really been considered until Sternberg. Socialness has traditionally been viewed outside the purview of intelligence per se. Under the taxonomies of educational domains written in the 1950s, the cognitive was viewed as separate from the affective in schooling. In plain words, thinking and valuing belonged to separate realms and were not connected. Is it a wonder that we have a values crisis at the same time we have an educational crisis?

When business, law, and medical people are measured by standard intelligence tests, they come out as higher than teachers. I suspect that if one applied a social intelligence test to both groups the results would be reversed. Before judging the two groups, one needs to be sure that the criterion are fair to both groups.

The Matrix

When the two groups are inserted into the Matrix, we find them generally in opposite quadrants: teachers in the Communicative on the Ideal side and the professionals in the Authoritarian on the Real side. It is not surprising to find them diametrically opposed in the Matrix, given the other differences. Businessmen absolutely make or lose money while doctors apply the accepted medical practice or face law suits, and lawyers base litigation on the weight of the authority of precedent. In contrast, teachers are not original thinkers, but are charged with conveying the original thoughts of others in terms which students can understand.

When Sternberg's view of intelligence is applied to the Matrix, one finds analytic intelligence in the Authoritarian, creative intelligence in the Inspiriting, and social intelligence in the Communicative. The Physical has a combination of Social and Analytic intelligence sufficient to get along and do the required work; creative intelligence would be a detriment to the routine of physical work and thus, we find it opposite.

Teachers and Professionalism

Clearly therefore, applying the same standards to teachers as to other professionals is incorrect; the groups are simply too different. This does not excuse lax teacher education, poor preparation, inferior individuals in the profession and the host of other accusations made about teachers and education; it simply means that we should apply appropriate criteria to the situation.

When we hear one more strident call for greater professionalism in teaching, we shouldn't equate that with trying to fill the teaching ranks with those who might otherwise become doctors, lawyers and businessmen. The commonly held belief that greater pay will attract those individuals who are "more competent" is at best a red herring, and at worst, a misdirection of gargantuan proportions. Although some very competent individuals have rejected the idea of being a teacher simply because the money has been so poor for so long, these people are the exception.

Implications for Teachers in a Communicative School

Greater pay should be a reward for greater professionalism in teacher terms - not in doctor, lawyer, or business terms. Professional personalities in each area will remain. Anyone who has ever held a job knows what was good or bad about that job and whether they would like to, or could, remain indefinitely. Although human beings are greatly adaptable, by and large, assembly line workers would not be happy in sedentary desk jobs, musicians would not be happy as businessmen, and university professors would not be happy as mechanics.

Arnold Mandel in studying professional football players found that, physical attributes aside, players played a position according to personality. The chaos and rage which makes a defensive lineman great was completely unsuitable for an offensive lineman who needs precise, organized movement. Mandel could walk into a locker room and see who played offense and defense by the way the locker looked. In short, a coach could change a player's position in high school or college and the player, being a good athlete would play it, but that eventually by the time that person got to the professional level, very few people played outside their personality.

For education, the implications are clear: teachers themselves will not change. The changes must occur in teacher education, from acceptance into a basic program to course demands to intern program.

Changing Teacher Education

The changes in education must begin with the most basic perception of what teaching is as an activity and a profession. If education is as important as we hear constantly in the press, that we must have better education to compete internationally, that we must have better education to keep our economy going, and that we must have better education to create a better society for all Americans, then teachers have to be the key ingredient and should be respected and paid accordingly. We can't expect young children to want to be teachers as they desire to be firemen, but when as teenagers looking for a college to attend and choosing a profession, teaching shouldn't be considered a last resort when all else fails. Adolescents can name entertainment and sports greats that they would like to emulate - but they, by and large, cannot name physicists, biochemists, social scientists or critics as professors or teachers that they want to emulate.

Such perceptual changes will take time, and the first step is to raise standards for teacher education. A young acquaintance from Texas recently chose to go into teaching because she didn't want to take math in college and teacher ed. was the only course of study which did not require any further math. That is not the way for us to recruit future teachers. Suffice it to say, I wouldn't want my children taught by such present and future ignorance, let alone someone who has such a slide-by view of education. Unfortunately, as long was we have colleges of education with such abysmal standards, we will find future teacher attitudes to match. Where the lowest common denominator may be appropriate for working with fractions, it does little to raise the standards of educational half-wits.

Colleges of Education

The idea of abolishing colleges of education is hardly new, but before getting carried away with reformer's zeal, perhaps we should look at the question from the perspective of undergraduate versus graduate study. There is a vast difference between the two.

Undergraduate Education

Educating teachers is rather like talking about language. Both language and the study of education of themselves are contentless in one sense, and unbroken wholes in another. When we speak, there is a presumption that what we are saying has meaning and purpose. However, where speaking conveys personal meaning relevant to a given situation, teaching assumes that the teacher possesses the knowledge of an external subject matter which is presented in such a manner that students can apprehend it. That is, the teacher knows both teaching and subject matter.

Unfortunately, when an undergraduate student enters a university and takes roughly fifty hours of general courses before specializing in teaching for the other 60 hours, that student knows very little about anything. Even, if in those 60 hours they became masterful in teaching technique, they don't know enough subject matter to fill their technique with meaning. If one is to be a biology, physics, English or history teacher under such a plan, then one can take 20-25 hours in the specialty while fulfilling other area requirements. Thus, one takes the six or eight hour introductory course leaving roughly 18 hours of sophomore or higher level material which translates to 6 courses of content material. Mediocrity is guaranteed under such a limited system.

The other typical teacher training arrangement has students taking a regular academic major and also getting certified in education. While having a regular academic major subject area ensures some knowledge to fill his or her class, the number of hours required for teacher certification precludes that person getting a broad education. It heightens specialist isolation and has, therefore, no more place in communicative education than the previous model.

In keeping with the raising of standards for the profession as a whole then, students should pursue an academic course of study to a B.A., after which they could become teachers by graduate education. It is the only way to have deeply and broadly educated teachers able to teach their own subject matter and extend that knowledge into other areas to show students that knowledge is related, not isolated.

Graduate Education

At first glance, it would seem logical that teachers should have expertise in their subject matter areas and teach according to the pattern of their academic subject. This, however, is precisely the specialist pattern we want to break in a communicative school. A math teacher should be as aware of language and language teaching as the language teacher is of math and math teaching. Leaving teacher education to the academic subject areas, ensures that breadth will be missing as an English department is not equipped to teach English teachers about math, anymore than a math department is equipped to teach math teachers about English.

If we agree that teachers should be broadly and deeply educated, then we could follow the pattern of the other professions or modify them for our own use. Medical schools ask for a minimum of two years of course work with a national test certifying basic knowledge, followed by clinical rotations for several years and then state certification - *before* beginning internship and residency. Law on the other hand has three years of coursework and state certification tests before entering a firm on the bottom level. Because teaching is a performance activity, an adaptation of the medical and legal models would seem to be appropriate. With modification, we might posit a two year course of study before a year of clinical teaching, followed by a probationary period of full-time teaching with close supervision.

For admittance to graduate schools of education, prospective teachers should be able to demonstrate broad education. Whether one were to use a currently available, test for graduate students or design one exclusively for teachers as medicine and law have done for themselves is of little consequence. The important point is that prospective teachers should know that they must know something.

Organization of the Graduate School

Currently, teacher education is as fractured as any other academic graduate subject. If a student is lucky enough to have a course in developmental psychology, it is usually taught from the perspective of developmental psychology and not as the basis for determining the curriculum on one hand, and the teaching methodology or instructional strategy on the other. Without such integration, why bother? It means nothing if one knows Piaget's four levels of development or Vygotsky's "zone of proximal development" and doesn't see that they are only worthwhile as used in the classroom. In like manner, a class on curriculum has to demand that a student know the range of educational philosophies and psychologies in order to make an informed choice - for that class and later in his or her classroom. We need students to know that the choice between Skinner and Bruner as a classroom psychology will affect everything else done, and they had better know why.

Because of the huge range of knowledge tapped by education, the integrated coordination of courses must be critical. One should know philosophy, the history of ideas, cognitive and developmental psychology, management in terms of organizational goals and classroom dynamics, curriculum development, and instructional strategies and methodologies. Each of these areas contributes to the whole and must be taught in those whole terms. Developmental psychology is a fascinating area of study, but is largely useless as taught in most schools of education because of being taught in isolation. When it is used to inform the teacher as to appropriate class materials and instructional strategies, it comes into its proper role in a college of education.

A command of the full range of educational knowledge is not asking too much if we are going to consider teachers true professionals in the communicative school. We expect doctors and lawyers to have knowledge of the full range of their professions, why should teaching be different? Obviously, doctors and lawyers have specializations and so do teachers. Where doctors might specialize in geriatric oncology, they must do clinical rotations in cardiology, immunology, and obstetrics as students. In like manner, teachers should know how to teach math, science, or language in elementary school or high school even if they specialize in middle school social studies. Only in this pattern can teachers see the linkage between the elementary schools and high schools.

The Communicative School

When we consider the vastly expanded role of teachers within a communicative school, we see that they must know instructional strategies, management techniques, and curriculum development. Without such comprehensive knowledge, teachers cannot effectively work out school policy with administrators, parents and the local community.

In current circumstances, teachers are not expected to know much, and they don't. As our expectations of teachers rise, so will the levels of education and knowledge. Without this increase, all the federal and state programs in the world are merely so many political band-aids.

When we have more educated teachers, working in good conditions with a limited number of students, teaching materials which allow students to learn about their world in a meaningful manner, then we will not have to keep wringing our hands about a rising tide of mediocrity - our children will get the education they deserve.

CHAPTER 16

The Final Exam - Healing the Wounds

The malaise and universal mistrust so prevalent in current society cannot lead to the changes needed in education. The feds don't trust the states, the state boards don't trust city school districts, and the local school boards and people don't trust the teachers. Change will come in large part because the present system is not working, and people will realize there is really nothing to lose when things get bad enough. At that point, a few educational leaders with the courage of a Menachem Begin or Anwar Sadat will step forward and begin to direct the change, healing the wounds in the process. The specific suggestions contained in this book are cursory at best and need a great deal more explication before any possible implementation; however, the overall pattern of the matrix should provide both a view toward the direction of change and a way to monitor the progress of that change.

When we look at the events of the decade of the Eighties, we find fundamental social changes in the U.S. occurring. The Sixties and early Seventies tore asunder the complacency at the peak of the industrial period in America. The prosperity of the Fifties and early Sixties (the Physical) of itself was no longer enough. The kids and a few radical adults realized openly that we had left the Real side and moved into the Ideal side of the Matrix. The bulk of the workers realized it in their personal self-definition, but not in their conscious life. Through the consolidation of the Seventies, America learned it could no longer control the world by the Physical sector brute force as had worked before. Politically and militarily humiliated in Vietnam, shocked when Iran and the Arabs decided to control their own oil and their own economies, and increasingly losing technological battles with the Japanese, the U.S. vacillated between despair on the one hand and the self-deluding aggrandizement so characteristic of the British and French Imperialists in looking back to the "good old days" of God and Empire.

The Eighties were dominated not by Smokestack industry production but by Smokestack restructuring and the communication revolution arriving in the Physical sector of production. With the competition from abroad, U.S. industry regrouped, becoming leaner and in the process throwing workers out as though they were disposable diapers. Bottom-line madness fueled by the boom on Wall Street ushered in information domination. The new producers of the Relative-Real could almost be viewed as market traders except for the fact that they deal only in information. Whether foreign exchange, commodities, or the stocks of Fortune 500 companies, 24 hour trading from Tokyo to London and finishing in New York assured that U.S. companies ended their isolation and joined the world if they were going to be successful.

Educationally, the Eighties spelled an endpoint. People throughout the country realized that the system was fundamentally flawed and book after book addressed causes. With Bloom, Hirsch, Smith, Farrell, or Schor to name a few, it is interesting (providing the impetus for this book) that within its stated confines, each author makes his own internal sense, but the views are mutually exclusive. With the exception of Smith, each takes a linear/analytic industrial view of education which would seem to indicate that the authors were not out in the schools or listening to teachers and students. This voids their validity for anyone who is looking at the classroom instead of the state capital.

Education is changing and will continue to change in the direction of personal autonomy and choice, just as the Matrix turns in the gyre. This would appear inevitable as personal choice, based on increasing variety and awareness of the world, has been the direction for some years in so many other areas: food, medicine, and retail to name a few. Such autonomy demands that the consumer be connected to and knowledgeable about the product consumed. Thirty years ago the medical profession and general public would have scoffed at the average person on the street knowing about cholesterol, let alone the danger levels, and the sub-parts of HDL and LDL. Now, it is not uncommon to know something about cholesterol, and it has not noticeably damaged the average person's brain. It is simply part of the information explosion and people learned about it. There is no reason that the average person cannot learn about education and begin to exercise control over local education just as they have improved their medical outlook and demanded appropriate choice of care, and second opinions.

Education and the Shift

When we stop the clockwise versus the counterclockwise movement within the Matrix at the present moment, we get a rough gauge as to where we are and if we will soon have resolution. Remembering that cultural change begins in the Inspiriting and moves through the Communicative and Physical to rest finally in the Authoritarian, we must find where communication is taking place. Clearly, communication is established in the Physical sector in manufacturing and production. In like manner, service industries are information users whether with the word processors, databases, and spreadsheets of the typical business office, or the computer aided design of an architectural office, or the bar code readers in any retail outlet. Information use in education is not even.

Cultural Progression at One Time: Information Use Moving into the Authoritarian Sector

Information use in the Authoritarian sector has provoked genuine physical fear, paranoia, and the general mistrust of the Orwellian "Big Brother." We seem to have chosen to look at the bleak, manipulated unfertile side of information control rather than focus on the potential for elimination of physical ill, the controlling of population, and the creation of world harmony. This is in keeping with the industrial worldview of looking at the downside, at the limits, and accountability - rather than looking at potential and limitlessness.

The Authoritarian sector is only beginning to understand the shift to information as a process rather than a product because Authoritarians see their power as an end rather than a means. Information manipulation has always been useful; however, it has usually been seen as a product. We see this clearly in the Big Lie mentality of Hitler and his fellow Authoritarian, Stalin - firmly within the Industrial framework. Such physical use of information is representative of the Industrial period.

The far more important political use of information in recent years, has been polling, which has only been really useful for prediction since the Sixties. A stratified random sample of roughly one thousand people can answer the general public's mood on any given question. While not as overtly insidious as Hitler and Stalin, we now have politicians who consult a poll before taking a political position on an issue rather than consulting their own hearts and values. Given the fickleness of politicians in the present condition, is it any wonder that education is skeptical of support?

The most general use of information in the Authoritarian sector, however, is the use mentioned in Chapter 1: that of the monitoring capability of computers. Whether attached to a recording device in a classroom, the monitoring of production speed at a given workstation, or the surveillance of the world by satellites, computers give an instantaneous update of any specified behavior. This accountability capacity grows as does the development and availability of computer power.

Computer monitoring, however, is two edged. On the one hand, personal privacy can be invaded by anyone with access to the computer - legal or not. On the other hand, the very availability of information from many sources assures that the public is better informed than it used to be. Both monitoring uses of computers will probably keep growing despite the best efforts of gatekeeping watchdogs on each front - simply because greater amounts of information has always created greater access to that information.

While we have not reached a limit of information use in the Authoritarian sector by any means, and, in fact, it has been widely noted that we are only really beginning to understand how to use it fully, it is clear that information use as a way of life has completed its rotation through the four sectors.

Cultural Progress Over Time:
From Industrial to Inspiriting - We *Are*   the Transition

Where information and communication have become well established in the Physical, and are becoming increasingly understood in the Authoritarian, showing that the idea has come to fruition at the present time, the progression through the Communicative quadrant gives us a slightly different view of our time position. The very acceptance of the idea into the Authoritarian shows that we are moving toward the height of its practical use. With the height of a cultural period, we are already looking at the next cultural shift to come along. With Moses as the exemplar of the Inspiriting, the stage was set for the kings and emperors of the Authoritarian. With the British Empire spanning the globe as the greatest geographic domination in history, the stage was set for the Physical sector and corporateness to reign. With the industrial organizational peak in the Fifties, we moved to Communication; now where are we?

If we entered the Communicative sector of the Relative-Ideal in the late 40s with the dropping of the Bomb, the development of transistors, and the rise of cognitive psychology, then we must have progressed somewhat beyond by now. Each of those events has evolved in numerous directions. The A-bomb gave way to multiple generations of H-bombs, clustered in MIRVs and carried in various delivery systems. The transistor gave way to the integrated circuit and multifunction chips. Cognitive psychology has moved from non-directive therapy to artificial intelligence and the realization that the world we perceive is largely constructed by us.

As we move through the Communicative sector, realizing that Communication has been accepted in the Authoritarian quadrant and is moving into power, are we already seeing signs of the next change? In Chapter 7, we noted that power is derived from the next clockwise quadrant, i.e., the Absolute-Ideal in our present case. We also noted that power appeared to split in the next clockwise quadrant, i.e., in this case into religion and information science, both of which are dichotomous in the new quadrant. Are religion and information science already affecting us, leading us into the Absolute-Ideal for the second time in human history, and if so how?, i.e., are the next set of ideas ready to move from the Absolute-Ideal into the other quadrants of the gyre in counterclockwise manner? If so, then the first move will be into our present sector where we will meet them head on in the largest conflict of our cultural era.

Religion in the Absolute-Ideal

Religion in the Absolute-Ideal splits with the schism of cultural time choice: from fundamentalist to New Age. Good old time fundamentalist religion has made a dramatic resurgence in recent years much to the consternation of politicians and commentators alike who see the move as regressive in time rather than progressive. Politicians in particular have seen the move as a move backward to traditional values rather than as a progressive realization of the barrenness of Industrial life. Just as the radicals and hippies distanced themselves from the industrial catastrophe twenty-five years ago, middle America has spent the Eighties seeking a goal of value.

The same politicians and commentators who grope for answers with the fundamentalist revival are at a loss to explain the rise of the New Age movement, calling it unscientific hocus-pocus which reflects the inability of the American people to think. It is obviously difficult for people so firmly entrenched in the Industrial-Physical mentality to conceive of people living in the diagonally opposite quadrant in the Ideal.

Within the Matrix both religious groups appear to fit normal cultural progression. Given that a lot of people will choose what they are familiar with over what they don't know, it should be no surprise that many people are going to fundamentalist religion as it provides absolute known answers to issues of being in a time of chaos.

Characterizing New Age religion is difficult because people draw from so many sources and literally are constructing from the consciousness of the believer with one central idea being that each person creates the world, i.e., that the world is a manifestation of our own consciousness. Eastern religion, American Indian ceremonies, tarot, astrology, crystals and mystics down through the ages all lend bits and pieces to the whole. Unscientific? Certainly, as is all religion. Unthoughtful? Certainly not, though the thought pattern does not fit the linear Aristotelian logic of engineering and Western thought. To the degree that we become what we think we are, there is little disputing the creative capacity in our own lives. Behavioral psychologists have worked with such notions of patterning for a long time though from a vastly different angle. Success motivators and cognitive psychologists alike know that when people think they can achieve a goal - they usually can, and that a negative thought can kill the possibility of achievement.

Where fundamentalists view God as the center of their universe, having created the world in his own image, New Age people see the world as their domain - a gift from God, from which they can create their dreams. The ramifications will play out in most interesting educational fashion as their children mature.

Information Science in the Absolute-Ideal

The developing information science of the next quadrant is taking two apparently quite different paths which may intersect in ways barely discernible at this time. Biologic science with the molecular genetics of recombinant DNA hold one key in the future while cognitive science in hardware and software hold the other key.

Biologic Science

With genetically altered plants and bugs, artificial hearts, lungs, and blood, and in vitro fertilization, it is abundantly clear that we currently have the capacity to create mutant higher life forms. As technology becomes more common and accessible, the use and misuse will grow. Just as the cheapness and universal accessibility of microcomputers changed how computers could be used, so the new biotechnology will change the face of biology. When computers meant gigantic mainframes, the idea of an individual hacker sitting alone at home with a laptop computer breaking into the Pentagon seemed preposterous - and how few years ago that was. Biology is just entering that era. What happens when a maverick biologist creates a new lifeform? How this plays out will be determined not by the physical controls that used to be put on scientists in the form of monies and physical plant, but by ethical concern alone. Just as access to a giant mainframe could be limited in early computer days, and clearly cannot be limited in a day of PCs and modems, experimentation in genetic alteration is moving from highly sensitive closely guarded labs to college campuses. One cannot stop a renegade biologist anymore than a computer hacker until after the fact. It is fitting that it is only ethics that can control the new-era biologist - as we will be in the Absolute-Ideal.

Cognitive   Science

The other scientific force in the Absolute-Ideal will be cognitive science in its many manifestations. As microprocessing chips have developed, computing power and price have come down to where a present laptop has the power of an old mainframe. Dramatic power increases appear constantly, and the new technologies promise further power gains as silicon gives way to the developments of materials science. However, the hardware is only one aspect in artificial cognitive development. Along with the development of greater memory and faster switching, software must keep pace to use the new power, and different models of information processing will necessitate different hard and software.

Computers have typically used a linear processing model with a central processing unit (CPU) to handle the chores because industrial thought dominated the early development of computing. It has become clear though that the circuit lines running to a CPU can only handle so much information before becoming overloaded. The alternative is to use multiple processors which necessitates the dividing of information for processing and then the reintegration of the processed information into usable output. Potentially, this will give an exponential increase in power.

At the cutting edge are two developments: neural networks and genetic network designers. Neural networks have trainable 'neural' pathways which fire off much as do natural synapses in nerve bundles, depending on the probabilities occurring in separate, external stimuli. Genetic computer designers have extended the concepts of artificial language, artifical intelligence, and artificial reality into the realm of artificial life where multigenerational entities exist in self-defined evolutionary patterns.

Computing power and development will continue to grow and feed on itself. The very idea of computers designing newer computers designing still newer ones gives a speed of change and growth never before seen. Never has a technology fed itself. Industrial technologies remain what they are as a physical reality and develop slowly because each part has meaning of itself. A steam engine remains a steam engine. It can be developed for the railroad, or a ship, or a factory, but each of those uses must then remain as a fixed use with a fixed meaning. The computer, like language, has no obvious meaning - it is simply a vehicle in helping to convey meaning. It can be used for words, or numbers, or processes, and the very use gives it meaning just as with language.

Not since the Greeks has a change affected all of life so comprehensively. When the Greeks turned language from the oral to the written form and brought self-consciousness to the act, they began the shift that is now playing out in our time.

Computer use presently is no more developed than early Greek writing. We have people searching for boundaries and definitions just as Aristotle tried to define rhetoric and poetics within the new concept of self-conscious language. We have debates on the use and misuse of computers just as Plato sought limits on the rhetoric and poets who stirred "wrongful passions." Clearly, we can have no static resolution, and because of that, we had better become educated to help guide the evolutionary process.

Harnessing the Power for Education

Realizing that education reflects the need of a given period, but at the same time lags the leading thought of that period, we are clearly in transition in the Communicative Age. The value education of traditional society was insufficient to power the vocational need of Industrial Society, just as the hierarchic limitations of industrial mentality are pointlessly constraining in a Communicative Era. In content and psychologic approach, we have left the rigid limits of industrial thought, but not in the administrative hierarchy. We must end the conflict.

The suggestions in this book call for education in a Communicative Age to have a core of content taught in a unified, comprehensive manner by truly professional teachers, supported by an administration which knows that its job is to support teachers, students, and meaning. This should not seem radical - only a change from the status quo.

In contrast, whether viewed from religion or information science, education in the Absolute-Ideal will shift further toward responding to the whole individual - toward *consciousness*. Because this quadrant deals with wholes, as opposed to the fragmentation of industrialism, education will become an issue of personal discovery of wholes quite apart from a core of information we see as our need in the Communicative quadrant. Where we need comprehensive education at present to deal with the vertical chunks of information which make up our industrial content system, the next quadrant will have that information at our fingertips arranged as we desire, as well as the means to access it.

In the expansion of education in the next quadrant, we may see the integration of the now current technologies of biofeedback, brainwave synchronization, and sensory isolation (float) tanks, animated by the techniques of Zen and Sufi masters, and unified by the discovery mechanisms of modern rhetoric to form a realm of meaning - allowing the individual to merge with the whole in what appears to us in our limited view to be a religious gnostic experience.

EPILOGUE

My Thoughts on a Last Trip Around the Matrix

I would like to discuss some of the issues which were raised and then either did not fit neatly into appropriate chapters, or were really tangential to the book as a whole. The Matrix, in particular, raised many ideas which were not directly applicable to a book on education, but the logical extension of these ideas under the general rubric of culture is not only appropriate, but a fitting close to a book on education in culture. If education is to be comprehensive, one will never tie up the loose ends, but rather keep trailing them off forever.

On the Inversion of Hierarchy

I wonder if there is something about the communicative use of information which inverts the patterns established in the industrial world? The Communicative is diagonally opposite the Authoritarian on the Matrix so it is not surprising that the truths are different for each sector. When bosses ask workers to think and take responsibility - and profit sharing appeals to greed and taking charge in workers, we are clearly not in the Authoritarian sector. Extending the thought...

Frank Smith looks at Bloom's Taxonomy of the Cognitive Domain (Knowledge, Comprehension, Application, Analysis, Synthesis, Evaluation) and says it is completely backward. People do not learn facts and build to evaluation, rather they value something, and therefore learn it. The idea of finding and starting from the smallest component is the very essence of reductionist thought. Reductionism looks for the smallest verifiable bit, not with meaning, so of course, a taxonomy for behavioral objectives will follow the pattern of facts first, building to complex thought.

In like manner, it makes far more sense for education when one inverts the hierarchy, placing teachers at the top as the producers and the state and city boards of education at the bottom, serving the needs of students and teachers in the classroom.

Increasingly, we see similar inversions of power. Shareholders in corporations, workers in dangerous industries, and consumers are all demanding action and getting it. To take only one as an example, the shareholders of America are demanding that the corporate world be responsive. Rather than the CEO and his personally named Board of Directors telling the shareholders what is going to happen to the company, shareholders are saying to the "bosses", "We want this and this or we'll vote you out and the company will go to someone who is responsive." We see this in response to politics, pollution, and the issues of social responsibility. The populist groundswell demands performance because the general public can now get information easily that was privileged before. The shareholders are saying, "We want our share." Essentially, power is shifting. Cultural change is always lagging as we saw in Chapter 7 with certain groups consistently leading the others. The Authoritarians are always last to understand the changes as the conservative nature of the group is usually looking backward to other times. In each of the cases, the Matrix helps explain as we see cultural shift toward the Communicative and away from the Authoritative.

Frank Smith inverts the Bloom Taxonomy because Communicative Education must be driven by meaning and not by facts. Students are responsive cognitive organisms, not empty vessels which need filling.

I inverted the school hierarchy because the importance of school is that of students learning - not administrators being bureaucrats.

Stockholders are demanding social responsibility and good financial return because they can read about their company very easily. They know when the company has a toxic waste problem or an oil spill. They know what the return on investment is and what the norm is for other companies within the same production sector of the economy. Information is available in huge quantities, and it just takes someone to organize it into meaningful knowledge to be used by the shareholders. With that information comes power, and shareholders know it.

War and Peace

I think we can abolish the army, most of the navy and the Air Force, leaving, if we really feel paranoid, land missiles, subs and an elite ground/air/water strike force whether marines or special forces. War as it has been known is past tense, a relic of the Real side of the Matrix. The Physical forces of army, navy and air force are a holdover from a previous time. But then, the military likes tradition and relics, parading bands dressed as Continental Soldiers, cadets who shoot 150 year old field cannons, and sailors who get blown up shooting a 50 year old battleship gun with 35 year old black powder. Blackpowder in the 1990s, really!

Information replaces physical power at each cultural stage of war - right to the present. The foot soldier, so trusted from the days of Middle Eastern Empires until World War I, found the tank impermeable. The French built that monument to the past, the "Maginot Line," to keep foreign invaders out, not unlike the Chinese and their wall years earlier, and the Germans drove right around it and captured Paris as though they were on a Sunday outing. Bigger and bigger battleships, the "dreadnaughts" could suddenly be sunk with one plane and one bomb. Static fortification gave way to movement on land and sea just as fixed thought gave way to process thought. By the end of World War II, the Germans had jets flying past the Allied propeller planes and rockets hitting fixed targets such as London. With the advent of lasers, information is literally able to destroy physical entities. Planes, ships and rockets are all reduced to scrap metal in the face of high power "smart" light. Military thinking, that oxymoron, will have to change eventually.

At present, the powers of lasers have been restricted to military guidance systems and demonstrations of Star Wars defensive accuracy against missiles. It takes no great imagination though to see the day when the Star Wars satellites can be used for offensive rather than defensive purposes. Boost the power slightly and instead of shooting an enemy missile, one vaporizes Moscow, Baghdad, or Washington. The instantaneous quality of light precludes defense.

Everytime I see ads for the army and navy with smiling soldiers jumping ditches in their tanks, or sailors looking alert and intelligent at their command posts, I feel both sadness and outrage. What is a tank but a piece of scrap iron to a Vietnam era Cobra or A-10, let alone amodern Apache with missiles and laser guided smart bombs? We saw the carnage in Iraq. Likewise, we saw a cheap little Exocet missile blow the British carrier right out of the water in the Falklands and our own cruiser severely damaged by a cheap Silkworm missile in the

Persian Gulf. Billions of dollars of essentially static hardware is as vulnerable to death by information, as the French were by sitting behind the Maginot Line waiting for the Panzers to spearhead the Blitzkrieg. It is absurd.

Modern war is essentially economic, i.e., informational. Only those countries unable to secure economic victory, resort to physical war. That means liberation movements, countries using surrogates, and terrorists. The Persian Gulf War is a brilliant example of economics and politics. Iraq, with a huge debt to Kuwait, and a large old-style army invaded and seized the Emirate, thereby voiding Iraqi debts and gaining oil fields. The U.S. and coalition forces could have blockaded Iraq and waited successfully. However, because this might have taken several years, it was not politically feasible for President Bush who did not want to get mired in the Middle East as former President Carter had previously. When actual war erupted, there was little question that smart weapons would destroy static formations. Tuned into CNN from Atlanta via Baghdad, Riyadh, Tel Aviv, and Washington, the world watched in amazement as laser bombs went into front doors and cruise missiles flew down streets, turned corners, and delivered their loads down air shafts.

It was a beautiful demonstration of technology, but was it necessary? While the U.S. lost very few military personnel, we didn't need to lose any. The question revolves around people who want "real" power vs. those who seek the ideal. In the aftermath, we see the "reality" that nothing has changed: Saddam Hussein of Iraq remained in power and the Emir of Kuwait is back on the throne.

Religion, Thought, Cognition and the Matrix

The Eastern Western or, Will the Quantum Cowboy Ride into the Sunset on Multiple Processing?

Do the Japanese have an advantage over Westerners because they have two writing systems? - not just two alphabets, but two processing systems. When one looks at the different processing mechanisms of a linear alphabet such as ours and their Heragama system, and the holistic sign processing of their Kanji writing derived from the Chinese sign system, I wonder what the implications are for being able to handle different kinds of information in multiple manners based on brain processing of discrete versus whole information. Do they grow up using the two hemispheres of the brain in discrete manners, or do they switch back and forth, or can they combine forces?

Especially intriguing are the parallels between linear and non-linear thought and creativity in areas such as subatomic physics and computer processing. *The Tao of Physics* and *The Dancing Wuli Masters* both looked at parallels between Eastern religion and physics, and the world has expanded greatly since those were written.

Does our right and wrong, dualistic, binary, linear view of thought obstruct our ability to see wholes? Has our linear expertise given rise to industrialism and yet, now gotten to the point where most people are at an endpoint? As physicists loop into non-linear thought, will they drag us along?

In terms of the Matrix, the Inspiriting deals with Absolute-Ideal Wholes, not with enabling objectives and Authoritarian accountability. Physicists, such as Hawking, are looking at wholes and trying to unify the extant theories of matter.

For this kind of mentation, linear patterns are not only not useful, they are positively limiting. One needs to open to varied thought patterns, not be confined in one. Can we move into this open field with our schools?

God and Geography and Thought

If one considers that there is one place where the three major monotheistic religions come from, i.e., North Arabia and all from Semitic people, perhaps we can examine the thought process. In the desert, there is one traditional way to live (anthropologically speaking) which is the hard life of a bedouin, moving with herds. Variation of thought is not an accepted pattern (as with all oral peoples). There is only one-way to live, and one power rules all. In a variegated climate, one finds multiple ways of sustaining life (hunting, gathering, herding, farming) *and* polytheistic religion, whether in Greece, Rome, Amerindian, East Indian or African animist.

Desert Semites did not have the luxury of choice of lifestyle. If they did not like being a bedouin, they could not shift and decide to be a farmer or businessman. One way to live; one God to be appeased. In areas with a variegated climate, people could grow crops, be herdsmen, or be hunters, and they reflected the diversity by worshiping a variety of gods.

That we are still bounded by desert Semitic thought of two thousand years ago poses an interesting limitation. In a different context, the anthropology professor to whom the book is dedicated once used the phrase, 'the shepherd's crook over the smokestacks of Detroit' to describe this limitation of view.

West versus the World

Examining the various characteristics which have separated the West from the rest of the world, beginning with the Greeks, it is amusing to wonder about life if the West had gone with Plato rather than Aristotle.

West	East
Aristotle	Plato
Definition and Classification	Whole Forms
Diversity	Unity
Well-tempered music	Microtonal Music
Salvation Religion	Religion as life

If we go back to the Mosaic period at the beginning of the Early Iron Age Period in the Eastern Mediterranean, we find that Judaism has one dominant God by which the people live or die. Life is migratory and the metaphoric imagery is that of the ethnarch/shepherd leading his flock. Life's commandments are codified by Moses, but it is a very different life than one finds several hundred years later in Isaiah when the city is beginning to rise and, by Amos, we see an entirely different view - urban man - the prophet must leave the city to have a vision. About this time in the development of the Near East, Zoroaster introduced the dualistic concept of an active good (Ahura Mazda) and an active evil (Ahriman) who must fight to the end. The Old Testament does not deal in active evil. Those people who disobeyed God, got a plague of locusts or a firestorm or became a pillar of salt and the retribution was for disobedience of God's will - not temptation by the devil which is New Testament imagery. Obey, or God will get you - no running, no hiding.

During this period of war and trade when Alexander conquered the Persians, the dualistic Zoroastrian thought spread through the Greek world. With Greek/Persian thought influencing the Romans, Christianity picked up on active evil, blending it with traditional Semitic thought and adapting the combination to the necessities of the city. The imagery of the New Testament remains pastoral, in contrast to Christianity's actual setting in the city and the precepts of how to live in the city. All this is set forth in general, but urban, vague terms of "Love thy neighbor...", "Do unto others...", - The Good Shepherd is already anachronistic; imagery for city people should have shown the honest businessman, not a shepherd.

Six hundred years later Islam came sweeping up out of Arabia, taking the thought of how to live in cities and codifying it in the Hebraic tradition of Deuteronomy in the Old Testament. There are no wishy-washy, "Do unto others..." just strict rules of "do this" and "don't do that" which look just like the Old Testament.

In the gap between Judaism and Islam, Christianity had escaped the Semites and fallen on fertile ground in the Greco-Roman world. Had Christianity been codified in the Semitic manner, it would not have had the appeal to the West, just as Judaism and Islam have never made large inroads in the West. Forging one's own definitions and questions in an Aristotelian manner has always been central to Christian thought. When the basic questions are answered by a set code, Aristotelian thought is pointless.

Definition and Classification

When Aristotle set down his logic, rhetoric, and poetic, he introduced classification and definition as essential to understanding, explaining and developing new patterns. By setting down these analytic procedures, Aristotle fixed a *method* of discovery and organization which could be applied across any range of information, rather than prescribing a content. However, if a social rather than an informational pattern is unalterably set as in the Old Testament or Koran, then one can only interpret; there is nothing to discover, explain or develop. Questioning is circumscribed, in contrast to the West where questioning is the central issue. What does one do to save one's self or soul? Let's define it anew, examine it anew in a different light; perhaps, if we classify it a bit further we'll find out that last irreducible step. Develop a tight enough formal system, and we've got it, right? Just ask Gödel. By the ultimate extension of logic in physics and math, we have gotten back to the Tao.

Music of the Spheres

Extending these thoughts into the realm of music, the same pattern holds. Rhythm is a constant in the world, but why does the West have a melody/harmony pattern and the rest of the world have a microtonal, developed melody? It would seem to come back to the idea of European people not being satisfied with an open ill-defined microtonal system in 1700 and seeking a closed well-tempered device.

Rather like Aristotle setting the limits of how an argument can be framed with rhetoric and logic, setting abstract limits so that specifics can be debated ad infinitum within a known established framework of discourse, the well-tempered clavier bends the tones to form a whole and then sets them forever, allowing infinite development within a set fixed system. The twelve tone scale allows recursion and the vertical development of melody and harmony in contrast to a microtonal system. To use another analogy, we might compare the fixing of musical tones to the defining of limits in a given geometry which only holds for a defined space. That this process of musical formation happened at the beginning of Rationalism is more than coincidental. It allowed for melodic development and the vertical augmentation of harmony as the music moved through chords of a given key at one time, rather than finding horizontal development over time in a microtonal chant form.

In developing the well-tempered device, the logic of Aristotle came to the fore; with analytically derived reductionism, science and well-tempered music blossomed in Europe but nowhere else in the world, developing vertical musical structures at every turn along the way.

Thoughts from Teaching English as a Second Language, or Is Language Both Physical and Symbolic?

Anyone who has ever taught international students has myriad stories of strange expressions and twisted "very foreign" language. Going back to the discussion of Kaplan in regard to contrastive rhetoric, we can extend his thoughts considerably. What is interesting to note is that having worked with a number of multicultural language classes, I found an almost exact parallel between Kaplan's ideas of writing patterns and the "physical rhetoric," of body language in talking, i.e. proxemics: that the more linear the paragraph development the farther one stands when talking to another person and vice-versa. As has been pointed out numerous times Americans stand 36 inches from one another when speaking. Anything closer and our physical space is infringed on. That can mean intimacy or threat depending on the circumstance. In contrast, Latins feel comfortable at 24 inches (English speakers back off at this range) and Arabs talk at 18 inches, but with their faces at a 45 degree angle.

When the distance in physical presentation is compared to the type of thought pattern in paragraph development, we find that the more linear the paragraph, the more distant the physical stance when talking. We have 36 inches of distance and a linear English paragraph. 24 inches finds a discursive Romance paragraph pattern. With the Arabs standing at 18 inches, but at a 45 degree angle, we find parallel development of pros and cons before resolution. The vortex of the Oriental pattern gives an inclusive sort of physical pattern, depending completely on relationship: equals are close, but with superiors, one doesn't even make eye contact.

Where will we stand when the new thought/expression pattern becomes common?

What do the Prophets Know that the Rest of Us Do Not? Or is There a Cosmology of Language?

Form

The idea of a prophet, religious or secular, keeps coming to mind in the sense of Kierkegaard's *Purity of Heart is to Will One Thing* with regard to the clarity of vision. Form seems to emerge from the certainty of vision, rather than coming out of conscious thought about a how to approach a subject. For mystics, the ultimate form is formless and the apprehension of that form is a totality: the things on Earth being mere representations of otherly attributes. For artists - physical, musical and literary - form is one representation of all that is possible at a given time, bringing together the relation of parts to the whole to shape the meaning. To say "I understand" in these terms means being able to "see" with the same comprehensiveness of a good experienced architectural drafter, knowing a whole reality behind the representation on paper or computer.

Form in writing appears to be a nonrational direct apprehension of thought. When we attempt to teach heuristics, the art of discovery of thought, we show the outward forms much as did the structural, linguists of a previous period show the structural forms of the language. We can show these patterns very well indeed, as did the structuralists, but just as they failed to consider meaning and the use of language, teaching heuristics shows the way of framing the subject matter rather than the framing of the meaning of the subject. In other words, if we write a composition several ways, we may find a center where we are meaning what we mean; then, the problem becomes discovering how to extract that core meaning, just as a sculptor extracts the form from the rough rock which conceals the perfect image of La Pieta or David.

In essence, we should teach "seeing" and then the person will be able to apprehend "form" in whatever field. The comments in the last chapter about education in the Absolute-Ideal shows us the idea of "seeing" as education. The idea of comprehensive education is as close as we are at present....

That is not very close, though we have glimpses beyond - mere intimations in Wordsworth's words of, 'that which having been must forever be'. We do not even have a terminology for trying to discuss the idea of form at a conceptual level. We need to agree on enough ideas to recognize terms on their own power and then, from the new perceptions, be able to expand the ideas. This is not unlike the idea of inventing a new geometry; however, unlike a brilliant individual such as Descartes, writing in universally recognizable mathematical denotations, we have to write out in natural language the ideas contained therein - and that means establishing a recognized, agreed upon, vocabulary.

Such discussions of form will happen when one looks at the progression of ideas; the only issue is when. We routinely have perceptions that were quite beyond the ancient world, whether in describing the physical world or human emotions. Discussing the abstractness of form will simply take some thought-time to develop.

Structure and Words

When we speak of meaning from form, we really get to the heart of a cosmology of language. How does English express the world in ways that are not easily expressed in other languages and how does that reflect English/American/International thought? Quite apart from the lexis or active vocabulary which only expresses the surface meanings of a given group, we should look at the ways of expressing relation. People who have taken Anthro. 101 will recognize the Sapir-Whorf postulate saying that Eskimos have X number of words for snow and Bedouin Arabs have X number of words for camels, and we don't. Without being sarcastic, one could say that any specialist knows many words for his specialty. Pizza makers know pizza words; four year olds know four year old words; and academics know academic words, but only within their specialty. Of course, one knows one's environment unless one is subverbal. The words are easy though; the real question is - how are the words related?

To adapt an example from Trimble's discussion of technical discourse, "Academics attend colloquia, symposia, and workshops. Such meetings allow for dissemination of information." Overtly the two sentences are a description of academic behavior and no educated native speaker has a problem with the meaning. Second language speakers have a problem with such usage though. They can know every word (or look them up) and yet not understand the meaning. When examined closely, we see that the marker "such" alerts us to a reference, i.e., we have to look backward to find what is going to be discussed in the future. Then the person has to understand that "meeting" is a general classifier for "symposia, colloquia, and workshops." If one misses either the reference marker, or the implicit classification, then the meaning is lost even though all the "content" words are known. Though this is a relatively direct example which occurs throughout technical writing, it illustrates the problem of relation in language as opposed to simple words.

To work with such problems, English as a second language developed a subgroup known as English for Special Purposes which examines limited use English whether in technical or social fields. Because the typical grammatically sequenced syllabus makes little sense for training purposes, why not teach the students only what they need for training? Rather than sequencing the syllabus by grammar, one can sequence it by the notions and functions of the language itself. In other words, if one examines the notion of time, and how it relates to a particular work situation, then one can teach the grammar and vocabulary that is appropriate for that situation. Similarly, a function is how the language is used in a situation; for example, "asking a question" is a function as is "giving directions". These are ways language is used informationally. In such a syllabus, one proceeds to teach the range of language need in notions and functions in the job place until the person is competent. Notional/functional syllabi have been a boon to training, but need a detailed needs analysis and skilled writers to bring the work to fruition.

Applying the notional/functional approach to other language situations makes sense instead of getting caught up in mere words or syntax which lack discourse meaning. Notions demand meaning be used. A discussion of time has to occur in a meaningful context where the traditional definition of words or grammar can be context-free. Let's look at a couple of examples.

The Japanese, the very same people who are supposed to be so intelligent now, could not break the Navajo language in World War II. In addition to standard forms of code, the Navy in the Pacific used Navajo Indians speaking Navajo. Each ship had on board some of the Code Talkers, as they became known, who used Navajo for ship to ship communication. The structural linguists knew Navajo to be extraordinarily arcane for its relational system. The Japanese never cracked Navajo even though the military subject matter of the conversations had to be quite specific. Military position, timing and coordinates are known limited pieces of information, but for understanding, one has to know how time and place relate. The Japanese never did figure out Navajo.

When we look at simpler examples of the notion of time relation, does a Frenchman or German "see" the English use of the present perfect, "I have gone to the store." as opposed to the simple past, "I went to the store." Or, in fairness, does an English speaker "see" the tense difference between "fut" and "etais" for the past tense of "to be" in French. Bilinguals, in each case, see relational differences, but people learning the languages rarely do.

In a different sort of relation Walter Ong commented that the 70s were the "Me" generation, not the "I" generation; the objective form rather than the subjective form says everything about perception - of things being done to the self, rather than the self doing. There is certainly an implicational active and passive, but hero and victim are left for the audience to decide.

In like manner, Yetta Goodman has pointed out that language is constantly vibrating between invention on one side and convention on the other. The new is constantly emerging within the bounds of the accepted in a dynamic equilibrium for the native speaker while the second language learner is just trying to discover the bounds.

Meaning, let alone the form of the meaning, is rarely clearly defined.

People

The discussion of ethnicity, race and school brings up many thoughts which did not fit earlier in the book.

All People Should Be Minorities for a Year.

I wish all people could be minorities for a while. I note a year, but that is flexible. The point is that one sees the world differently as a minority: one cannot simply be invisible on the street and blend in with everyone else.

Working in Africa in the Peace Corps, I found the issue of having no annonymity so pervasive, that I did not even think of it until much later when I was walking down a street in Amsterdam and suddenly had the thought, "Nobody even sees me! I'm just sort of blended into the group." This is not a racial breakthrough, but it provided an understanding that I could not possibly have gotten from books. It has nothing to do with intention, or tolerance, or spirit, it is simple beingness.

The pervasiveness of race cannot be fully understood by someone who has not had a such an experience. It changes the very perception of what can be done or not and the desire to do or not do. When I found my male students in Senegal wanting to be like their President who had a white French wife, or the pecking order of lighter students being more "enlightened", or the blanching that African photographers did to make people look more white, I could say from a purely intellectual point of view - "This is the final harvest of colonial evil" but equally, I can never "know" that sense in fullness. It is easy to spin out the implications for the women of Senegal and extend that to the reality of the men who then join with these women.

A communicative school should promote *being* in the simplest sense. Integration of self, allowing integration with the world.

All People Should be Teachers for a Year

I wish all people could be teachers for a while and then they would see what goes on in this profession: both good and bad. Teachers would get a great deal more support if people saw the reality of teaching. We wouldn't hear about teachers only working part-time and getting paid for doing nothing.

The Mommy Track: Or Did We Jump the Rails Somewhere?

I salute the idea that mothers can choose fast-track or "slow-track" careers. Why does one sound inferior rather than both being equal alternatives? We should have such flexibility - but aren't we missing half the populace? Men are people too. Should we have a People-Track and a Fast-Track? This looks rather like the previous discussion of being versus doing. Those who define themselves by being in relation with others as opposed to those who define themselves doing in work.

Typically, with this sort of thought, we keep defining ourselves into differences rather than similarities. We could simply talk of "leave time", "continuing part-time", "on-going flextime" or any of a host of other nondivisive terms, but when we say slow-track vs. fast-track, we add a great deal of cultural baggage to the discussion. In school fast track is smart; slow track is dumb. Fast track is going places; slow won't ever amount to anything. Fast is better, it's progress, advancement, moving to the top. Slow is not. The industrial metaphor returns a final time to point out the pervasive nature of language and image in our thoughts.

A Final Thought on the Matrix

We need all four quadrants for completeness, no matter that we probably find the quadrant opposite our own to be a pain. We can look at the matrix several ways which will change our perception of four equal parts. If we looked at the world's population as a balance in the matrix, the Inspiriting would be ever so tiny and the Physical ever so large. But, if we looked at it by the change agents, the Ideal would be large, and the Real would very small except during revolutions. If we looked at it from a Communist or Capitalist point of view, we'd find contradictions between the Absolute-Ideal and the formulation of ideas against the Physical of "The Workers" and "The People" respectively.

Because the Matrix demands comprehensiveness and each part of the Matrix needs the others, it would be nice if there was a bit more understanding. The intellectual/religious/aesthete of the Inspiriting quadrant would not be damaged if a year or two of late adolescence was spent in the Physical sector, nor would the Communicative or Authoritarian folks. In like manner, those who see themselves as Physicals would probably profit from being placed in other sectors.

Such mixing regularly happened in the draftee army where people from all walks were thrown together willy-nilly. We might use this mixing idea as a springboard for having a universal national service which could accomplish several comprehensive tasks. A new infrastructure could be built just as FDR reshaped America during the depression; job skills would be learned by those who had none; and socially, all the groups would get to see each other and have to live together. The actual building, and then the servicing, of the new communicative schools could be a starting project for such a service, keeping costs down for the public benefit at the same time job skills were learned. An equal benefit would be the bringing together of rural and urban, Black, White, Hispanic, Indian and Asians who would have to see each other as people and not as stereotypes when living with each other on a project. With such a national service, the Matrix could become more than just a conceptual device, it could become a new Reformation.

Bibliography

Aristotle. *Works*. Princeton, N.J.: Princton University Press, 1984.

Asher, James. *Learning Another Language Through Actions*. 2nd ed. Los Gatos, CA.: Sky Oaks Productions, 1982.

Barzun, Jacques. *The House of Intellect*. New York: Harper Collins, 1959.

Bertalanffy, Ludwig. *General System Theory*. New York: Braziller, 1968.

Bloom, Allan D. *The Closing of the American Mind*. New York: Simon and Schuster, 1987.

Bloom, Benjamin. (ed) *Taxonomy of Educational Objectives*. New York: Longmans,Green, 1956.

Bloomfield, Leonard. *Language*. New York: H. Holt and Co, 1933.

Buber, Martin. *I and Thou.*. New York: Scribner, 1970.

Byron, George Gordon. *The Works of Lord Byron.*. New York: Octagon Books, 1966.

Capra, Fritjof. *The Tao of Physics* . Berkeley: Shambala, 1975.

Chomsky, Noam. *Syntactic Structures*. The Hague: Mouton, 1957.

-----------. *Aspects of the Theory of Syntax.*. Cambridge: M.I.T. Press, 1965.

-----------. *Language and Mind.*. New York: Harcourt, Brace & World, 1968.

Dewey, John. *Democracy and Education.*. New York: The Free Press, 1944.

Dresselhaus, Mildred, Committee Chairperson
  Women in Science and Engineering. National Research
  Council (U.S.) Committee on Women in Science and Engineering.
  Washington, D.C.: National Academy Press, 1981.
Ebbinghaus, Hermann. *Memory.* New York: Teacher's College,
  Columbia University Press, 1913.
Eliot, T. S. *The Wasteland and Other Poems.* New York: Harcour,t
  Brace, Jovanovich, 1934
Ellis, Albert. *Humanistic Psychology: the rational-emotive approach.*
  New York: Julian Press, 1973.
Freire, Paulo. *Pedagogy of the Oppressed.* Translated by M. B. Ramos.
  New York: Herder and Herder, 1970.
Fries, Charles. *English Sentence Patterns.* Ann Arbor: University of
  Michigan Press, 1958.
Gardner, Howard. *Frames of Mind: the theory of multiple
  intelligences.* New York: Basic Books, 1983.
Ginsburg,A. *Howl amd Other Poems.* San Francisco: City Lights
  1956.
Goodman, Kenneth. (ed.). *The Psycholinguistic Nature of the Reading
  Process.* Detroit: Wayne State University Press, 1968.
Hirsch, E.D. *Cultural Literacy: what every American needs to know.*
  Boston: Houghton Mifflin, 1987.
Holt, John. *Freedom and Beyond.* New York: E.P. Dutton, 1972.
--------------. *How children fail.* New York: Pitman, 1964.
Illich, Ivan. *Celebration of Awareness.* Garden City, NY: Anchor
  Books. 1971.
Jaynes, Julian. *The Origin of Consciousness in the Breakdown of the
  Bicameral Mind.* Boston: Houghton Mifflin, 1976.
Jordan, Hoover. *Bolt Upright.*: The Life of Thomas Moore. Salzburg,
  Austria: The University of Salzburg Press, 1975.
Jung, C.G. *Archtypes and the Collective Unconscious.* 2nd ed.
  Princeton, NJ: Princeton University Press, 1968.
_____ *Man and His Symbols.* Garden City, NY: Doubleday,
  1964
Kaplan, Robert. *.The Anatomy of Rhetoric: Prolegomena to a
  Functional Theory of Rhetoric.* Philadelphia: The Center for
  Curriculum Development, 1972.
Kierekegaard, Soren. *Purity of Heart is to Will One Thing.* NY:
  Harper and brothers. 1938.
Lado, Robert. *English Pattern Practices.* Ann Arbor: University of
  Michigan Press. 1964.
Marshall, John. *The Hunters.* Chicago: Films Inc. 1989.
Neill, A.S. *Summerhill..* New York: Hart Publishing Co., 1960.

National Education Association of the U.S.
  Commission on the Reorganization of Secondary Education,
  Cardinal Principles of Secondary Education, Washington:
  Government Printing Office, 1918.
------- Committee on Secondary School Studies (Committee of Ten)
  U.S. Bureau of Education Washington, 1893.
National Commission on Excellence in Education *A Nation at Risk:*
  The Full Account. Cambridge, MA: USA Research., 1984.
Ong, Walter. *Interfaces of the Word.* Ithaca, NY: Cornell University
  Press, 1977.
----------------. *Orality and Literacy.* London;New York: Methuen, 1982
----------------. *The Presence of the Word.* New Haven: Yale University
  Press, 1967.
Pei, Mario. *How to Learn Languages and What Languages to Learn.*
  New York: Harper and Row, 1966.
Perls, Frederick S., Ralph Hefferline, Paul Goodman. *Gestalt therapy.*
  New York: Dell, 1951.
Plato. *Phaedrus.* Translated by W.C. Helmhold and W.G. Rabinowitz.
  New York: Liberal Arts Press, 1956.
---------. *Republic.* Translated I.A. Richards. Cambridge: Cambridge
  University Press, 1966.
Politzer, Robert C. *Linguistics and Applied Linguistics: Aims and*
  Methods. Philadelphia: The Center for Curriculum Development,
  1972.
Rogers, Carl. *Client-centered Therapy, its current practice, implicatons*
  and theory. Boston: Houghton Mifflin, 1951.
Salinger, J.D. *Catcher in the Rye.* New York: Bantam Books, 1964.
Schlafly, Phyllis. editor *Conference on Comparable Worth.*
  Washington, D.C. The Fund, 1984.
Schor, Ira. *Culture Wars.* Boston: Routledge& K. Paul, 1986.
Selinker, L., Lackstrom, W., & Trimble, L. "Technical Rhetorical
  Principles and Grammatical Choice." *TESOL* 7 (3). 1973.
Selinker, L., & Trimble, L. "Presuppositional Rhetorical Informational
  and EST Discourse." *TESOL* 10 (3). 1976.
Selinker, L., Todd-Trrimble, M. & Trimble, L. "Rhetorical-Function
  Shift in EST Discourse.". *TESOL* 12 (3) 1978.
Shaw, Bernard. *Complete Plays.* New York: Dodd, Mead, 1962.
Smith, Frank. *Understanding Reading.* New York: Holt, Rinehart and
  Winston, 1971.
Smith, Frank. *Psycholinguistics and Reading.* New York: Holt,
  Rinehart and Winston, 1973.

Sternglass, Ernest, *Secret Fallout* New York: McGraw-Hill .1981
-----------------------*Phi Delta Kappan* Fallout and SAT Scores: Evidence
  for Cognitive Damage During Early Infancy April 1983.
Thompson, William Irwin. *At the Edge of History*. New York: Harper
  & Row, 1971.
Toffler, Alvin. *Future Shock*. New York: Random House 1970.
--------------------. *The Third Wave*. New York: Bantam Books, 1980.
Trimble, Louis. *English for Science and Technology*. Cambridge:
  Cambridge University Press, 1985.
Yeats, W.B. "The Second Coming." *The Collected Poems of W.B.
  Yeats.* New York: Macmillan. 1956.
Young, Richard, Alton Becker, and Kenneth Pike *Rhetoric: Discovery
  and Change* . New York: Harcourt, Brace and World, 1970.

Index

Biographical Sketch

While the author has spent his professional life in Education, the world has been his kindergarten. At Oberlin College in the Sixties, he tutored inner-city kids during the year and taught in Upward Bound in the summer.

In the Seventies, he taught in the Peace Corps in West Africa before moving to Paris as an illegal alien and teaching English to French businessmen. Other contracts took him to Riyadh, Saudi Arabia with the U.S.I.A., Rasht, Iran with the School for International Training/ Imperial Iranian Navy, and to the United Arab Emirates with the Abu Dhabi National Oil Co.

In between contracts, he got his M.A. in Journalism at Syracuse, got his photographs listed at agencies in New York and Paris, selling one for a national ad for Bank of America, played one summer with the Rochester Lancers of the North American Soccer League, and after a try-out with the Kansas City Chiefs was invited to the L.A. Rams Rookie Camp.

The Eighties found the author getting his doctorate at the University of New Mexico and contract teaching all over the Southwest. For fun he was a featured extra in Oliver Stone's movie *Born on the Fourth of July* after a five year stint on the *Dallas* tv series, spent two years as an on-air TV and FM film critic, rebuilt a truck and motorcycle, studied shiatsu and helped run a flotation center with sensory isolation tanks.

The Nineties find him teaching teachers, playing rock and roll, and studying clairvoyance and healing at the Berkeley Psychic Institute. At 46, the author feels almost ready for college. This book marks that transition.